Gratitude Communication at Work

Gratitude Communication at Work

Research-Based Tools to Build Relationships and Get Results

Ross Brinkert
Penn State Abington

SAN DIEGO

Bassim Hamadeh, CEO and Publisher
Todd R. Armstrong, Publisher
Tony Paese, Project Editor
Abbey Hastings, Production Editor
Abbie Goveia, Graphic Design Assistant
Trey Soto, Licensing Coordinator
Natalie Piccotti, Director of Marketing
Kassie Graves, Vice President of Editorial
Jamie Giganti, Director of Academic Publishing

Cover image: Copyright © 2020 iStockphoto LP/smartboy10.

Printed in the United States of America.

3970 Sorrento Valley Blvd., Ste. 500, San Diego, CA 92121

I dedicate this book to the Sminkerts, with whom I have been fortunate to share a Catskill mountain home: Colby, Emily, Eshen, Faith, Hannah, Kevin, Sagan, Sydney, and Trey.

I am grateful for our many good times together. I am grateful for the kindness you have shown me in the ebbs and flows of life. I am grateful for the futures we have yet to create.

My love and appreciation,
RB

About the Author

Ross Brinkert was an associate professor of corporate communication at Penn State Abington, where he also served as program chair and the campus's faculty ombudsperson. A native of Canada, Dr. Brinkert earned his bachelor's degree in communication studies from Concordia University in Montreal and completed his MA and PhD at Temple University in Applied Communication Management.

Dr. Brinkert was a past co-chair of the National Communication Association Training and Development Division and held appointments as editor of the *Organization Studies Research Network* and chair of the International Conference on Knowledge, Culture, and Change in Organizations. In 2020, he received the Lifetime Achievement Award from the NCA Training and Development Division and the division's Rising Star Award was renamed in his honor.

In addition to this book, he is the co-author of *Strategic Corporate Communication: Core Concepts for Managing Your Career and Your Clients Brands* (with Lisa V. Chewning) and *Conflict Coaching: Conflict Management Strategies and Skills for the Individual* (with Tricia S. Jones). His work appeared in such journals as: *Conflict Resolution Quarterly, Journal of the International Ombudsman Association*, and *Group Facilitation*.

From the Publisher

Unfortunately, Ross Brinkert died of glioblastoma, an aggressive form of brain cancer, in August 2020, right as this book was beginning its production process. The research, study, and teaching of gratitude was indeed Ross's life's work, and Cognella is extremely humbled and proud to be the publisher of his lasting contribution to the field and to the betterment of people's interactions.

Todd Armstrong
Publisher, Cognella

Contents

Introduction

A Better Way at Work

*"The deepest craving of human nature
is the need to be appreciated."*

—William James

Work. It can be a struggle. But maybe it doesn't have to be. This book is about a sometimes-simple act of communication—expressing gratitude—that can go a long way to making our work lives better. Yes, gratitude communication can be a byproduct of an already healthy organizational culture, but it can also be the way that we create that culture and alter our more immediate work experience. The 100 in-depth interviews on which this book is based tell us that gratitude communication offers the promise of not only feeling better about ourselves and our professional relationships, it can also play an essential role in increasing internal organizational effectiveness and realizing client breakthroughs. Best of all, innovative, yet straightforward, research-based solutions give us the power to put gratitude communication to work in new ways so that we can experience new gains in our own professional worlds.

Overall Organization of the Book and Chapter Preview

This book is divided into four parts: Part I—Making the Case for Gratitude Communication; Part II—Mastering the Basics of Gratitude Communication; Part III—Charting the Boundaries of Gratitude Communication; and Part IV—Becoming a Grand Architect of the Gratitude Communication Opportunity.

Chapter 1: Striving for Breakthroughs in What Can Feel Like a Tiring, Mean, and Lonely World

This first chapter identifies three broad social challenges to which the remainder of the book provides a partial response. The speed of change and other aspects of present-day work have caused many people to feel overwhelmed or worse, burned out. And, unfortunately, many are not feeling the support of others in their workplace. Incivility and other forms of workplace negativity are well-documented and have considerable costs for organizations as well as individuals. Finally, the rise of loneliness in society in general and, specifically, in the workplace is concerning. Increased energy, a stronger sense of positive meaning, and better connections to others are some of the themes weaving their way through the narrower findings presented in this book. This chapter highlights Kahn's (1990) Theory of Workplace Engagement.

Chapter 2: A Brief History of Gratitude and the Birth of Gratitude Communication and This Project

While gratitude is an ages-old religious and spiritual concept, it was not until the late 20th century when it began to be widely explored in other ways. This chapter considers gratitude as a psychological concept before tracing efforts to position it as gratitude communication in the workplace. The chapter also explains the theoretical orientation and research design that provided the original findings shared in the remainder of the book. This chapter puts special emphasis on appreciative inquiry (Cooperrider, 1986).

Chapter 3: Why Do We Send Gratitude Communication?

It turns out there are five main reasons professionals send gratitude inside and outside organizations. Some expressions of gratitude fall squarely within one of these five categories while other expressions of gratitude check the boxes of two or more categories. *Essentials* refers to individuals, individual entities (such as organizations), or qualities closely linked to an individual's or individual entity's identity as the subject of gratitude communication. *Potentials* refers to the promise of performance in the receiver as the subject of gratitude communication. *Efforts* refers to the actual activity of the receiver as the subject of gratitude communication. *Outcomes* refers to the specific achievements of the receiver as the subject of gratitude communication. *Recognitions* refers to the fact that senders will quite often express reciprocal gratitude—gratitude for the past recognition of the sender by the receiver. This chapter features Dweck's (2006) mindset theory (as it relates to feedback), which suggests that gratitude for efforts may be most effective in reinforcing future positive behavior.

Chapter 4: How Do We Send Gratitude Communication?

In response to prompts about interviewees' most positive and memorable gratitude communication episodes, respondents revealed that senders often but not always used more than one communication medium. Senders most frequently use the spoken or written word. Senders sometimes involve senior leaders, extend gratitude in front of an audience, use special gratitude events, include some kind of financial expenditure, and are aware of the use of touch. Examination of the subcategories and different patterns between sending and receiving as well as between doing so inside and outside organizations reveals even more. This chapter highlights media richness theory (Daft & Lengel, 1984) to explain how professionals choose to send gratitude.

Chapter 5: What Are the Benefits of Gratitude Communication?

The 100 gratitude communication interviews used for this book revealed numerous possible benefits of gratitude communication. These are best represented by modifying a framework that was proposed in the conflict resolution community to describe the benefits of mediation. In short, the benefits of any act of gratitude communication can be simply, yet reasonably precisely, understood in the way the act 1) empowers (i.e., strengthens) individuals or entities and/or 2) recognizes (i.e., enhances connections between or among) individuals and entities. *Empowerment* and *recognition* can occur for an individual sender or receiver in a personal or professional capacity. They can also take place for a team, an organization as a whole, and an even wider collection of stakeholders. This chapter puts special emphasis on the Empowerment and Recognition Framework (Bush & Folger 1994, 2004) to broadly make sense of the many benefits of sending and receiving gratitude.

Chapter 6: What Makes Gratitude Communication Most Positive and Memorable?

Apart from being generally vivid, individuals reported the following reasons for specific instances of gratitude communication being positive and memorable: deep personal meaning; strong positive emotion; challenging overall situation;

recognition of notable effort; primacy involving the triggering event(s); high status involvement; gratitude rarely happening; key financial achievement or client outcome as triggering event; positive yet routine nature of the gratitude; receiver previously unrecognized; and shared aspect of gratitude reception. The frequency with which surprise and happiness and other closely associated emotions was mentioned was compelling. Individuals reported a number of specific ways that acts of gratitude communication could be made even more positive and memorable. This chapter highlights expectancy violations theory (Burgoon, 1993) to explain why receivers of gratitude communication love surprise.

Chapter 7: Reciprocation and Gratitude Communication

Reciprocation refers to mutual giving and receiving. It is regarded as one of the most powerful forms of influence. Reciprocation is relevant to the topic of gratitude communication because many receivers immediately respond to acts of gratitude communication with a direct "thank you" of some kind. More profoundly, all gratitude communication is positive reciprocation in that the act of sending implies a meaningful if indirect gift has already been received. Most boldly, a number of interviewees explicitly noted how gratitude communication and the positive benefits associated with it can gain terrific momentum in a relationship. This chapter explores compliance gaining theory (Cialdini, 2008) to give context to reciprocity as a strong and well-established form of influence.

Chapter 8: Philosophies of Gratitude Communication

Philosophies of gratitude are closely tied to a consideration of reciprocation. While the link between reciprocation and gratitude communication was not challenged, individuals differed as far as whether gratitude communication should cycle back to the sender. Essentially, a spectrum emerged with some plainly using gratitude communication as an instrument for self-related gain, some asserting that all sending of gratitude communication was done without any expectation of even simple acknowledgement, and most others expressing views somewhere in between. It is important for individuals—and organizations—to intentionally choose their spot on the spectrum and embrace the limits and potentials connected with doing so. This chapter features the Ethic of Care (Gilligan, 1982) as a way of contrasting individualistic, other-oriented, and hybrid/self-and-other philosophies of sending gratitude.

Chapter 9: Ethics of Gratitude Communication

There is no question that gratitude communication can do tremendous good. However, there is the potential for gratitude communication to cross ethical and even legal lines. Many professions, organizations, and even whole economic sectors have rules about receiving certain kinds of gratitude, especially those involving money. This means a clear view of the law as well as terms of employment and professional accreditation are important. General consideration is needed regarding the following: shared expectations between sender and receiver; any use of touch; acts that transcend the personal-professional boundary; and responsibility to your organization and those you serve in carrying out your overall job. It is not just about possibly breaking a hard and fast rule, it is about making sure that gratitude communication is enhancing rather than taking away from your individual reputation and the reputation of your organization. This chapter offers stakeholder theory (Donaldson & Preston, 1995) as a way of respecting all of the interested parties in a gratitude situation, regardless of a sender's particular philosophy.

Chapter 10: Personal and Professional Lives and Gratitude Communication

Well-intentioned work-related gratitude communication very often affects senders and receivers simply as human beings—a major finding of the research project underpinning this book. In addition, often personal and professional lives significantly overlap in the sending and receiving of gratitude communication. In so many of these instances, there is plenty of upside and little or no downside. Frontline workers are more committed to an organization that aligns with their personal values, as showcased with the sending of gratitude. The relationship between a manager and a direct employee can be fortified with an overall gratitude interaction that appropriately recognizes what matters to an individual beyond the workplace. This chapter offers the theory of relational dialectics (Baxter & Montgomery, 1996) and Communication Privacy Management (Petronio, 2002) to explain the ongoing and not necessarily negative tension between the professional and personal when communicating gratitude.

Chapter 11: Using Gratitude Communication to Transform Challenging Situations

The good feelings of surprise and intense joy that are often associated with gratitude communication can blind us to the fact that we can use it effectively in some of the hardest moments we face at work. An expression of gratitude can be used to offer reassurance and boost confidence. It can offer an effective segue into making a request, including seeking client referrals. Gratitude can be paired with an apology and otherwise mitigate negative conflict. It can even be used to transition individuals during a necessary downsizing or a voluntary but unwelcomed retirement due to illness. Gratitude communication can also go a long way in working through the grief related to the death of a beloved leader or employee. This chapter provides an introduction to facework theory (and especially "mutual face") (Goffman, 1955) to shed light on an important and common feature of effective gratitude communication in difficult times.

Chapter 12: Gratitude Communication as a Career-Spanning Commitment

This chapter shines light on the fact that some individuals interviewed stood out in their awareness-level associated with sending and receiving gratitude, their commitment to participating in gratitude communication, and the sheer dramatic power of their gratitude communication stories. I call these individuals "gratitude communication masters" and give four extended profiles, each from a separate industry. Two key themes are identified per master. The theory of structuration (Giddens, 1984) receives special consideration to make sense of these individuals' positive action orientations despite a world of limits.

Epilogue: The Gratitude Communication Opportunity Right Here, Right Now

Learning the power and practice of sending and receiving gratitude communication reveals the power of framing meaning—punctuating our professional lives by emphasizing what is most important in certain situations and, in some cases, creating positive meaning where it did not previously exist. Indeed, the most important point I took away from this project (and I encourage you to take away from this book) is that moments of gratitude communication may be some of the best moments of our lives. The immediate add-on reminder is that we are referring to work—or at least the hidden potential in our work. Think of what we can achieve with colleagues, clients, and communities when we advance our practice of gratitude communication. Most profoundly, I invite you to consider who you and your organization might become if you fully realized the gratitude communication opportunity that rests in your hands, here, in this moment. This chapter highlights framing theory (Fairhurst, 2010) to describe the process of shaping key moments with gratitude communication.

The Organization of Each Chapter

A relatively uniform chapter structure is intended to make the book easier to understand and navigate, especially as the material shifts among theory, research, and practice. The following sections are used throughout the book.

- Each chapter begins with a short quote reflecting the essence of the chapter.

- Each chapter also starts with a short crystalizing story to generate intrigue about one or more main points of the chapter.

- The book takes a concentrated approach to including academic theories. Each chapter highlights a particularly relevant theory from communication (main emphasis) or an allied field (e.g., business, sociology, and psychology) in a section called Theoretically Speaking.

- Each main chapter offers elaboration of research-based findings.

- Each chapter features a Return to the Opening Story section that draws tighter connections to the initial story given the research insights.

- The Chapter Conclusion closes out the chapter topic and creates a transition to the next chapter.

- A Real World Recommendations section states the chapter's main points in a prescriptive manner.

- A section titled Your Opportunity to Work with Gratitude Communication offers chapter-themed activities for students or other book study groups.

- The Questions for Reflection and Discussion section consists of prompts for additional scholarly exploration.

- The Recommendations for Learning More section suggests chapter-related scholarly and applied resources.

What This Book Is and Is Not

This book is concerned with gratitude as communication—*one or more people communicating appreciation and/or thanks to one or more other people*. Specifically, it is focused on gratitude communication in the workplace. While gratitude is more commonly understood as a feeling (or an intrapersonal psychological concept) and while this consideration of gratitude has been shown to be very important, this book does not concern itself with that approach. Justifications for taking a strongly communication-based orientation to gratitude include the value in exploring new aspects of its relational nature, strategic functions, and the complexities sometimes entailed in sending and receiving gratitude communication and in co-creating such moments.

This book is based on a unique and, arguably, uniquely-fitting approach to the study of gratitude communication. It is not only concerned with gratitude and appreciation as communication; it is dedicated to reporting on a study that was designed and conducted from an appreciative point-of-view. The appreciative research approach (Preskill & Catsambas, 2006) was derived from appreciative inquiry (Cooperrider, 1986), a philosophy and practice that aims to shift from an identification of existing strengths and past high point experiences as the basis for brainstorming, selecting, and developing positive futures, all the while emphasizing the co-construction of reality through language. The use of an appreciative approach to research can be seen as a strength and a limitation. It is a strength as it allowed for the collection and analysis of the most positive and memorable instances of sending and receiving gratitude communication by participants. It is a limitation as it meant the negative potential of gratitude communication was not thoroughly surfaced and probed here.

This book takes a qualitative approach. The in-depth interviews allowed for rich findings, thoroughly inseparable from contextual detail, to be shared. This can enhance clarity and validity as well as underscore the humanity contained in the subject matter and make the material more interesting for the reader.

Even as this book takes a qualitative approach, it has limits in this respect. For instance, even though the one-on-one research interviews asked some questions that addressed the interactional nature of gratitude communication episodes, future research could offer additional qualitative insights by working with recordings of multiple participants in a gratitude communication situation or even just include interviews with two or more participants to a given gratitude communication situation.

This book does not offer quantitative insights, including statistically significant findings about the prevalence of gratitude communication or the effectiveness of gratitude communication. The purpose of the study from the outset was to take a relatively foundational approach to establishing gratitude communication concepts and to demonstrate an appreciative approach to the topic, a fundamentally qualitative endeavor. It is important to also point out that the use of convenience and snowball sampling make a quantitative focus less appealing.

Broadly, this book is intended to enhance the understanding and practice of gratitude communication, illustrate an appreciative approach to research, and inspire theory, research, and application that moves beyond what is articulated in these pages. It is mainly intended for university students with scholarly and general career interest in gratitude communication, but is also written to be welcoming to others, especially professionals in formal or informal leadership roles, who may be captivated by the power and promise of gratitude communication at work.

May You Enjoy the Journey!

Whether you are reading this book as a university student or professional or both, or as part of a class or a professional group or on your own, I sincerely hope you find it engaging and immediately valuable in what it identifies and suggests. I also hope it encourages you to consider taking gratitude communication steps that possibly move far beyond this book in terms of advancing theory, research, or simply how you communicate with others in your work and overall life.

Acknowledgments

Thank you to the following individuals for generously providing their expertise to review the book proposal and/or early versions of the manuscript: Craig L. Engstrom (Southern Illinois University, Carbondale, Department of Communication Studies); Peter M. Kellett (University of North Carolina, Greensboro, Department of Communication Studies); Barbara A. Marusiak (Arizona State University, Edson College of Nursing and Health Innovation); Diane M. Monahan (Saint Leo University, Department of Communication Management,

Marketing, and Multimedia Management); Steven N. Pyser (Rutgers, The State University of New Jersey, School of Business–Camden); Laura E. Reimer (University of Manitoba, Arthur V. Mauro Centre for Peace and Justice). Of course, any shortcomings in the final volume remain my own.

This project was made possible, in part, because of Penn State Abington Faculty Development Grants and a sabbatical funded by the College.

My appreciation goes to Penn State Abington alumna Courtney Greenberg Foley who worked as a research assistant on this project, carried out many research interviews, and developed an Abington College Undergraduate Research Activities (ACURA) presentation and wrote her Schreyer Honors Thesis using some of the data. Courtney is a smart, talented, motivated, and kind individual. It was a joy to have her involved in the project. I am grateful for her important contributions.

I want to express my appreciation to all current Penn State Abington Corporate Communication students as well as all alumni of the program and all those I have taught and/or teach who are affiliated with other majors.

I am grateful to work at Penn State Abington and to have developed this project under the leadership of Chancellor Karen Sandler (now chancellor emeritus), Chancellor Damian Fernandez (incoming president of Eckerd College), Associate Dean and Acting Chancellor Andy August, Division Head Tom Smith (former), Division Head Roy Robson (former), Division Head Friederike Baer, and Corporate Communication Program Chairperson Lisa Chewning.

Thank you to my Communication and Corporate Communication colleagues at Penn State Abington, including Ellen Brennan, Carla Chamberlin Quinlisk, Melvin Gupton, Hannah Kliger, Diane Mitnick, and Surabhi Sahay.

Thank you to my many Communication and Corporate Communication colleagues across Penn State.

Thank you to Penn State Abington Head Librarian Dolores Fidishun (former), Interim Head Librarian Paula Smith, and the entire library faculty and staff.

Thank you to other Penn State Abington faculty and staff colleagues, including Howie Bogot, Joy Fraunfelter, Gina Kaufman, Eva Klein, Tina Vance Knight, Janet Mignogno, Beth Montemurro, Carol Millinghausen, Judy Reale, David Ruth, and Karen Weekes.

Thank you to my many supportive colleagues and friends in the National Communication Association, especially in the Peace and Conflict Division, Public Relations Division, and Training and Development Division.

Thank you to my colleagues and friends in the Organizational Studies Research Network, particularly Phillip Kalantzis-Cope.

Thank you to colleagues and friends in the Association for Conflict Resolution.

Thank you to colleagues and friends in the Philadelphia Public Relations Association, particularly Dan Cirucci.

Thank you to other colleagues and friends who have been steady supporters of this project, including Marc Balcer, Angela Wilkins Drake, Kevin Kruse, JSM, and Christo Schutte.

Thank you to Peter Kellett and Thomas Matyok for inviting my participation (Brinkert, 2016) in the edited volume *Transforming Conflict through Communication,* which included an early version of what became the Gratitude Communication in Challenging Situations chapter found in this book.

Thank you to the incredible team at Cognella Academic Publishing who were vital in bringing this book to fruition. I am most grateful to Publisher Todd Armstrong. This is my third book project with Todd. I always regard it as a pleasure and a privilege to work with him. Todd comes to his work with head and heart. He has a well-earned reputation as a top publisher for scholarly communication titles across sub-areas. He is universally admired by those who have worked with him over the years.

Others on the Cognella team for whom I am grateful include Vice President of Editorial Kassie Graves, Project Editor Tony Paese, Copy Editor Melissa Brown-Levine, Production Editor Christian Berk, and Production Editor Abbey Hastings.

I extend my deepest gratitude and love to my family: Colby, Eshen, and Sagan. Thank you for your love as well as your appreciation of and allowances for my professional life.

A note on the dedication: I dedicated this book to a group of people comprised of my own immediate family and the Smith family of Greenville, New York, who have become family to me over the years.

PART I

Making the Case for Gratitude Communication

1

Striving for Breakthroughs in a Sometimes Tiring, Mean, and Lonely World

"I am saddened by how people treat one another and how we are so shut off from one another and how we judge one another, when the truth is, we are all one connected thing. We are all from the same exact molecules."

—Ellen DeGeneres

Your Work Is About More Than Pushing a Rebounding Boulder

The myth of Sisyphus is the Greek tale of one man's complicated and now largely forgettable life and his well-known eternal punishment. In his life, Sisyphus was said to have upset the god Zeus. Therefore, in death, Sisyphus is forced to repeat endlessly the process of rolling a boulder up a hill and, upon reaching the hilltop, watch the boulder roll down to the base of the hill. Roll the boulder up. Watch the boulder roll back down. And so on. And so on. And so on.

The Overall Social Context and Gratitude Communication

In popular culture, the story of Sisyphus is largely taken to represent the absurdity that some experience in their work life. Unfortunately, many feel fully consumed and exhausted with their solitary, hard, and seemingly meaningless efforts. We may laugh at greeting card images or Facebook® memes of people attempting to push massive boulders, but it is really a sad situation for those who are, metaphorically, trapped like Sisyphus.

Because few, if any of us, live in fear of Zeus, perhaps we need to question what may be driving any sense of Sisyphean struggle in our lives. Perhaps we would do well to attempt to remedy the situation and, ideally, make the feeling of demoralization entirely go away. In this chapter, I argue that three forces, or trends, go a long way toward explaining what may feel like the "big boulder," "daily grind," or "rat wheel" of disempowerment and disengagement in people's work worlds and that gratitude communication may play a positive and important role in making it more manageable.

Whether we are focused on the individual or organizational level in our professional lives, pressure is often felt to put our elbows up, get our heads down, and attempt to burrow through our ever-expanding task list. We know there is something bigger than that task list and just skating by in our interactions with others, but oftentimes we feel we just cannot quite get there. A quick examination of three major trends shows us why a strong commitment to gratitude communication in the workplace may be a worthwhile quest. We will begin to explore how gratitude communication might help us manage feelings of being overwhelmed, counteract the incivility many of us encounter, and decrease feelings of loneliness with a better form of connectedness. First, though, we will explore theory and research that provides insight into the Sisyphus myth, explaining that it highlights the value of human meaning and more.

THEORETICALLY SPEAKING

The Struggle of Sisyphus Is the Struggle for Meaning and More

Dan Ariely is a behavioral economist well-known for designing novel experiments that provide insight into how people make all kinds of everyday decisions. Notably, Ariely (2010) named part of an experiment after Sisyphus. In a study to examine worker motivation under different conditions, he used the expression the "Sisyphean condition" to describe a research participant who not only was offered de-escalating pay for completing a mechanical assembly task but also, and this is the main Sisyphean component, had to endure a researcher de-assembling the assembled object in front of them before being offered the chance to build the object once again (pp. 68–74). The overall finding of the research project was not just that participants accomplished more when the work was meaningful but that they accomplished a lot more. Those for whom the work lacked meaning produced only 68% of what the others produced.

Ariely's (2010) clever study essentially reinforced earlier, allied findings on the importance of meaningful work. For instance, research has shown that purposeful work—a function of transformational leadership—may lead to worker wellbeing and may be amplified when humanistic expectations about the importance of meaningful work are present (Arnold et al., 2007). Ideally, meaningful work is closely linked to a meaningful overall life (Chalofsky & Cavallaro, 2013). It is reasonable to suggest that a competent leader will make sure workers understand the purpose of their efforts, a smart leader will foster a sense of meaning across the work environment, and a wise leader will encourage a sense of meaning that encompasses not only the work environment but people's personal lives as well.

Perhaps the application of the Sisyphus metaphor to work life is about meaning and something more. An exploration of the term *workplace engagement* may be helpful in this respect. The concept of workplace engagement began with William Kahn (1990) who generated a theory of it through in-depth participant observation in two contrasting organizations, a camp for teens and an architecture firm. For Kahn, engagement means to express and use our authentic self while disengagement means to withdraw or defend our authentic self. Kahn was most concerned with the psychological conditions under which people engaged or disengaged in their work lives. He found three conditions to be important: (a) meaningfulness, (b) safety, and (c) availability.

Meaningfulness is the feeling that our work is worthwhile, that it advances what we hold dear (Kahn, 1990). Meaningful projects draw on both our existing talents and push us further in our abilities and accomplishments. The most meaningful roles are those that are central to an organization—positions with influence that seem necessary.

Safety is the feeling that there are not negative consequences, such as threat to self-identity or career, in freely expressing ourselves and participating in workplace change (Kahn, 1990). Supportive and trusting relationships create safety. Our position in informal, often unconscious, group dynamics can be a major factor in making us feel safe or unsafe. Support from management and other leaders can make us feel safer. Safety also is more likely when organizational norms about inhabiting roles align with our own sense of what is right and natural for us.

Availability is the feeling that we have the personal resources to get work done at a certain moment (Kahn, 1990). Availability relates to physical energy, emotional energy, a sense of security about our work and status, and the level of demands from our outside lives. Sometimes our physical energy is spent. Sometimes we become emotionally drained. Sometimes we lack confidence as new members, are self-conscious, and are unsure of how we fit in the organization. Sometimes the goings-on in our personal life carry over into our work life and make us less effective.

While Kahn's initial (1990) writing on workplace engagement was completed in the early 1990s, it only took off in the 2000s. A big reason for its ballooning influence is its considerable practical importance. In increasingly complex workplaces where individuals cannot be bluntly mandated to care and commit themselves, the mysteries of engagement are front and center. While research on engagement has mainly concentrated on its positive relationship to job satisfaction and its negative relationship to burnout, engagement remains something different (Anthony-McMann et al., 2017; Saks & Gruman, 2014), particularly if we consider defining it and studying it from a social constructionist standpoint, essentially opening the concept to theoretical recontextualization.

On the General Need to Pursue Higher Levels of Workplace Engagement

The following trends are offered as a broad argument for the need to foster more engagement in organizations and suggest how gratitude communication can play a role. Subsequent chapters will provide more focused theory-research-practice connections concerning gratitude communication as a form of engagement, especially in relation to the social constructionist perspective and the original research that are the backbone of this book.

Trend #1: A Lot of People Are Overwhelmed

Change is happening more and more rapidly. In 1981, the designer, inventor, and author R. Buckminster Fuller wrote that it probably took 1,500 years for all human knowledge at 1 CE to double. The next two doublings took approximately 250 years and 150 years, respectively, bringing us to the beginning of the 20th century. By the middle of the 20th century, knowledge was doubling every 25 years (Fuller, 1981). A more recent estimate of knowledge doubling suggests that human knowledge is doubling every 13 months (Schilling, 2013).

But the knowledge doubling metric may simply be losing meaning in an era of an Internet of things with massive amounts of data being generated, analyzed by computers, and making a difference in the human world beyond what humans are directly contributing.

A more familiar measure of the speed of change in recent decades has been Moore's law. Moore's law, first proposed in the 1960s and revised slightly in the 1970s, states that transistor counts on an integrated circuit (i.e., microchip performance) will double approximately every 2 years (Brock & Moore, 2006; Moore, 1965). Moore's law entails exponential growth that is experienced in the ongoing evolution of electronic devices such as smart phones, tablets, and laptops. Although Moore's law is in its final throes with chip technology facing barriers at the atomic size level, it is reasonably speculated that this will lead to a transformative breakthrough from sequential computing to parallel computing (Fuller & Millett, 2011). This would mean yet another level of computing power and associated human change.

A few years ago, *New York Times* columnist Thomas Friedman (2016) wrote a book *Thank You for Being Late*. As the title suggests, the book broadly normalized the sense many of us have of living in a world that has quickly changed (and continues to rapidly change) and sometimes catches us on our heels, despite our best intentions. More vivid for Friedman and more directly related to the naming of his book, when someone is late, it can be a relief because it gives us time to think. Many of us are so incredibly busy with the world. Friedman described the top three factors of change as technology, globalization, and climate change, and argued that they are all accelerating and adding to the accelerations of each other. While Friedman recognizes that many of us feel overwhelmed, he takes a positive view about things ultimately working out.

One of the ways a feeling of being overwhelmed is genuinely hurting people is with workplace burnout. It has exploded as a widespread global phenomenon with the emergence of the service economy (Schaufeli et al., 2009). A psychological approach to the study of burnout involves three dimensions: emotional exhaustion; cynicism or depersonalization; and reduced personal accomplishment (Maslach et al., 2001). Although defined somewhat differently in different cultures, since the turn of the century burnout has increasingly been broadly described as the loss of engagement (Schaufeli et al., 2009). A meta-analysis found that one of the two strongest established associations involving burnout was between low workplace support (i.e., emotional support at work) and increased emotional exhaustion (Aronsson et al., 2017).

Arguably, one of the reasons we may feel overwhelmed is because we are not taking time to appreciate the good things we are doing and accomplishing. No doubt we are making progress. It is highly probable we are doing good work. And, perhaps most importantly, we are likely working with some great people—people who make us feel good about our work contributions and ourselves as human beings. What might it mean to express those feelings with our colleagues? How might those expressions be especially powerful if we are in a formal or informal leadership role?

Trend #2: A Lot of People Are Experiencing Incivility and Worse

Workplace incivility was defined, by the originating authorities on the topic, as low intensity workplace behavior that goes against positive norms and is delivered with ambiguous harmful intent (Andersson & Pearson, 1999). Example behaviors offered by these authors included ignoring others, cutting others off, and talking down to others. As summarized by Schilpzand, De Pater, & Erez (2016), the suffering related to workplace incivility is considerable with 50% experiencing it on a weekly basis (Porath & Pearson, 2013). The financial costs are considerable too with the estimated price for distractions and delays at $14,000 per year per affected employee (Pearson & Porath, 2009) and additional costs associated with behaviors such as employee withdrawal from work and decreased service quality for customers (Porath & Pearson, 2013). Kunkel et al. (2015) documented other specific negative outcomes of workplace incivility including increased turnover (e.g., Giumetti et al., 2012), decreased job satisfaction (e.g., Lim & Lee, 2011), decreased performance (e.g., Porath & Erez, 2009), decreased organizational commitment (Blau & Andersson, 2005), and decreased organizational citizenship behavior (Porath & Erez, 2007).

Incivility is a concept that exists within a larger category known as workplace negativity, an area that has seen explosive growth since the early 2000s (Schilpzand et al., 2016). Workplace bullying is a concept in that same category. Bullying behavior is mistreatment that occurs across time, involves formal or informal power by the perpetrator over the target, and may cause severe social, psychological, and physical problems for the target (Hodgins et al., 2013). As summarized by Wall et al. (2017), 27% of U.S. workers are bullied (Scholten, 2005), and 21% have witnessed the bullying of others (Branch & Murray, 2015). There are deep costs for those bullied, those aware of bullying, and the organizations in which bullying occurs. As compiled by Hodgins, MacCurtain, & Mannix-McNamara (2013), the direct experience of bullying is strongly associated with anxiety and depression (e.g., Hauge et al., 2010). Even witnessing bullying results in decreased health and well-being (e.g., Niedhammer et al., 2006), and, therefore somewhat unsurprisingly, exposure to bullying is worse than all other forms of workplace stress put together (Zapf et al., 2003). The costs to overall organizations can be charted in terms of absenteeism and pre-senteeism, employee turnover, litigation expenses, and damage to organizational brand and reputation (Wall et al., 2017). A review of the research on workplace incivility and bullying concluded that these conditions need to be addressed at the individual, job, organizational, and even societal levels (Hodgins et al., 2013).

Perhaps incivility and even more ugly variants of workplace negativity are largely reinforced behaviors that need to be destabilized and overcome with a groundswell of positivity. Could the development of competencies in a topic like gratitude communication and the promotion of gratitude communication make a difference?

Trend #3: A Lot of People Are Lonely

Loneliness is usually experienced as a mix of negative feelings, especially sadness, and is caused by a gap between perceived social relations and desired social relations (Peplau & Perlman, 1982). Basically, to be lonely is to be less connected to others than we want to be. Loneliness has been associated with various neg-ative health states, including depression (Cacioppo et al., 2010), risk of high blood pressure and high cholesterol (Hawkley & Cacioppo, 2010), stroke and cardiovascular disease (Valtorta et al., 2016), and decreased immune function (Jaremka et al., 2013). Loneliness can quite literally be deadly. For example, research has shown that those who are lonely and suffering from cardiovascular disease are likely to die early (Olsen et al., 1991) and, in general, individuals who are lonely are at increased risk of mortality (Penninx et al., 1997).

Loneliness is an epidemic in the United States with patterns that stretch across decades. The General Social Survey (GSS) is a regularly used measure of U.S. attitudes. An analysis of GSS data from 1985 to 2004 revealed considerable changes in social isolation in the span of 2 decades (McPherson et al., 2006). These changes included a tripling in the number of individuals who indicated they had no one in their lives to confide in and a decrease in kin and non-kin social ties.

The problem of loneliness in the modern United States first gained wide visibility with the book *Bowling Alone* by Robert D. Putnam (2000). Putnam chronicled how involvement with others, especially in civic associations, had decreased significantly since the 1950s. He anchored his argument in the concept of social capital or the practical value of humans having strong social bonds with others. For Putnam, one of the main drivers of the loss of social capital was the changing technological landscape in which people have become more removed from rich contact with others.

A more recent champion of the need to address loneliness is former U.S. Surgeon General Vivek Murthy. In a *Harvard Business Review* article, Murthy (2017) not only described the contours of loneliness as an epidemic in our broader society, but he also addressed its implications in the workplace. For Murthy, social capital is vital to workplace engagement, and high self-reports of loneliness, even among CEOs, indicate it is lacking. Murthy attributed the high rate of workplace loneliness to the transient nature of the gig economy, even for salaried professionals, and the magnetic pull of our individual technologies, even when we are in the same physical space. The answer for Murthy included creating opportunities to share more of who we are as well as to recognize the value of others more deeply.

Returning to the Opening Story: The Importance of Meaning in Connection to Others

Metaphors can be interpreted in different ways. Such is the case with the application of the Sisyphus story in this chapter. Perhaps the most basic interpretation of the Sisyphus story to the work world is that we should stop performing and stop instructing others to perform certain tasks. While it makes sense to stop useless, wasteful, and demoralizing practices, this interpretation of the story is probably not the most pertinent when it comes to the topic of this book. For starters, there is no getting around the fact that most people are paid for work because it involves effort. In addition, we can reasonably expect work to remain hard in some fundamental respects even if the conditions around it and even, to some extent, within it are transformed. So, maybe the metaphorical boulder does not go away even if we confront the trends outlined above.

From another point of view, the boulder may represent the sometimes-inescapable struggles of work and life that are well-supported and made meaningful with gratitude communication and other forms of positive engagement. The challenge is not to avoid suffering but to find meaning by taking an assertive approach. To be alive is to encounter big obstacles from time to time and take on big goals, even purely on our own initiative, that will require great effort. We are not going to make hard work disappear. However, perhaps we can make it meaningful by, in part, confronting the three trends and cultivating the practice of gratitude communication.

Even at its origins, the concept of workplace engagement was about more than individual meaning and not just because the aspects of safety and availability were set out alongside meaning (Kahn, 1990). Each of these aspects, meaning in the Kahn's own sense included, are based at least in part on the importance of connection. Engagement, as elaborated by Kahn, involves meaning predicated on value within the relational context of the organization, safety on supportive and trusting relationships in our workplace, and availability to feel that we can develop relationships with others across our life.

The challenge for Sisyphus and most of us is not the hard work (the suffering) but developing and keeping a sense of meaning and meaningfully connecting to others. In a way, each of us does face considerable repetition in our work life. The physician and nurse treat one patient and then immediately must address another patient in need. The insurance agent writes a policy for a client and moves on to securing another client and writing another policy. The teacher graduates one student, and another student enters their classroom. On the one hand, this can be maddening in its infinite continuity. On the other hand, this can be beautiful if the healer, insurer, and teacher find their work engaging, including being full of meaning and human connection. Overall, I propose in this book that gratitude communication is an important way to create engagement that is meaningful, deeply connects us to others, and is more than just individually motivational. ▬▬▬▬▬▬

Chapter Conclusion

In this chapter, I have suggested that the experience of three trends can make people feel as if they were pushing a Sisyphean boulder uphill only to have it roll back down. I have also pointed out how gratitude communication can play a role in countering these trends. In all, promoting engagement efforts and, specifically, gratitude communication can minimize the reach and impact of the three trends.

Real World Recommendations

- Whether working independently or collaborating with others or leading others in getting work done, try to make it meaningful so it is intrinsically satisfying, and more is accomplished.

- Whether working independently or collaborating with others or leading others in getting work done, try to eliminate or better manage perceived workplace threats as these can stifle engagement.

- Whether working independently or collaborating with others or leading others in getting work done, try to create ways to increase feelings of availability and capability to get the work done and otherwise satisfy the interests of relevant stakeholders.

- For you and others, recognize that it is quite common to feel overwhelmed.

- For you and others, recognize that it is quite common to experience incivility.

- For you and others, recognize that it is quite common to feel lonely.

- Work-related meaning, workplace engagement, and general engagement in life are about individual perspectives and choices, but they are also about living well in relation to others.

Your Opportunity to Work With Gratitude

- Describe an instance in which you felt most engaged in an organization.

- Think of someone who was instrumental in helping you feel more engaged. What did this person do that made a difference for you?

- Think of a time you made someone else feel more engaged. What did you do that seemed to make a difference for the person who felt your support?

- What resources are available to you inside or outside your organization to positively address feeling overwhelmed, experiencing incivility, and feeling lonely?

Questions for Reflection and Discussion

- What is a literature-based argument for the aspect of engagement that is most important to you?

- Engagement has often been studied as the opposite of burnout. Does that seem reasonable? Explain.

Recommendations for Learning More

- Explore William Kahn's (1990) foundational article on engagement and reflect on whether his theoretical framing is applicable in additional ways to matters of engagement beyond those presented in this chapter.

- Read Murthy's (2017) Harvard Business Review article on loneliness and the workplace and decide whether you agree with the breadth of the loneliness issue.

- Consider Brooks's (November 24, 2018) perspective on loneliness as an epidemic (expressed in a *New York Times* opinion article): Brooks, A. C. (November 24, 2018). "Loneliness Is Tearing America Apart." *New York Times*, Section A, p. 25.

- Read Klinenberg's (February 11, 2018) critique of loneliness as an epidemic and decide whether this argument has merit and, if so, its implications for the need to explore gratitude communication: Klinenberg, E. (February 11, 2018). "Is loneliness a health epidemic?" *New York Times*, Section SR, p. 8.

2

A Brief History of Gratitude and the Birth of Gratitude Communication and This Project

"To know an object is to lead it through a context which the world provides."

—William James

The Man in Need of Shoes

There is an old Taoist story (Moody, 2008) about a man in need of shoes. Before leaving home, he carefully traces his feet and measures them. He then journeys quite a distance to the market. Upon approaching the shoe salesperson at the market, he realizes he forgot to bring the outlines and measurements of his feet. He immediately returns home, gathers his important papers, and hurries back to the market. Unfortunately, when he arrives, he learns he is out of luck. He will not be able to get new shoes because it is closing time.

Toward an Understanding of Gratitude Communication as an Excellent Fit

The opening story has no direct relationship to the topic of gratitude, let alone gratitude communication! However, I argue that the story offers some vital takeaways for the experience and study of gratitude communication. This is a story of recognizing the importance of experience and of keeping the value of quantitative measurement in perspective. Regarding the first point, the experience of gratitude and gratitude communication can be as obvious as a shoe that fits. Someone in the day-to-day world might vigorously and reasonably, in the eyes of many, insist, "I know it when I experience it. Nothing more is needed."

Regarding the second point, the measurement of shoes and gratitude communication can be related in that the measurement or assessment of gratitude communication has an important qualitative aspect. This is not to say that it makes no sense measuring our feet or seeking to measure gratitude or gratitude communication in numeric ways. After all, knowing our shoe size and then, accordingly, trying on shoes likely makes the process of finding a good fit more efficient. However, with shoes and with gratitude and gratitude communication, the qualitative aspect is also valuable, even essential, for finding a good fit.

In this chapter, we explore the concept of gratitude, the emergence of gratitude communication, and then the research design used for the study reported in this book. Before starting down that path, we will first get acquainted with appreciative inquiry, a philosophy and practice highly resonant with the concepts of gratitude and gratitude communication.

THEORETICALLY SPEAKING

Appreciative Inquiry as a Type of Gratitude Communication and a Way to Study It

Appreciative inquiry was developed by Cooperrider (1986) as a philosophy and group process. It involves considering what is best in organizations to develop a more desirable future. *Appreciative inquiry* begins with a recognition of the positive already present in individuals, relationships, and communities. Appreciative communication about what is currently desirable becomes the basis for considering, selecting, and creating more positive future conditions for all involved. Appreciative inquiry has been used extensively in workplace settings.

Appreciative inquiry (Cooperrider, 1986; Cooperrider & Whitney, 2005) emphasizes the asking of carefully crafted questions to structure the overall conversation. The typical use of appreciative inquiry involves a large group conversation organized around four stages:

1. Inquire—appreciate what is.

2. Imagine—explore what might be.

3. Innovate—determine what should be.

4. Implement—create the desired change.

Participating in an appreciative conversation is often refreshing and transformative for participants. Appreciative inquiry tends to work for the following reasons:

- It promotes positive reflection and action.

- It allows people to decide how to contribute.

- It provides an opportunity for people to speak and be heard.

- It builds relationships.

- It allows people to share and make progress toward major goals.

Appreciative inquiry is a kind of overarching gratitude communication framework. It entails a general posture of gratitude by facilitators and participants. It frequently involves the direct sending and receiving of gratitude messages when, for example, a group is recognizing the strengths of others and past positive experiences with others. It regularly involves the co-creation of gratitude communication when collaboratively generating a positive vision for the future along with plans for, commitments to, and acknowledgements of efforts for making that vision a shared reality.

Appreciative inquiry has been variously adapted to improve the everyday lives and work experiences of individuals, dyads, small groups, teams, and organizations. Appreciative inquiry has also been adapted to create a unique approach to research that involves deliberately seeking positive examples of human performance (Preskill & Catsambas, 2006). This articulation of appreciative inquiry inspired the design of the research project reported in the remainder of this book, a study that sought participants' most positive and memorable examples of sending and receiving gratitude communication.

It is important to point out that the original formulation of appreciative inquiry and its numerous subsequent manifestations arose from a social constructionist perspective. *Social construction* is concerned with reality as created and continually reformulated in the shared use of language (Gergen, 2015). This is a fundamentally communication-based paradigm that values the importance of context and human relationships for making sense of the meaning of concepts and the identities of individuals.

Background on Gratitude and Gratitude Communication

Gratitude is as least as old as history—and almost certainly older. Gratitude has been written about in religious and spiritual texts for over 2,000 years. Although human knowledge began expanding greatly in the early 20th century with the growth of universities and various forms of media, not until the late 20th century did gratitude come to be interpreted, studied, and applied in other ways. These approaches have centered mainly on gratitude as a secular phenomenon and as a positive emotion experienced by individuals in their personal lives. Considerable benefits have been associated with gratitude as a personal psychological phenomenon. In comparison, my interest in gratitude as gratitude communication is relatively unique given that it frames gratitude as (a) an interaction (and often a strategic interaction) between two or more people and (b) places it within the professional sphere. My orientation to gratitude is anchored in the communication discipline in which I work as a professor and in which I have worked as a consultant and training development professional for more than 20 years.

Emmons and Crumpler (2000) completed important foundational work on the concept of gratitude, primarily aimed at advancing gratitude as an emotion, but also supporting those exploring it from other perspectives. They noted that gratitude has been depicted as an emotional state, but also as a moral virtue (e.g., Roberts, 1984). Citing Roberts (1991), they suggested that gratitude contains a paradox of feeling indebted for something that cannot be repaid. They noted how gratitude is strongly emphasized in many of the world's great religions, including Judaism, Christianity, and Islam (Emmons & Crumpler, 2000).

Since the 1990s, gratitude has become recognized as a major positive emotion (Lopez & Gallagher, 2009) and studied extensively in people's personal lives within the field of positive psychology, mainly as a state of gratitude and a concept of therapeutic importance. For example, gratitude is important to clinical psychology because it explains a great deal about well-being, and it offers the potential to improve well-being with straightforward exercises (Wood et al., 2010).

Working from a psychological standpoint and taking a broad view of the concept of appreciation, Adler and Fagley (2005) acknowledged it can be learned and its expression can build social bonds. The concept of appreciation for them entails observing and recognizing its value and meaning as well as feeling a related positive emotion. They demonstrated that appreciation was significantly related to life satisfaction and positive affect, even while controlling for many related concepts.

The psychological concept of *gratitude* has more general visibility and may be defined as the emotion someone experiences when something good has happened and someone else is judged to be largely responsible (Watkins et al., 2009). However, in this book, the main concept used is *gratitude communication*, defined as one or more people communicating appreciation and/or thanks to one or more other people.

Some psychological research and related applied approaches have had a strong focus on gratitude as communication. Writing gratitude letters increased the writers' happiness and sense of life satisfaction while decreasing depression-related symptoms (Toepfer et al., 2012). Carefully crafted experiments by Grant and Gino (2010) showed that when individuals receive thanks for their efforts, they increase their prosocial behavior because they feel socially valued. A research study on gender and gratitude revealed notable differences between men and women (Kashdan et al., 2009). In general, men were less likely to feel and express gratitude, were more critical of it, and experienced fewer benefits. These researchers found women had a more straightforward understanding of gratitude. They were less likely to find it complex, uncertain, and conflicting, and more likely to find it interesting and exciting. They were less likely to feel a burden and obligation and more likely to feel gratitude. Other research addressing gender and gratitude did not find large differences. For example, both men and women, and both benefactors and recipients, experienced increased relationship satisfaction and connection the day after a gratitude interaction in a romantic relationship (Algoe et al., 2010). Also, neural research has established that the writing of gratitude letters resulted in behavioral increases in gratitude and lasting neural sensitivity to gratitude (Kini et al., 2015).

A psychological approach to gratitude and appreciation has at times addressed workplace communication. Chapman and White (2011) adapted Chapman's (2010) work on love languages from family therapy to consider different ways that individuals express appreciation in the workplace, basically words, time, service, gifts, and touch. Research on this family therapy approach in the workplace showed an increase in employee engagement, decrease in staff turnover, increase in customer satisfaction, and a better sense of organizational purpose (White, 2016).

In another publication on appreciation, White et al. (2014) distinguished between recognition and appreciation by arguing that recognition is primarily concerned with external behavior and is seen by many employees as contrived.

He recommended that appreciation be seen as communication that occurred regularly, was individualized and personal, paid special sensitivity to the language desired by individuals, and was perceived as authentic.

This book highlights the linkage between gratitude as a workplace emotion and expression and the concept of engagement, particularly inside organizations. An engaged employee is someone who fully embraces their work roles (Bakker, 2011). According to Albrecht (2010), engagement involves two aspects: (a) a positive and energized motivational state about work and (b) a willingness to act for work role and organizational success. As Albrecht has summarized, engagement has been connected to increased employee commitment (Hallberg & Schaufeli, 2006), in-role and extra-role behavior (Bakker et al., 2004), and service climate, employee performance, and customer loyalty (Salanova et al., 2005). Behavioral strategies for developing engagement in organizations include expressing gratitude (Albrecht, 2010) and, specifically, writing gratitude letters (Schaufeli & Salanova, 2010).

Gratitude as an emotion and communication has also been linked to some external organizational concerns. Expressing gratitude has been acknowledged as a tactic for retaining donors (Birkner, 2012; Merchant et al., 2010). Research on consumer brand engagement demonstrated that feelings of gratitude are tied to community involvement (Brodie et al., 2013), and acts of corporate social responsibility have been shown to trigger feelings of gratitude and reciprocation in those consumers who hold altruistic values (Romani et al., 2013).

Approaching Gratitude With a Strong Communication Emphasis

Scholars with a predominantly communication orientation have made many decades-old contributions to gratitude communication. Advancing Pomerantz's (1978) pragmatic approach to gratitude communication, Herbert (1986) summarized responses to compliments, such as "thank you," as having 12 different types, including comment acceptance, scale down, reassignment, and disagreement.

A longstanding concern with gratitude as communication has been part of the symbolic interactionist tradition, a perspective in close relation to social construction (Brinkert, 2016). Within the symbolic interactionist tradition, facework theories, as noted by Shimanoff (2009), employ the metaphor of face for identity and are most closely associated with the work of Goffman (1955) and Brown and Levinson (1978). Gratitude has been considered as facework (Shimanoff, 2009) and is seen as co-constituted in social interaction.

Other communication-based theoretical areas with possible relevance to gratitude communication given their intersections with facework theories include, but are not limited to, the following: accounts and account giving (Braaten et al., 1993), attribution (Manusov & Harvey, 2001), communication privacy management (Petronio, 2002), compliance gaining (Cialdini, 2009), ethics (Gilligan, 1982), expectancy violation (Burgoon, 1993), framing (Fairhurst, 2011), impression management (Goffman, 1956), and media richness (Daft & Lengel, 1986). The application of many of these theories will be explored in more detail in subsequent chapters.

Non-workplace gratitude research with a strong communication emphasis has started to emerge. There have been a few studies of gratitude expressions in dissertation acknowledgments, including Hyland's (2004) work. Research into Japanese thanking, known as *o-rei*, revealed that participants have a goal of "debt-credit" equilibrium that goes beyond simple expressions of gratitude (Ohashi, 2008). Pragmatic research in Hong Kong showed that expressions of gratitude are typically brief, and responses to thanking are rare with only a few strategies used (Wong, 2010).

A notable examination of workplace gratitude communication was Beck's (2016) study that combined focus groups and quantitative surveys to specifically address managers' expressions of gratitude to employees in a sales and marketing company. Findings included a preference by employees for verbal one-on-one gratitude that demonstrated sincerity. Results also emphasized the dark side of gratitude, organized into the categories of over-communication, withholding, undeserved, unfair selection, unequal opportunity, lack of relationship, and insincerity.

A communication-centered approach to the study and application of gratitude communication is justified by various research findings as well as various calls for better organizations. For instance, a stewardship-based approach to brand reputation during a crisis (Byrd, 2012) suggests the value of cultivating gratitude communication among external stakeholders. A study employing both quantitative and qualitative methods to study the impact of managerial communication on workers' attitudes and behaviors found that people-centered managerial communication practices are needed to have employees who are happy and contributing at a high level (Dasgupta et al., 2014). The continued development of gratitude communication can contribute to the advancement of the virtuous organization (Froman, 2009), organizations that are ethically principled and are committed to positive human as well as economic goals.

Approaching Gratitude With a Strong Appreciative Emphasis

While the conceptual distinction between gratitude and appreciation is debated within the positive psychology literature (Fagley, 2012; Wood et al., 2008), gratitude and appreciation are thoroughly intertwined within social constructionist appreciative inquiry writing. For instance, Whitney and Trosten-Bloom (2010) note, "Appreciation has to do with recognition, valuing, and gratitude" (p. 2). Accordingly, any scholarly effort to advance the notion of gratitude communication in the workplace needs to acknowledge appreciative inquiry. As noted above in the Theoretically Speaking portion of this chapter, appreciative inquiry started as a philosophy and group practice. It generally provides a gratitude frame and encourages direct expressions of gratitude in some instances. Appreciative inquiry (Cooperrider, 1986; Cooperrider & Whitney, 2005) and an appreciative approach to the evaluation (Preskill & Catsambas, 2006) formed the foundation for the study shared in this book.

The Study on Which This Book Is Based

The purpose of this section is to give an overview of this gratitude communication interview study, including the initial aim and details of its execution.

Rationale and Research Aim

Work in positive psychology and appreciative inquiry has established gratitude as a secular phenomenon in organizational life. Further, research in communication (Goei & Boster, 2005) has demonstrated that gratitude is a distinct concept (e.g., separate from obligation when considering compliance issues). Given scholarly and applied concern with engagement and calls to research expressions of appreciation in organizations (e.g., Fagley & Adler, 2012) and develop gratitude interventions in organizations (Waters, 2012), comprehensive study from a scholarly communication standpoint is warranted. The aim of the study was to provide a basic understanding of individuals' work-related sending and receiving of gratitude communication inside and outside their organizations. The study used the definition of gratitude communication shared earlier in this chapter: one or more people communicating appreciation for and/or thanks to one or more other people.

Human Subjects Consideration

The research proposal was submitted to the Office of Research Protections at Penn State University and was granted exempt status given its low risks to participants.

Participants

Convenience sampling and snowball sampling were used to identify prospective participants. Participants were required to be at least 18 years old, to have worked in a full-time capacity (35 hours or more per week) at some point in the past year, and to have been predominantly based in the United States while carrying out their work. No more than five individuals from a given organization were permitted in the study. The study consisted of 38 female participants and 62 male participants.

Research Method

The study used semi-structured qualitative interviewing (Kvale & Brinkmann, 2009) and an appreciative approach to evaluating human performance (Preskill & Catsambas, 2006) in seeking positive and richly detailed examples of sending and receiving gratitude communication.

Procedure

Major questions related to participants' most positive and memorable experiences sending and receiving gratitude communication inside and outside their organization over the past year. For example, participants were asked, "Please think back over the past year and describe the most positive instance of you expressing gratitude to one or more other people inside your organization (e.g., to an employee, manager, or senior leader and/or owner in your organization)." An additional major question asked for the participants' most positive and memorable gratitude experience from across their entire career. Each major question was followed by eight or nine follow-up questions. A series of demographic questions were also asked.

All interviews were audio recorded and professionally transcribed. QSR NVivo® software (versions 10 and 11) was used to organize and manage the transcripts while carrying out a structural approach to coding (Saldana, 2016). Data were initially categorized and coded by question. Categories and codes were later developed across the larger data set.

Findings

The initial design (i.e., focusing on sending and receiving in the internal and external organization and highlighting instances that were most positive and memorable) along with emergent patterns in the data analysis process resulted in the chapter topics and subtopics that are shared in the remainder of this book. The considerable amount of data allowed for rich examples of categories that can be probed in the future with quantitative methods as well as additional qualitative approaches. The content of this book maps an initial appreciative exploration of gratitude communication while placing a premium on theoretical explanation and practical insights for readers' own careers. Overall findings are offered in the epilogue.

Limitations

Any study has limitations. As noted in the book's introduction, this study was especially limited in terms of not providing statistically significant findings. Additional limitations and some ways to address limitations are presented in the epilogue.

Returning to the Opening Story

The opening story in this chapter and the research approach used as the basis for this book are both concerned with the context or circumstances of an object or event in life. The man in need of shoes story is associated with a Chinese school of legal thought known as the Han Feizi (Moody, 2008), which stressed the contextual over the purely rational. Likewise, the remainder of this book is concerned with the context of gratitude communication, the details of it in particular people's lives, because of the immediate value in that approach. While a qualitative approach can establish conceptual distinctions and relationships for quantitative approaches in the future, there is also merit in closely hewing to individuals' circumstances.

Chapter Conclusion

In Chapter 1, I made the case for the value of gratitude communication given some of the broad social trends of our time. In this chapter, I shared some of the history of gratitude and gratitude communication. I also shined a light on appreciative inquiry and how it was used to give shape to the research project, the results of which comprise the remainder of this book. These first two chapters formed the first section of the book, Part I: Making the Case for Gratitude Communication. Now we will move on to the next section, Part II: Mastering the Basics of Gratitude Communication. The first chapter in this section is Chapter 3: Why Do We Send Gratitude Communication?

Real World Recommendations

- Appreciative inquiry is a philosophy and group practice that involves working with existing strengths to bring about positive change.

- Appreciative inquiry has been adapted as an approach to evaluating human performance by focusing on what is already most positive.

- Appreciative inquiry and its various formulations are built on a social constructionist foundation that assumes a language- and context-based view of the human experience.

- The concept of gratitude has its deepest history in religion and spirituality.

- Gratitude as an emotion has received considerable attention and is linked to many positive benefits.

- Gratitude as communication, especially as workplace communication, is a less developed concept that, nonetheless, has important implications.

- A qualitative and appreciative approach to the topic of gratitude communication is valuable for sharing the detail and meaning of individuals' extraordinary moments and also for developing categories that can form the basis of subsequent quantitative studies as well as further qualitative studies.

Your Opportunity to Work With Gratitude

- Reflect on your own most positive and memorable experience of sending, receiving, or co-creating gratitude communication with one or more other people. Who was involved? What was the context? What were the notable verbal and non-verbal behaviors? What made this instance especially positive and memorable for you? How could it have been made even more positive and memorable for you and others involved?

- Select any one-on-one or group situation in your life and develop at least four questions that surface the already positive aspects of the situation or that help develop an even more positive future. Ideally, the questions will be helpful to anyone involved in the situation.

Questions for Reflection and Discussion

- Other than the topic of gratitude communication, what is another topic for which an appreciative approach to evaluation might be especially valuable?

- What are the limits of an appreciative approach to research, and are there any research topics for which it just would not work? Explain your response.

Recommendations for Learning More

- The Appreciative Inquiry Commons at www.appreciativeinquiry.champlain.edu is the most comprehensive site for appreciative inquiry resources as well as resources on the broader topic of positive change.

- David Cooperrider's site at www.davidcooperrider.com is the personal site of the founder of appreciative inquiry and includes news about appreciative inquiry developments, including new books.

- The Taos Institute at www.taosinstitute.net is a community of scholars and practitioners using the social constructionist perspective to positively address different societal issues.

PART II

Mastering the Basics
of Gratitude Communication

3

Why Do We Send Gratitude Communication?

> "No one who achieves success does so without acknowledging the help of others. The wise and confident acknowledge this help with gratitude."

> —Alfred North Whitehead

Gratitude for Searching All Day or the Search for the Missing Lamb

One morning, a mother with a small homestead was feeding the family's animals and noticed that one of their lambs was missing. She gasped but, with no signs of an attack by a predator, felt hopeful that the lamb had simply wandered off and was still alive. Because she had a full day of obligations on the farm, she enlisted her two daughters, 15-year-old Isa and 13-year-old Aniella, to search for the lamb and bring it home. She instructed the girls to search hard but be sensible. She emphasized that the lamb was unlikely to survive if it was not found by nightfall. Before the girls departed, she provided each with a sling-like sack made of strong yet soft material. It would be helpful to carry a few provisions and even hold the lamb if it was found tired or injured. The girls set off in different directions.

The morning passed. The afternoon passed. Both girls returned and met their mother who was laboring in the vegetable garden. Both were empty-handed. "It is okay you did not find the lamb," the mother said to her two daughters. Then she asked, "But why do you look so odd? Isa, you look unusually clean and rested. Your sack looks brand new. Aniella, you look completely filthy and exhausted? Your sack looks like it is 100-years old." Then she added, "What did each of you do out there?" As is often the case with teenagers, each spoke shamelessly. Isa determined that the search would be futile, so she found a meadow close to their home and relaxed and enjoyed the day. Aniella marched hard through the woods and fields all day getting dirty and scraped up along the way. Having had a long day herself, the mother sent the girls into the house and told each to keep hold of their sack, perhaps as a memento of their day. Isa, with much energy, shot off in a sprint. Aniella, extremely tired, plodded along. The mother quietly spoke, "You showed your good character today, Aniella. Thank you." Aniella registered a spark of a smile and walked on.

Just then the mother heard rustling behind her. The lamb had returned on its own. It was roughed up by the world but fine. It was stronger than probably anyone had realized. ▬▬▬▬▬▬▬▬▬▬▬▬▬▬▬▬▬▬▬▬▬▬

Stepping Into the Terrain of Gratitude Communication

The Search for the Missing Lamb is a story relevant to the topic of this chapter because it involves a clear example of gratitude communication when the mother expresses her thanks to her daughter Aniella. As the original research, on which this book is based, demonstrated, thanking someone for their character (or another "essential") is an example of one of the major reasons people send work-related gratitude messages. The story is also useful in this chapter because it offers a chance to apply the theory offered in the next section and, arguably, improve the story.

It turns out there are five main reasons professionals send gratitude inside and outside organizations. Some expressions of gratitude fall squarely within one of these categories while other expressions of gratitude check the boxes of two or more categories. *Efforts* refers to the actual activity of the receiver as the subject of gratitude communication. *Outcomes* refers to the specific achievements of the receiver as the subject of gratitude communication. *Essentials* refers to individuals, individual entities (such as organizations), or qualities closely linked to an individual's or individual entity's identity as the subject of gratitude communication. *Potentials* refers to the promise of performance in the receiver as the subject of gratitude communication. *Recognitions* refers to the fact that senders will quite often express reciprocal gratitude—gratitude for the past recognition of the sender by the receiver. The Theoretically Speaking section in this chapter presents Dweck's (2016) mindset theory (as it relates to feedback), which suggests that gratitude for efforts may be most effective in reinforcing future positive behavior.

THEORETICALLY SPEAKING

Sometimes Great Gratitude Reflects and Reproduces a Certain Mindset

Carol Dweck is a professor of psychology at Stanford University whose work spans developmental psychology, personality psychology, and social psychology. Dweck (2016) is best known for proposing and establishing mindset theory, a theory that can help guide us in more effectively communicating gratitude in organizational settings, especially in leadership roles.

Dweck's (2016, 2017) research on mindset theory has mainly addressed children's implicit theories of intelligence in relation to succeeding or failing at tasks in school but has also been more generally elaborated. Those with a *fixed mindset* attribute their successes and failures to trait-based or inherent abilities and limits. These individuals view themselves as born with certain strengths and weaknesses in learning and achievement. When faced with serious setbacks, these individuals often pull back on the activity or give up completely. They explain success as evidence of character or natural ability. Those with a *growth mindset* attribute their successes and failures to their own efforts. These individuals emphasize their ability to generally learn and overcome obstacles on the path to achievement. When encountering challenges, these individuals tend to demonstrate resilience and push on. They explain success as evidence of hard work, good strategies, and/or good instruction. The good news is that not only do some have the growth mindset from an early age, but others can be taught it. And those in positions of influence can learn to better provide feedback to promote a growth mindset.

Mindset theory has been extended in some fascinating ways. For example, students with a growth mindset are more likely to successfully navigate school transitions and complete challenging math courses as well as exhibit lower aggression and stress related to victimization and exclusion from peers (Yeager & Dweck, 2012). Those who hold a growth mindset regarding empathy are more likely to be empathetic in challenging situations (Schumann et al., 2014). Students from economically disadvantaged backgrounds are less likely to hold a growth mindset compared to peers from wealthier backgrounds. But those from some of the most economically disadvantaged backgrounds who hold a growth mindset experience a buffering effect on test performance placing them on par with students with a fixed mindset from relatively wealthier families (Claro et al., 2016). Additionally, parents need to be aware of how they may influence their children's mindsets with their views about failure (Haimovitz & Dweck, 2016). Basically, parents' philosophy of "failure as a normal part of life" is connected to a child's sense that growth is possible, while parents' philosophy of "failure as debilitating" is linked to a fixed mindset.

Ways to Apply Mindset Theory

Although mindset theory has not been thoroughly investigated and applied to the world of work, it can be reasonably expected to apply as follows:

1. Expect that your learning and others' learning is possible, even for tasks that are challenging initially.

2. Do not overlook the importance of positively acknowledging effort, even if outcomes are not yet achieved.

3. Resist the tendency to tie recognition of achievements to inherent ability rather than effort because that can stifle positive risk-taking by those who have previously demonstrated high competence.

4. Regarding gratitude specifically, consider your ability to develop your gratitude communication competencies beyond where they are right now.

5. Consider sending and receiving gratitude even in situations that involve failure.

6. When sending gratitude, make it your default to attribute effort rather than attribute permanent characteristics in an individual, team, or organization. Expressing gratitude for stable characteristics may be appropriate; just be aware of thinking through the context before making this move, though.

One caveat about mindset theory—it possibly faces a limit when applied to gratitude communication because there may be times to confirm personhood and, therefore, most appropriately and effectively thank a person (or team or organization) for their being.

INSIGHTS BASED ON ORIGINAL RESEARCH

The Five Big Reasons People Express Work-Related Appreciation

What follows are examples of themes uncovered in the research.

Efforts

Effort gratitude means giving or receiving thanks for behavior such as going above-and-beyond, showing hard work, doing work with extra care (apart from delivering an overall outcome), demonstrating initiative, and/or demonstrating perseverance. Efforts gratitude was sometimes general and sometimes specific.

- Making It Rain Despite the Snow

It was Saturday morning, typically the busiest day for car sales, but there was a blizzard the night before, and the storm would have heavily blanketed the cars making it difficult to make any sales. However, when Mac, the owner of the car dealership, arrived at 9 a.m., he saw that all the approximately 100 cars had been cleared of snow. Mac recalled:

> *I have one gentleman who cleans all the cars and gets all the snow off the cars so that we can do our business for the day. And I remember that he got in at 7 in the morning. He doesn't have to be in till 9. And when we came to work at 9 in the morning every car was cleaned from the snow, and we were ready to sell.*

The dealership sold at least three cars that day. Soon after, Mac and the sales team expressed gratitude for the detailer's efforts, most notably, thanking him verbally.

- Great Effort Over Many Years Needs to Be Recognized

Charles is the founder of a technology company that recently sold out to a larger company. He learned that some key employees were retiring, and the new company was not going to recognize their departure. He knew he had to take action so he organized, hosted, and paid for a getaway and party for the retirees and those close to them at one of his out-of-state properties. He explained:

> I think it was that I appreciated their efforts 'cause I wouldn't have gotten to where I was [or to] benefit from the sale of the company without their hard efforts. So, it was really a token of my appreciation that the employees know that I support them, and I appreciate their efforts and that it hasn't gone unnoticed. I think that's the message. And the company wasn't gonna do anything so I just … went ahead and decided to do it.

- You're Good Along the Way

A communications director, Jasper, recalled how he received a very meaningful thank you from an employee who appreciated the way he worked with her and their overall team. The director remembered her basic message, "It was really thank you for understanding our perspective, always being understanding of where we're coming from … on behalf of the group." The other thing the director recalled hearing from this employee was her appreciation of his clarity:

> [T]hey appreciate the clarity with which I'm assigning them. In other words, I'm not dumping something. … I'll say, here's what we need. I can suggest to you ways to get there, but if you want to do it a different way I'm good with that.

- A Simple "I See Your Effort"

Sharon, a director of legal and business affairs, put in considerable extra effort—working on nights and weekends and being on call—to play a key role in her company's acquisition of another company. Her CEO reached out by phone to acknowledge her hard work:

> It was to thank me for working so hard and going above and beyond in terms of hours and days; and for just being responsive and helpful and helping get the deal done and looking forward to doing more things like this in the future.

- Doing So Much at the End of the Year

Madison is a recruiter in an engineering firm that unexpectedly needed to fill a senior finance position, a difficult task, especially at the end of the calendar year and with her company wanting to move quickly on it. Madison put in considerable work to make it all happen. She was processing background check items for a top candidate right up until the Christmas party. Madison described how she was thanked for her efforts by her supervisor:

> When I got to the Christmas party, she [said] 'I just got your emails, thank you so much, you worked all day and even all the way through to the Christmas party.' A week later I had received a phone call from her, and she said [she] just wanted to tell [me] this in person before [I] receive this and before it's announced publicly. ... At the management meeting this morning she [said] 'I let all the managers know that I was presenting you with an Above and Beyond Award. And it's because of all the effort you put in filling this accounting position. I just want to thank you so much for all the personal time that you took out of your life to fill this role and I couldn't be happier with this person. I think she's gonna be a great fit.'

Her formal award noted that Madison "went above and beyond and demonstrated dedication coupled with personal sacrifice."

- Appreciating Efforts Without Likely Outcomes

Darren is a pharmaceutical representative with pressure to show results. While he is more likely to reach his company's main metrics by focusing on physicians, he cares about his work and the various professionals he serves. Darren shared an example of receiving thanks from a nurse practitioner:

> [The nurse practitioner said] 'Thank you for your help, thank you for all the resources you've provided me, thanks for answering my calls when I call, thanks for coming out.' She could call me and say 'hey, do you have any of these or do you have any of that?' Yes, I do and I'll be out either later on today or tomorrow, so I've been quick with response. And [she] just [said] thanks for the time. I think that she probably just gets overlooked in the office, ... and she was appreciative that I make her feel important and that I make her patients, even though they're few, feel just as important as somebody who sees a lot more patients.

- Efforts Acknowledged Despite an Overall Business Failure

Greg was one of the principals in a boutique investment firm that was closing its doors because the business was continuing to lose money. It was a difficult time as Greg reached out to friends, clients, and close industry colleagues to share the news. However, when an acquaintance heard secondhand about the upcoming closure, he contacted Greg with a note to express admiration and appreciation for Greg's efforts despite things ultimately not working out. Greg explained:

> We're both kind of entrepreneurial. He's tried entrepreneurial efforts, and they just haven't worked out his way so he knows what I've been through. He wrote a note saying it sucks when your plan doesn't work out exactly like the vision, but I know you have the proper mindset for taking this all in stride and I'm sure you'll end up somewhere great in the future. He wasn't trying to get anything out of it; he was just trying to do something nice for somebody. I don't know if you define that as gratitude or appreciation or thanks, but that's how I interpreted it.

Outcomes

Outcomes gratitude refers to giving or receiving thanks for clear results, for successfully completing a project, or for reaching end goals. Three main categories here were outcomes for a team, outcomes for the organization, or outcomes for the sender or receiver specifically.

- The Sweet Smell of Success

Brian, a fragrance company vice-president, along with his team delivered a presentation on industry trends to an existing client and the results were impressive. Brian described the increased demand for their work: "We went from opportunities [to develop for them], every six to eight weeks [and then] they turned around and dropped like 14 things in my lap inside of two weeks." The VP explained the thank you he extended to the three other team members,

> It was a total team effort. Each person knew their role and responsibility; everyone executed flawlessly, congratulations and thank you for all of your help.

- Thanks, Because We Did This Together

Rick, a social networking professional, was one of a handful of high-profile contributors in his public relations firm invited to present at an end-of-the-year internal showcase event. The organization tasked him and the other featured presenters with providing the highlights of their work in achieving client goals over the past 12 months. From the outset of his presentation, Rick chose to share the success and express appreciation to his team:

I opened up my presentation, the first line was, 'it takes a partnership,' and I was talking about our agency and the clients. My second line ... was, 'it also takes a team.' From there I said something along the lines of 'I know I'm a social media guy, I know I'm the one giving the presentation but it's important to note that it did take a team and everyone pulling together to keep all of this, the different gears spinning.'

Rick went on to talk about the team's success in not only designing and launching a client's Facebook campaign but also blogging and performing media relations work to increase traffic, overall visibility, and overall success. He literally pointed to and named his blogging and media relations colleagues on the project.

- Thanks for Being a Contributor to Achieving the Best Nationwide Results

In her work with Human and Urban Development, Liz works with contractors in an assigned area of the country to build, renovate, and sell properties. Although she is technically only supposed to monitor the contractors, she finds it much more effective to relate to them as partners. This makes it easier for her to be influential in steering their work and it makes it a smoother process for the contractors' relationship with the government, including getting paid by the government. Liz went through a stretch in which she was first in the country in terms of breaking sales goals, and she had done so for 14 straight months. She knew she did not accomplish this on her own. She expressed her appreciation through the contracting manager to the various contracting staff:

The staff's diligence had made us all look so exceptionally good. Again, for 14 months—nobody else has managed to do this across the country—we've exceeded sales goals. So, I just said, it was due to their diligence and their hard work, and they're exceptionally communicative with me, whereas some of the other contractors were really kind of secretive, as opposed to communicating.

- Thanks, From Clients for Providing Us a Way to Achieve Our Business Goals

Theo is a managing director in reinsurance for a global insurance company. His line of work does not typically encounter much gratitude communication, but his team and organization occasionally receive this type of positive feedback from clients. For example, Theo recounted the words of an economic client and business unit client communicating by email about a recent reinsurance partnership:

One email in particular, from the economic buyer, [said] more or less, 'thanks for achieving all our goals, our renewal goals, and allowing us to continue to grow in this space.' And then the business unit head, who is the day-to-day person, [said] 'The team's really excited about what all you guys accomplished in allowing us to execute our business plan.'

- Your Generous Gift Was a Sacrifice, But It Is Making a World of Difference

Christie, a university president, learned that a major donor had fallen on relatively tough times with his business portfolio. She was concerned that the donor may have had some regret about what he had given the university. She contacted him with a message of appreciation for the results his gifts were achieving:

I wrote a long email and just said, 'You may be thinking, but I can assure you that this is the best thing that has ever happened to our students and you're not just helping one person, you're helping, maybe 1,500 students a year, forever.'

- You Helped Land Me a Terrific New Job

Dr. Griffin oversaw a veterinary medicine group at a major pharmacy company. Unfortunately, for Dr. Griffin and her team, the entire group was eliminated during a major company restructuring. After the announced downsizing, but before the individuals in the group were let go, Dr. Griffin took steps to prepare her team members for the transition. She brought in speakers to talk about topics such as job searching and interview skills. It was gratifying for Dr. Griffin to be thanked by a former team member for what she had helped this team member achieve:

Dr. Griffin, I really want to get back into the workforce; I need to get a job. I remember the interview workshop that you hosted for the department when we got this message [of being let go], and ... I had a copy of the book. I rewrote my resume using some of the guidance [the presenter] had given us and some of the messages that you gave us. I went in and I was able to secure a job and I thank you because ... no one had ever spoken to me about how to write a resume; no one had spoken to me about interviewing ... and no one gave me constructive feedback. I took that to heart and I was able to get a job; I was able to get more money than I could have ever imagined.

Essentials

Essentials gratitude refers to giving or receiving thanks for one or more of a person's fixed or stable qualities, a collection of people's fixed or stable qualities, or the overall nature of the person or group. Main categories here were a person's qualities in general and a person's qualities in the organization.

- A General Manager Generally Appreciated

Antonio, a restaurant owner, received a five-star, all-expenses paid trip for two to Grand Cayman from a major vendor. Rather than take the trip himself, he decided to give it to the general manager at one of his locations as an overall thank you for that person. The restaurateur's message to the general manager was the following:

> We appreciate you and since I was given a gift, I'd like to share it with you; give you that gift.

- Deeply Appreciated and Loved as a Professional

David, the top communications executive for a large legal organization, has warm memories of recently receiving thanks when he received a career achievement award from his professional association. The association dedicated the entire event to honoring David. One speaker's words stood out for him. David recalled what his current boss and the head of his organization had to say about him:

> I think the items that resonated with me were that he felt [that]with me around, he never has to worry; he knows that things will get done. He ... said there's a level of professionalism that he felt was a hallmark of my career work, and also that I had an eye for detail that he's never seen before. But, the one thing he said, above all the others, that really stuck in my mind, which I did not expect, was in the speech he built to an ending where he enumerated some of my qualities, and he said, he appreciated me, he valued me and 'Yes, in fact, I do love David.' So that was very nice to use the love word, which really was very touching and moving.

- Thank You for Being Like Close Family

Desiree is a young professional who worked in the career office of her university prior to graduation. Desiree has faced considerable obstacles in her life, including having her mother die when she was a child. Accordingly, it meant a great deal to her to work in an environment that made her feel so comfortable. She extended gratitude to several people in the career office, most notably her direct supervisor. Desiree shared,

> *I'm blessed to have you in my life. Even though you're not my blood mother, I still consider you my mom.*

- I Appreciate You as a Close Friend

Angela, a senior information technology director, became friends with Janice, a junior colleague, over 15 years ago. Although they do not currently work in the same company, it is possible they will again work together in the future. Whether or not their professional paths will so directly cross again, they have continued to enjoy a wonderful friendship. Angela expressed appreciation for three things: a recent gift, their friendship, and also for who Janice is as a person:

> *I had gone on a trip, not long after Christmas, and sent [Janice] a long letter and told her how much I appreciate her friendship, how much the [recent] gift meant to me, [and] just the time and the friendship over the years, especially this past year, and how much I really appreciated her.*

Potentials

Potentials gratitude refers to giving or receiving thanks for the capabilities seen in the receiver but not yet fully evidenced in past behavior. Potentials tended to relate to both the individual and the organization.

- The Business of Bringing Toys to the World and Growing as an Employee

Axel, the president of a small toy manufacturer, chose two employees for year-end monetary bonuses in addition to verbal year-end reviews. One of these individuals was the import manager who not only demonstrated results in terms of growing international business but also showed additional promise. The president explained the reasons he extended his appreciation:

> *It was to reinforce the growth in her position and to encourage continued growth.*

- You Have It in You to Earn Your Degree

Gwen, the executive director of a preschool, met with each of her employees for an annual evaluation but also to simply "get together and talk." Gwen expressed positive feedback and appreciation about what one young woman was accomplishing with her students in the classroom. And she combined this with appreciation for how the young woman was capable of developing herself further:

> I believe in you and that you can do this, I know that you have the capabilities to do this, and I can help you get this done.

- Potential Recognized in a Highly Competitive Environment

Theo, the managing director in the reinsurance business who we met above, works in New York City. For the most part, Theo operates in an "eat what you kill" culture because he is with a major publicly traded company. Nonetheless, he received gratitude from his boss along with a discretionary bonus. The verbal expression of gratitude included strong recognition of his potential:

> His message was 'Keep up the good work, you're one of our future leaders here; obviously this is what we're trying to do—make sure that we don't tempt you to go anywhere else.'

- The Potential to Move From Sales to Management

Cody is an investment advisor who was asked to visit his company's main office in New York City. There he spent a day with management learning that side of the overall business and exploring the possibility of him transferring from the sales side to the management side. Cody remembers their message as,

> We've heard good things and we think you might be good on a different level.

Recognitions

Recognitions gratitude refers to giving or receiving thanks in response to a previous recognition, including a previous thank you. There is a connection to reciprocation, which is explored in Chapter 7.

- Your Recognition Got Me Promoted, and So I Am Recognizing You

Chantal is a senior relationship manager at an annuity and life insurance company. She had a major victory when she organized and led a training session for over 200 people. Her management team was very impressed by what she had done and formally reported their appreciation for her great work in writing to those higher up in the organization. Chantal was so very grateful in return because this directly led to her winning a promotion. Chantal explained:

> *If management teams don't recognize you then you pretty much don't get promoted. Because my managers had recognized me I was able to get a promotion through that. I, in turn, did a write-up for them just to express my gratitude and my thanks for that.*

- Thank You for Your Gesture of Appreciating What I Can Bring

Matt is a corporate recruiter for a logistics and supply chain company. As someone very early in his career, he was thrilled and felt very appreciated by his company when they invited him to visit some of their facilities in Canada and paid for his expedited passport application. In recognition of the gesture and the incredible experience of the trip itself, Matt shared his gratitude with his supervisor, the director of talent acquisition:

> *It was just a great time and a great experience for me, and I expressed it throughout the plane ride and back home; how awesome it was to see what it was like up there. Everybody learned more about the company and more about what I was doing for recruiting up there and learning different laws.*

- I Appreciate and Literally Held on to Your Appreciation for Me

Andy, the owner of an automotive repair business, was the unexpected recipient of gratitude when Wayne, an employee at his business, came into his office and sat down opposite him. Andy explained the wonderful way they mutually shared appreciation:

> *I had written [Wayne a letter], showing my appreciation to him, and his dedication for his service over the years. Out of the clear blue, [Wayne] opened up his wallet and took the letter out that I had actually written to him. [The letter was] letting him know how I felt about him and showing my [gratitude] to him. He, in turn, made me feel great by showing me that he saved that letter and kept it in his wallet.*

Combination Situations

It is important to note that many gratitude communications involve two or more reasons for sending gratitude. Theo (above) received both verbal accolades and a financial bonus. Combination situations are important because they are more complex and, at least theoretically, demand more resources such as time and money, the latter for material manifestations of gratitude. In the next chapter, you will meet Carmen.

Returning to the Opening Story

The opening story of *The Search for the Missing Lamb* includes an expression of thanks from the mother to her daughter Aniella. When Aniella returns, she says, "You showed your good character today, Aniella. Thank you." As noted earlier, this is gratitude concerned with an essential or fixed aspect of the receiver. At least within the immediate confines of the story, the mother was not able to express thanks or appreciation in the form of a recognition or outcome. However, Dweck's (2016) mindset theory clearly supports the case that the mother would have been more effective by commenting on her daughter's effort instead of an essential. For example, the mother might have commented, "Even though the lamb is not (yet) back, I see the hard work you demonstrated today in searching for it. I am grateful for your effort, especially since I was unable to help out." The mother might also add a statement related to her daughter's potential, but, notably, this would have to be done with care because this should not be stated in a fixed manner. One good possible addition here, given what can be extrapolated from mindset theory, might be, "I realize you are ready for other opportunities to grow."

Chapter Conclusion

The research study that is the foundation for this book uncovered an incredible variety of gratitude communication examples. An analysis of those examples revealed five main reasons senders initiate gratitude communication. Sometimes it is the case that more than one reason is an option for a sender. In these instances, the sender can combine types or select among them. And sometimes one or more types just do not apply to the situation and the choice is limited or, perhaps, there is just one way to go. In all, this chapter examined the "why" of gratitude communication. The next chapter addresses the "how" of gratitude communication.

Real World Recommendations

- Remembering the five basic reasons for composing and sending gratitude communication can help as you scan for opportunities to express thanks.

- Remembering the five basic reasons can also guide your decision of which type(s) to use in structuring your gratitude message, as sometimes you face choices on attributions.

- Efforts gratitude means giving or receiving thanks for behavior such as going above-and-beyond, showing hard work, doing work with extra care (apart from delivering an overall outcome), demonstrating initiative, and/or demonstrating perseverance. Efforts gratitude was sometimes general and sometimes specific.

- Outcomes gratitude refers to giving or receiving thanks for clear results, for successfully completing a project, for reaching end goals. Three main categories here were outcomes for a team, outcomes for the organization, or outcomes for the sender or receiver specifically.

- Essentials gratitude refers to giving or receiving thanks for one or more of a person's fixed or stable qualities, a collection of people's fixed or stable qualities, or the overall nature of the person or group. Main categories here were a person's qualities in general and a person's qualities in the organization.

- Potentials gratitude refers to giving or receiving thanks for the capabilities seen in the receiver but not yet fully evidenced in past behavior. Potentials tended to relate to both the individual and the organization.

- Recognitions gratitude refers to giving or receiving thanks in response to a previous recognition, including a previous thank you. There is a connection to reciprocation, which is explored in Chapter 7.

- To promote learning and greater achievement, Dweck's (2016) mindset theory suggests that senders of gratitude communication should generally strive to attribute efforts rather than essentials, and attribute efforts along with other reasons such as outcomes.

- A global expression of appreciation for a person, team, or organization may on occasion be ideal, as it can convey a deep level of confirmation.

Your Opportunity to Work With Gratitude

- Craft one expression of gratitude reflecting each of the main reasons for sending gratitude (i.e., efforts, outcomes, essentials, potentials, and recognitions).

- For one possible gratitude sending situation in your life, craft two different options for expressing your sentiment in this instance. The two options should relate to two different reasons for sending gratitude (i.e., efforts, outcomes, essentials, potentials, and recognitions).

Questions for Reflection and Discussion

- How might you design a study of gratitude communication in the workplace that tests the application of Dweck's (2016) mindset theory?

- Consider when the gratitude communication implications of Dweck's (2016) mindset theory should be put aside for the sake of offering emotional confirmation by expressing appreciation for a person (i.e., not concentrating on efforts or even outcomes, potentials, or recognitions but embracing gratitude communication for one or more essentials). What criteria might help to determine the appropriateness and effectiveness of such a decision?

Recommendations for Learning More

Here is a terrific book to learn more about mindset theory: Dweck, C. S. (2016). *Mindset: The new psychology of success.* Ballantine.

4

How Do We Send Gratitude Communication?

"Silent gratitude isn't very much to anyone."

—Gertrude Stein

Gratitude Goes Nuclear

The Cold War started soon after the end of World War II and extended until the fall of communism in Eastern Europe in the early 1990s. The United States and its allies and the now-former Soviet Union and its allies had a strained peace that involved the proliferation of nuclear weapons. The height of these tensions was the Cuban missile crisis that occurred in October 1962. Soviet leader Khrushchev sought to strengthen his country's nuclear strike capability by positioning nuclear weapons in Cuba, approximately 100 miles from the continental United States. U.S. President Kennedy would not have it and ordered a naval blockade of Cuba. The brinkmanship between leaders, the presence of a high number of U.S. and Soviet personnel and vessels, difficulties with communication, and the potential to launch nuclear weapons made it a very volatile situation. Fortunately, the situation was resolved when an agreement was made between the United States and the Soviet Union that included the Soviets backing down from deploying nuclear weapons in Cuba (Dobbs, 2009).

The situation in President Kennedy's White House was tense during the period of the crisis, especially as U.S. leaders met to decide whether to rely solely on the blockade or more actively engage militarily. Shortly after the crisis passed, President Kennedy chose to thank those who had helped in the endeavor. The White House commissioned commemorative plaques from

Tiffany & Co.® that featured an engraved October calendar page with the dates of the crisis in bold. Also, each recipient's initials were engraved at the top of the silver calendar along with the president's initials. The president presented the plaques in person at the beginning of the National Security Executive Committee Meeting on November 29, 1962. First Lady Jacqueline Kennedy received the first plaque, and then each member of the president's cabinet received one as well (John F. Kennedy Presidential Library and Museum, n.d.). ▬▬▬▬▬▬▬▬▬▬▬▬▬▬▬▬▬▬▬▬▬▬

Lots of Ways to Hit "Send" on Gratitude

The President Kennedy Cuban missile crisis thank you story is about expressing appreciation with a financial expenditure in the form of a plaque with writing, spoken appreciation between the sender and each receiver, and the incorporation of an audience, at least of fellow gratitude recipients. This chapter considers the individual media that senders use and how these individual media are often rich. This chapter also highlights how senders create richness in frequently using multiple communication channels.

In the research study discussed in this book, respondents revealed that senders often but not always used more than one communication medium. Senders most frequently used the spoken or written word. Senders also sometimes extended gratitude with a financial gift or reward, incorporated an audience, and used touch. Before exploring actual examples of sharing gratitude with different communication media, let's first consider media richness theory (Daft & Lengel, 1986) to inform the "how" choice of sending gratitude.

THEORETICALLY SPEAKING
────────────────────

Media Richness as a Strong Explanation for How Gratitude Communication Is Shared

Media richness theory (Daft & Lengel, 1986) provides a framework for organizing different communication media based on their relative abilities to convey information with clear meaning or without allowing for different interpretations. Media richness theory was developed in recognition that organizations are more challenged by the ambiguity or equivocality of data rather than the lack of data or information uncertainty. A *richer* medium is often one that incorporates multiple channels (e.g., face-to-face communication is both non-verbal and verbal), is the same as or close to an originating medium, is personal, and allows for immediate feedback. Some common media ranked in descending order of richness include: (a) face-to-face communication; (b) video calls and videoconferencing; (c) telephone calls; (d) personalized emails and letters; (e) impersonal emails and letters; and (f) number-based written communications.

A richer medium is not necessarily a better medium in a particular circumstance. Generally, richer media are the better choice for non-routine communications while leaner media can be the most appropriate choice for routine communications. Routine communications involving high amounts of data are well-suited to leaner media. The unique contexts of certain organizations can help frame how messages in certain media should be understood and, therefore, alter the standard understanding and application of media richness theory. Sometimes a richer medium will be used even with relatively routine messages to address relational issues more effectively (Sheer & Chen, 2004). To be an effective manager is to be someone effective at determining and executing, based on media richness requirements (Lengel & Daft, 1988).

Media richness theory informs the sharing of gratitude communication because it highlights how richer media are often used, richness is often maximized within particular media used, and richness is often generated within a specific gratitude episode with the use of multiple media.

INSIGHTS BASED ON ORIGINAL RESEARCH

Communication Choices When Sending Gratitude Communication

Those interviewed for this book project most often recounted the sending of gratitude communication via the spoken word (face-to-face and phone), written word (email and hardcopy correspondence), financial expenditure (various forms), audience-involved events, and touch. Often two or more communication forms of media were used.

Spoken Word

Spoken word gratitude mainly entailed face-to-face oral communication or conversation over the phone with the clear majority occurring face-to-face. Face-to-face was extremely common inside organizations and somewhat less common when sending or receiving gratitude with someone outside the organization. Face-to-face spoken word communication includes considerable nonverbal communication as well but, in the examples below, the verbal aspect seems to be foregrounded. A couple of instances involved face-to-face gratitude communication that was televised (a township manager getting appreciation in a township meeting and a restaurateur getting appreciation from a celebrity on national TV).

Face-to-Face

• Construction Business Owner Immediately Thanks Carpenter for Job Well Done

Leo owns and manages a construction business specializing in interiors. He and some of his workers finished a home theater project. When the homeowners walked in to see the completed work, their jaws dropped in amazement. The carpenter responsible for much of the work was with Leo at the time, and Leo immediately took the opportunity to extend his gratitude. Leo explained:

> *I pulled my carpenter aside and said, you know, this is a job well done, you do amazing work and that's why I'm glad that you're working with me. Keep up the good work and, make us look good.*

• Thank You for Your Message of Hope

Sharon is the senior director of legal affairs for a media company in New York City from Chapter 3. She watched as her company stagnated and was relieved when a private equity firm purchased it and installed new top-level leadership. Sharon was so pleased to have the chance to have a one-on-one meeting with the new CEO. Sharon described how she shared her appreciation for her:

> *[The CEO] asked me what she thought the best asset of the company was and what would be our best chance going forward of having success. I told her that she was. She was kind of taken aback by my comment, but I just told her how much I appreciated her energy, her new ideas, her willingness to think outside the box and was hoping that she would help us along to become a successful company again.*

- Building Bridges With Those Who Run Bridges

Rodney is the manager for a staffing company with various government contracts. In taking over the supervision for workers running bridges, he met face-to-face with each group to offer appreciation and reassurance. Rodney described:

There were four bridges and I met with each shift, roughly anywhere from three to eight people at a time. I gave the same message of stressing my gratitude for the [importance of the] work that they had done and [for] the company, as well.

Rodney further explained how it all seemed to go:

Very positively, especially the ones that didn't have much contact with me until then. ... [O]nce I began to speak, you could see them relax and be very receptive to what I was saying.

- Thank You for Not Dismissing a Contracted Worker After an Incident With a Permanent Employee

Another time that Rodney used the face-to-face communication of gratitude was when one of his contracted workers got into a dispute with a permanent employee. These kinds of situations can easily result in the contracted worker losing their position when the government-employed manager of the permanent employee backs their own. Rodney described what he did: "[Y]ou thank [the government manager] for [not firing the contracted employee]." He went on to explain the logic of how he expresses gratitude in these situations:

[A] lot of those types of conversations happen face-to-face, and actually I think you get a better result doing it face-to-face because then they can look at you, and they can tell whether or not, you're sincere. Body language, eye contact; it's hard to really gauge your message over the phone. Sometimes you can but not all the time; face-to-face is always better. It's more personable.

- Great Job on Your First Successful Client Pitch

Saoirse is a media planner for an advertising agency. Recently, her junior media planner returned after giving his first solo client pitch. It went great. The client decided to invest in all that he offered. Saoirse explained: "I walked up to him after he got back and I said, 'How did it go?' We talked about it for like 15 minutes. I said, you did a fantastic job, thank you very much."

- We Appreciate What You Have Done, and You Don't Have to Carry the Load

Dominic owns a wholesale food distribution company that supplies restaurants and other retailers of prepared food. Health care costs have escalated considerably during the many decades he has been in business, and they have especially grown in recent years. Regrettably, Dominic had to announce to his employees that he had to introduce a co-pay medical benefits model to share costs with his employees. After making the announcement, he returned to his office. He described what happened next:

> *A few of my older, senior employees came up and said, 'Dominic, enough's enough, you've done enough for us for all these years. Stop tearing yourself apart, it's time that we started kicking in.' It took a burden off my shoulders and it let me know that ... it's ok.*

Phone

- Thank You From the CEO for Working Extra So We Could Execute an Acquisition

Sharon, from above and in Chapter 3, had been experiencing a lot of turnover at her NYC media company. Her CEO changed twice in the previous year. One of the initiatives of the newest CEO was to acquire another company. Sharon and her team put in a considerable amount of work and, to thank her, her supervisor let her know that the CEO would be contacting her by phone. Sharon explained:

> *Our team had to work nights, weekends, be on call for information and it was a harried and crazy time. The gentleman I report to called me and said, 'Are you going to be home this evening, the CEO is gonna be calling you.' And he did, he called me. He thanked me for all my hard work, said how much he appreciated me and our team. I thought with all that was going on, I don't really know him that well. It was very, very nice of him to reach out to me personally and express his gratitude.*

- Thank You for the Great Designs That I Get to Build

Chad, the owner and head designer for an interior design company, was on the phone with his main cabinetmaker discussing an ongoing project. Chad was happy to receive an unexpected gratitude message from his cabinetmaker. He recollected,

[H]e was just giving me high marks on my design abilities and I interpreted it as a very sincere compliment.

- I Appreciate Your Help Solving a Crime

Manny is the director of security for a home improvement store. To complete an internal theft investigation, he needed the help of the local police commander. With the commander's assistance, Manny was able to identify someone on video who was stealing from his store. Manny phoned the commander—someone he went through the police academy with decades prior—to extend his "genuine appreciation."

- Thank You for What Smells Like Success

Brian from Chapter 3 is the vice president of fragrance at a global flavor and fragrance company. He earned the appreciation of a client who requested follow-up work combining two fragrances that were initially presented on their own. Brian and his team worked quickly and fulfilled her request. He described her reaction and what it meant for all involved:

> *She was incredibly grateful because she went back to her superiors and said, 'Hey look, I did this with the group, this is what they came back with, I think we're gonna have a better overall product when it's all said and done because of X, Y, Z.' She looked like a rock star; we were the beneficiary of that perspective. She called me [and said] 'Thank you so much, I really appreciate everything you guys did, it made my life so much easier.' It was nice to receive that communication back from the client 'cause oftentimes it's, 'Hey, great job, thanks, move on, what's next?'*

Written Word

Written word gratitude included all forms of verbal correspondence such as email, hardcopy correspondence (e.g., greeting cards, notes, and letters but not plaques; see Financial Expenditures), other electronic verbal communications (e.g., text messages, social media platform postings, intranet postings, and other web-related postings), and other hardcopy verbal communications (e.g., newsletters). Most written word gratitude communications took the form of email and hard copy correspondence. Notably, hard copy correspondence was the most common response for the question that probed for the most memorable example of gratitude communication across the interviewees' entire career. In other instances, email was more common.

Email

• Using Email to Nominate a Colleague in a National Organization and Blind Copy Her

Liz from Chapter 3 is a senior specialist with Housing and Urban Development, a department in the federal government. Liz sought to shine a light on the great work of her colleague Tracee on a shared project they completed. Liz made use of an organization-wide recognition program to thank Tracee. Liz nominated Tracee via email and blind copied her. Liz remembered,

> [S]he came to me, and this was before they had even told her that she had gotten anything, and she thanked me for going out of my way to stress that she had done a good job.

• Using Email Because Recipients Are Spread Around the World

Carmen is a senior director of compliance and culture at a global pharmaceutical and consumer products company. She was charged with introducing a revised code of conduct across the entire organization. Because the organization operates in over 20 different languages, Carmen had to rely on company contacts in many different countries to translate materials in a way that was unique to local operating environments yet still on brand with the overall organization. To thank these many individuals, Carmen contacted the senior vice president overseeing the initiative and composed and sent an email from that person to all involved in the translation process as well as the individuals' supervisors. Carmen recalled the message:

> I've known that we've called upon you numerous times to really help us with translations, in particular, [when] we re-launched our [code of conduct], and I know that there was a lot of effort in a short period of time, and we would not have been able to launch successfully globally without your help. Obviously, [I wrote] something around thanks for your continued support and help, I know we're going to call upon you in the future, and please know that I appreciate any effort that you give us.

Carmen explained the email that she sent:

[E]verybody saw who it was delivered to and then all the managers were cc'd as well, so it was an open communication to the group.

Carmen also lobbied the SVP to get permission and funds to provide each translator with a monetary reward.

- Using Email With a Colleague Because That Is Largely How We Communicate

Jay, a partner in public accounting firm, was organizing a team from the office to meet with a prospect. He included his junior colleague Melanie, which came as welcome but unexpected news to her. Melanie expressed her thanks to Jay via email. Jay described the message:

Her message was very thankful and appreciative [for] being included in the process, because she incorrectly assumed that she wasn't qualified for it. And I told her 'You absolutely are.'

Jay added,

"[Y]ou could tell by the tone of her email that she was very, very happy about it."

- Using Email With a Client Because That's Largely How We Communicate

Meara is the owner of a small, full-service travel agency. She was excited and nervous to win the business of an extended family who had worked with another agency for 20 years. In various emails, she let them know she was appreciative of their business. Of course, it also mattered to Meara and, presumably the family, that the agency designed a trip that was an overwhelmingly positive experience for the family.

Hardcopy Correspondence

- A Thank You Note to the Interviewer When Applying for a New Position

Ella is early in her career and works as a community liaison for a hospital. After her interview for her current position, she wrote a note to her interviewer. Ella recalled:

I think that I went above and beyond by sending that handwritten thank you note, and the woman who interviewed me, who is now my direct supervisor, expressed that that was really nice, that she often does not get a handwritten thank you note. I think that that might have made the difference in terms of her deciding that I would be a good fit for the team.

Ella also shared what she wrote:

The gist of it was that I really appreciated the opportunity, along with her taking the time to outline the job and consider me. I just said that I really thought that it was a great, potential fit for me as a professional and that I would hope to be a part of her team in the future.

- A Scrap of Paper With a Heartfelt Message

Jerry is a golf course manager. One of his seasonal workers, Miranda, is a young person whose mother died of cancer in the prior year. To honor the memory of Miranda's mother, Jerry and Miranda organized a charity golf tournament. Jerry handled the overall logistics, and Miranda handled the direct communications with those attending. It was a lot of work for both Jerry and Miranda, and it was especially tough for Miranda because she was still deeply mourning her mom. The day went well, though. It meant a lot to him to receive a note that Miranda left for him on his desk at the end of the day. He described the situation:

It was literally on a little [sticky note] that was just left on my desk at the end of the day. By the time we got out of there, [it was] 8, 9 at night [and] I went back to my desk to get my keys, and the note was just sitting there on my chair. And it was just a little note. I've received cards and I've received things but, you know, this was just a little, like almost a scrap of piece of paper, and it was really nice.

- A Thank You Note to a Manufacturer's Premier Client for a Large Project

Bill is the president of a small, steel heat-treating company. He thanked his main client for a substantial job by writing a thank you note. Bill explained:

There's a job that represents well over a million dollars' worth of sales to me in a period of five years, and it's a beautiful thing. I sent them a thank you note for that order specifically. I elaborated on, not just this, but thank[ed] them for each and every order.

- A Consultant Sends a Thank You Note When a Client Gives a Generous Go-Ahead

Roger is a political consultant. In recent months, he reached out to one of his clients who is a well-known elected official. Roger asked the official if taking on a certain new client would create a conflict of interest from his point of view. Roger did not want his current client to feel compromised in any way. Roger explained the official's reaction and his follow-up:

> I called the elected official to see if he would be upset if I were to undertake this new client that potentially created this conflict. And he immediately said that he would not consider it a conflict, that I was welcome to pursue it ... [and] it would not create any problems for our continued professional working relationship. Although I rarely communicate with him in writing handwritten notes, normally it's phone calls and emails, I sat down and wrote a detailed handwritten thank you note and sent it to his home expressing appreciation for his professional approach to the issue.

Financial Expenditure

Financial expenditure gratitude can be communicated in whole or in part with money and/or a direct money-related expenditure. Money-related gratitude included pay bonuses, pay raises, and loans on good terms. Direct money-related expenses included products, services, and experiences. When financial expenditures were a factor, bonuses and products were most common inside organizations, and products were most common when either the sender or receiver was outside the organization. Notably, a product can include something like a plaque, but these did not come up that often and, when they did come up, they were secondary or tertiary in their importance to the interviewee.

- Making Use of Standard Company Awards to Express Thanks

Monae is a vice president at a major bank and the person in charge of running the United Way Campaign within her division. To thank a colleague who worked closely with her on the campaign last year, Monae nominated the woman for the company's "way to go" award, which the woman won. This was part of a company-wide award system to recognize excellent work. Monae explained the process:

> *It carries a monetary value that the giver can decide on. So, it was an*
> *actual electronic notation that goes to her that says 'You've been awarded.'*
> *I think I gave her $50 in a gift card and she can spend it wherever she*
> *wants to spend it.*

- Thanks for Company Results Combined with Bonus and Promise of Raise

Axel, introduced in Chapter 3, the president of a toy manufacturing company, expressed appreciation to an import manager who had made significant contributions to the organization's growth in their international business. In extending his gratitude, the president awarded "a fairly respectable cash bonus for the year and the promise of a pay increase at the end of the first quarter and year end."

- Quarterly and Annual Gift Cards for Top Grocery Store Associates

Brendan is the general manager of a grocery store for a major chain. Each quarter, he recognizes an associate. Each year, he also recognizes one of the quarterly winners as associate of the year. The associate of the quarter receives a $50 gift card, and the associate of the year receives a $250 gift card. In the most recent year, Brendan awarded the quarterly and yearly honor to Derek. In doing so, Brendan essentially relayed and reinforced the thanks of a customer with special needs who regularly gets assistance from Derek. Brendan explained:

> *We have a blind customer that Derek works with every time she comes into*
> *the store, does personal shopping for her. And she has complimented Derek*
> *numerous times about going above and beyond. Derek makes sure she gets*
> *the items she wants, verifies dates, makes sure her pay is correct and ... then*
> *makes sure [things] actually ... get delivered to her house.*

- A Book With an Inscription to Show Appreciation at the Beginning of a
Professional Partnership

Grant is an independent management consultant who, over the past year, developed a professional relationship with a fellow management consultant, Jules. Part of Jules's business involves running executive retreats at remote locations around the world. They were in the early stages of involving Grant in Jules's retreats as a co-leader. Jules mailed a book to Grant and wrote inside the front cover. Grant explained what he received:

[J]ust out of the blue I received a book in the mail about some coaching stuff. He wrote in the book to me how much he appreciates me, how much he sees in me and how he's looking forward to walking this road with me.

- Appreciation in the Form of 32 Shirts for 32 Golfers

Jerry is the golf course manager we met above. His course is part of a larger resort. Other than course members, many of Jerry's golfers are out-of-towners who visit the resort and course on an annual basis as part of self-organized groups. Jerry was enjoying a group of 32 golfers who regularly came for four nights and were always a pleasure to host. On the second night of this stay, Jerry wanted to do something special to show his appreciation for their business and also their presence. Jerry went to a woman in the group and explained:

I said, here are 32 tickets. Tell [everyone in your group] that these tickets are good for one shirt in the clubhouse; any shirt they want. They're just to present these [tickets] to whoever's at the desk and pick up a shirt. They were kind of dumbfounded at dinner, to be honest with you. So right after dinner they all took their tickets to the pro shop, and they turned them in and every single one of them [got a shirt and] had them on the next day for golf, which was great. The next morning when I showed up to work, the head guy [in the group], Steve, said, 'You know, that was just an incredible act of kindness, and generosity.' I just told him why I did it. I said you know; you guys are great guys. And he said, 'Well, Jerry, if you're worried about us coming, don't worry about it because we're booked, you need to book me in for next year.' And I decided we feel we're friends with each other; they're not just customers.

- Gratitude With a Plaque for Supporting Students From the University

Tracy is a regional talent manager at a major rental car company. She recalled participating in an end of the academic year marketing department dinner at her alma mater and one of the universities at which she is active as a speaker and hiring manager for interns and full-time professionals:

They brought me up and gave me a plaque to recognize that we were a great partner throughout the year. I had two other alum that I brought to school with me, so we all, all three of us got recognized. They took some pictures, like I said, gave us a plaque, an award, and then just said that they really appreciate that we, again, were hiring their students.

Audience-Involved Events

Audience involved gratitude can be communicated in front of those beyond the direct intended receiver(s) and, therefore, involve an audience. Note that audience-involved gratitude communication is distinct from gratitude event communication. The latter involves an audience solely or primarily to communicate gratitude.

- Presenting a Sales Award in Front of the Whole Organization

Jeff is a sales and marketing lead at a small personal care products company. Jeff won approval to present a coveted year-end award to express gratitude to one of his sales supervisors, Julie. It was Julie's fifth year anniversary with the company, and she had a distinguished history of meeting and exceeding sales goals with her seven-member team. Jeff recognized her at a quarterly meeting in front of a group of almost 175 that included the organization's senior leadership, Julie's team and her peers, and others in the organization. Jeff described it in more detail:

> *I was up in the front of the room and she happened to be seated towards the rear of the room. … [I wanted her to] hear what I was saying … instead of being concerned about people looking at her, so I kept her back at her seat and then asked her to come up.*

- End of Global Meeting Formal Recognition

Sean is a director for a pharmaceutical company based in Europe. His entire group of 70 from across the globe gathered at the company's headquarters for 2 days of meetings. At the end of the meetings, the vice president overseeing the group presented several awards. Sean was surprised when he was called to the front of the room, thanked, and received an award for his work creating collaborations in the group over the previous few years and for organizing part of the meeting in which they were participating. Sean explained:

> *I received it verbally in front of a room of 70 people, and I had to get up in front of our vice president and shake her hand and say, thank you.*

- Informal Recognition in a Community Business Alliance Meeting

Brad is a township parks and recreation manager who attended a community business alliance meeting for the first time since many organizations represented in the alliance membership had recently participated in a community triathlon led by Brad. Brad was surprised when, as part of the informal self-introductions process, a handful of people expressed gratitude to him and his colleagues. Brad explained,

They were just very positive about the event and the work that we had done as an organization.

• Client Expresses Gratitude in Front of Contracted PR Professional's Boss and Others
Rick is a social networking manager for a public relations and marketing firm from Chapter 3. At the annual meeting with a longstanding client—a travel agency—the owner of the agency thanked Rick in front of all gathered including Rick's boss. Rick described:

She thanked me multiple times. [There were] a couple executives from the firm and the team that works on her account. She publicly thanked me there and went as far as to say she wanted to set me up a desk in her office so she could just keep me there all the time.

Touch

• The Professional Handshake That Builds a Relationship
Erica, a training manager, remembered running a recent nationwide learning and development series for emerging leaders at a large insurance company. On a particular occasion, she arranged for between eight and 10 executives to speak with the emerging leaders group. To close the session, the training manager orally expressed her thanks to the executives on behalf of the group but also made a point of shaking each executive's hand in front of the training participants. The way the training manager sees it, "[I]t's okay to stand up and shake someone's hand as a professional thank you." She views this as part of her "personal mission ... to resurrect the dinosaur of building relationships." She added, "I always like that personal contact, [the] handshake thank you ... some of the little things that help to build a relationship."

• The Professional Handshake as a Sign of Attention and Thought
Darren is a senior sales representative for a major pharmaceutical company from Chapter 3. He is very grateful to a particular physician prescriber who

routinely allows access to him. This physician was difficult for Darren's predecessor to access. Darren shared at length the importance of a handshake and related nonverbal as well as verbal communication for connecting with this physician and others:

> *I shake hands when I'm down here a lot, and I don't know that a lot of people do that. I think that has an impact. I think that any kind of contact in some way with somebody, whether it's a tap on the shoulder or shak[ing] hands ... has an impact, a lasting impression. But just good conversation, good body language, a focus on what he's saying and what he's needing and making sure that I'm giving him the attention that he needs ... I try to have open conversation and make it more about them than it is about the product.*

- A Great Big Hug for Going Above and Beyond

Barb is a national account manager at a large insurance company. One of her clients helps lead two charity golf leagues, including one for a boy who became paraplegic after a car accident. The client reached out to Barb and requested her help. With only one day's notice, Barb prepared and delivered two gift bags to be raffled off. This was the fourth year in a row that Barb had helped. Barb described the client's gratitude, including her hug:

> *She was so thankful because she knew that she had given this to me late; I was able to pull together these great gift things really quick and [with] short lead time and I took the time to do it. This was, I think, my fourth year I've done it for her. And she was very appreciative because the families of these two people look to raise funds annually, and anything that they can raffle off is obviously a help to them.*

Multiple Media Forms

The vast majority of gratitude communication used two or more media.

- We Want to Speak to You and Otherwise Show Our Appreciation for Your Talents

Mika is a vice president of marketing and communications for a company that specializes in physician services. Until recently, she was very happy working as a consultant but found herself won over with gratitude and took an unexpected professional leap. The owner and another senior executive invited Mika to join them for an all-expenses paid 3-night trip to a beautiful hotel in Florida. Mika had previously done consulting work for the executives, and now they wanted her to join them on a full-time employee basis having seen her great work. Mika described the situation:

> [T]hey wooed me. They flew me to Florida, put me in a really, really nice hotel and offered me whatever I'd like to eat or drink and let my voice be heard. They asked me my ideas and they praised my thoughts and my ability to think through things and said wonderful things about my ability to do things and break things down and simplify things. They wanted that skill set on their team, so they did it through nonverbal ways in terms of showing appreciation. And the dollar amount, 'I'm gonna treat you to a little vacation, I'm going to give you little material things.' But it's not the materials that were most meaningful.

Returning to the Opening Story

In terms of the President Kennedy Cuban missile crisis thank you story, it was likely even richer than was described at the beginning of this chapter. Although we do not know for sure, it is possible, perhaps likely, that the president shook the hand of each recipient when presenting the plaques. Although numeric information is typically considered less rich, the calendric numbers on the plaques were very possibly seen by recipients of the president's gratitude as rich reminders of tracking the crisis while it was an ongoing for 13 days. Unfortunately, all the participants in this gratitude communication episode are deceased now. It would have been fascinating to speak with them about not only the basic details of how they were thanked but also, related to the Chapter 6 topic, about the aspect of the whole episode that was most positive and memorable for each.

Chapter Conclusion

This chapter focused on the means of delivery. Positive and memorable gratitude communication was most often found to be communicated via spoken word (face-to-face or phone), written word (email or hardcopy correspondence), financial expenditure (various forms), audience event, and touch. Often two or more of these media were used. This meant that there was a general media richness theme in terms of individual media used and in the frequency with which multiple media were used for a single gratitude communication episode. The next chapter addresses the benefits of gratitude communication for those involved.

Real World Recommendations

- Face-to-face spoken word is a very rich form of communication and is most strongly associated with positive and memorable gratitude communication.

- Spoken word communication over the phone is considered a rich medium and is also strongly connected to positive and memorable gratitude communication. It is an especially good choice when face-to-face contact is not possible.

- Many instances of gratitude communication involve written communication, most often email and less frequently hardcopy correspondence. Email can make sense for senders and receivers spread across time zones or in companies that otherwise regularly use email.

- Financial expenditures can take various forms and can involve relatively large investments such as pay raises or bonuses or relatively small investments such as modest cash awards or gift cards. They can also take the form of plaques, trophies, or gifts such as books.

- Sometimes gratitude communication is made positive and memorable because it includes those other than senders and receivers as an audience. Audiences can consist of one or two individuals sharing the moment in person, a small or large group of people at an in-person event taking in the gratitude communication, or individuals copied on an email.

- Positive and memorable forms of touch-related gratitude communication include a handshake or a hug. Heightened discretion is needed around the possible use of touch.

- Upon selecting a medium for gratitude communication, give some thought to appropriately and effectively maximizing its richness.

- Many instances of positive and memorable gratitude communication involve multiple media, another avenue for richly communicating.

Your Opportunity to Work With Gratitude

- Create a concise, practical guide with suggestions for best communicating gratitude using different media, including at least three from this chapter and at least one not specifically covered in this chapter. For this activity, feel free to count a single social media platform as its own medium.

- Develop an extra special expression of gratitude communication for one or more valued individuals in your work or personal life. Consider how you can make the expression especially rich (and positive and memorable) by using two or more media and/or maximizing the richness of one or more media.

Questions for Reflection and Discussion

- Thank you cards and thank you notes are seen by some as uniformly old-fashioned and irrelevant and by others as polite and even necessary, at least in certain circumstances. Can the media richness theory account for a medium itself gaining or losing social standing? If not, can you provide another theory that explains this phenomenon?

- What is your single favorite medium for sending gratitude communication? What is your single favorite medium for receiving gratitude communication? Explain your answers.

Recommendations for Learning More

- Media richness theory has continued to develop from a theory and research standpoint and has continued to provide new practical insights and applications. Nonetheless, it has been challenged with media naturalness theory (Kock, 2005). Media naturalness theory suggests that face-to-face communication is optimal because it was dominant throughout human evolution and takes less cognitive processing. Therefore, media should be understood and evaluated in terms of their distance from face-to-face communication when, for example, creating online experiences. Learn more about media naturalness theory, and make a case for how it offers more, the same, or less usefulness for those wanting to practice gratitude communication successfully.

- Another interesting example of gratitude communication and President John F. Kennedy involved Kennedy receiving an inspirational plaque from Admiral Hyman Rickover and responding with a thank you letter. The episode is notable in part because the plaque sat on the president's desk for the remainder of his presidency.

  1. An image of the plaque and the basic details about it can be accessed at the John F. Kennedy Presidential Library and Museum at this link:

  2. The RAAB Collection web site offers more details and an image of the thank you letter at this link:

- Evidence suggests that even less rich forms of gratitude communication still leave receivers feeling great—and better than anticipated by senders. This *New York Times* article explains how gratitude messages sent by email leaves receivers feeling ecstatic. This article can only be accessed with a subscription; however, you can access it through a university library database by searching: Murphy, H. (2018). You should actually send that thank you note you've been meaning to write. *The New York Times* (July 20, 2018).

5

What Are the Benefits of Gratitude Communication?

*"No act of kindness, no matter
how small, is ever wasted."*

—Aesop

A Whale of a Thank You

In 2005, the *San Francisco Chronicle* reported on a group of scuba divers who were called into action when an adult humpback whale got horribly tangled in fishing line linked to crab fishing traps (Fimrite, 2005). As noted in the story, a fully-grown humpback is so large that a mere flick of its tail could kill a person. Nonetheless, several divers entered the water and tried to help. James Moskito, the first diver by the whale's side, saw the situation was very serious with fishing line wrapped around the tail, back fins, one of the front fins, and inside the whale's mouth. Fishing line had also lacerated the whale's blubber in places. Moskito and the others worked carefully with curved knives to free the animal. It may be impossible to know for certain what, if anything, the whale was trying to communicate to her rescuers, but Moskito described it as "an epic moment of my life" when the whale winked at him while he cut the line around her mouth (Fimrite, 2005, para. 14).

The divers continued with their work and were indeed successful at entirely freeing the humpback from its bounds. At this point, the whale swam to and "nuzzled" each of the four divers who had assisted in the hour-long effort. As Moskito reflected, "It felt to me like it was thanking us, knowing that it was free and that we had helped it" (Fimrite, 2005, para. 2).

Entering an Ocean of Benefits

It may seem crass to even consider the benefit of the thank you that Moskito felt he had received from the freed whale. The recollected moment has such a purity to it, a completeness to it that may defy words for some. Yet the profound impact of the thank you for Moskito, the other divers, and those who may read the account justifies the question of benefit. Perhaps the primary benefit was simply the seemingly clear sending of recognition to another being—a being in this instance separated by species type. Perhaps every feeling of appreciation in the purely human world, let alone act of appreciation in the purely human world, is positive recognition of another from whom we exist apart and yet to whom we are connected. Moskito certainly made the point that he felt the nuzzling whale was recognizing him and his diving partners for the empowerment they provided to the whale. Although this empowerment was not fostered by the thank you itself, it remained an important part of what was taking place in the overall encounter.

The 100 gratitude communication interviews used for this book revealed that gratitude communication has nearly innumerable benefits if benefits are narrowly defined. A more holistic approach to gratitude communication benefits indicated they are best represented by modifying a framework that was proposed in the conflict resolution community to describe the benefits of mediation. Accordingly, the benefits of any act of gratitude communication can be understood in the way the act (a) empowers (i.e., strengthens individuals or entities) and/or (b) recognizes (i.e., enhances connections between or among individuals and entities). In the context of the study used for this book, "empowerment" and "recognition" sometimes took place for an individual sender or receiver in a personal capacity and sometimes in a professional capacity. They also sometimes took place for a wider collection of stakeholders such as a team or an organization. Before considering empowerment and recognition in actual expressions of workplace appreciation, the Theoretically Speaking section presents the empowerment and recognition framework (Bush & Folger, 1994, 2004) to broadly make sense of the many benefits of sending and receiving gratitude.

The Benefits of Strength of Self and Connection to Others

Mediation is a dispute resolution process that involves a mediator or impartial third party working with direct parties to a conflict to improve the quality of their conflict communication process. Mediation is appealing, in part, because parties maintain a high degree of control of the conflict process and any outcomes. Also, because parties are in control, any solutions they agree upon are more likely to be integrative and creative (Billikopf, 2009). To protect against mediators pushing parties toward conflict resolution (when it may not be what the parties want or to what they will feel invested) and otherwise acting in dominating ways that run counter to known benefits of mediation, Bush and Folger (1994, 2004) proposed the empowerment and recognition framework for clarifying what should ideally be accomplished in the mediation process. More fundamentally, the empowerment and recognition framework makes sense to people who seek to account for both valuing individual strength and for valuing concern for others.

Empowerment is about strengthening the self. It can occur in terms of clarity of goals, awareness of options, development of skills, access to resources, and enhanced decision making. Empowering experiences are those that provide greater "self-worth, security, self-determination, and autonomy" (Bush & Folger, 1994, p. 87). *Recognition* is about strengthening concern for others. It can occur in terms of consideration of giving recognition, desire for giving recognition, giving recognition in thought, giving recognition in words, and giving recognition in actions. Recognition is when a person "realizes and enacts [their] capacity to acknowledge, consider, and be concerned about others" (Bush & Folger, 1994, p. 91). Notably, receiving recognition is, narrowly-speaking, an instance of empowerment because it is personally strengthening to be affirmed. Furthermore, empowerment and recognition are not mutually exclusive or zero-sum since, for example, the empowering reception of recognition could trigger a reciprocal act of recognition that could lead to an improved relationship, implying ongoing mutual recognition, that could enhance empowerment for all parties through the sharing of networks and material resources.

In positioning empowerment and recognition in relation to gratitude communication, it bears repeating (from the commentary on the opening story) that one benefit of any act of gratitude is recognition achieved by the sender. In experiencing the feeling of gratitude and acting on it (not necessarily in that order!), the sender experiences enhanced appreciation of and connection with another. Many other recognition benefits and empowerment benefits are also possible, as will be seen.

INSIGHTS BASED ON ORIGINAL RESEARCH

Empowerment and Recognition in Gratitude Communication

Results were found for both empowerment and recognition in the many accounts of sending and receiving gratitude communication. Benefits could be sorted in terms of benefits for the sender and receiver personally, the sender and receiver professionally, and for the wider organization. While the presentation of findings is done in a narrow manner, focusing on either empowerment or recognition in one particular sphere in one particular account, any given account virtually always contained a combination of benefits. Before presenting these discrete examples, a combination will be explored in one case.

Combination

• Many Benefits Extending Thanks to Front Office Staff With a Special Lunch
James is an executive vice president for a boutique investment firm owned by a much larger company. He and other investment advisors showed their appreciation to their front office staff by paying for lunch at the restaurant of one of their city's premier hotels and covering the phones so the staff could take their time enjoying themselves. James noted various benefits:

> *Well, it promoted customer loyalty. When you compliment someone, they try to live up to that expectation, in most instances. And obviously the more efficient that you have an operation the more profitable that you should be, and the better service that you can offer to clients if you have a happy employee. You can't have happy clients if you don't have happy employees—my opinion. … [W]hen the employees do something collectively, it encourages them working together and to have a positive attitude about each other when they share something nice.*

The expression of appreciation by James and fellow investment advisors was beneficial in functioning as an act of professional recognition by these senders. The lunch payment, office coverage, and opportunity to enjoy themselves outside of office activities was personally empowering for the front office staff. James directly noted how this expression of thank you also fostered a sense of professional empowerment among those at lunch (e.g., "happy employees") that would lead to continued or better empowerment for clients (e.g., "happy clients") and empowerment for the overall firm (e.g., "efficient" and "profitable"). Recognition was also fostered among employees (e.g., "a positive attitude about each other").

Empowerment

Empowerment benefits were most common for sender and receiver as individual professionals, then the wider organization, and then for the sender and receiver individuals in a personal capacity.

Empowerment: Sender and Receiver, Personal

These are examples of personal empowerment beyond typical work roles.

- Thanks and Keep Your Home

Alec owns a small automotive repair business. He learned that one of his most valued employees had fallen behind on his home mortgage payments because of all of the obligations he was juggling. Without the employee asking, Alec demonstrated his gratitude by offering to lend him money to get caught up on his mortgage. Alec described the benefit:

> He was happy. He seemed somewhat relieved that he didn't have that pressure any longer and he wasn't going to lose his house. … The benefit was that he would still remain in his house and he wouldn't have to worry about finding an alternative home and then finding a new place for his wife, his mother-in-law, his children. They all live under his roof.

Access to money empowered the employee in addressing his housing needs.

- Thanks, Provides Reassurance You're a Worthy Person

Paige is early in her career with a financial services company. Over the past 2 years, she has been completing exams covering different financial regulations. One exam she completed was the Series 6. Another was the Series 63. In preparation for each, Paige's company held test preparation training, with each led by a different outside instructor. Paige so enjoyed the first training and credited it with allowing her to easily pass the Series 6 exam. She did not enjoy or find the second training nearly as helpful, though she did manage to pass that exam too. After the second training, Paige located the email address of the instructor for the first event and wrote a message of appreciation. Paige articulated the benefit:

> I think the benefits were just the reassurance that … he's just a great, great guy in general and he really made a memorable experience.

Recognition from Paige to the instructor about being a good person is empowering for him as an individual.

- Thanks, With Bread Leads to a Belly Full of Good Feeling as a Human
Jordan has owned his dental practice for decades. Despite his many years in business, he is always moved when patients express their gratitude to him at the holidays. One patient who is a baker on the weekends brought in fresh rolls, bread, and sweet rolls for Jordan for taking care of him over the years. Jordan and his family get to enjoy the baked goods, but Jordan himself primarily recognized the benefit as the good feeling he experienced. Jordan explained:

> It's just a wonderful feeling that people go out of their way, when people treat them nice, to do something in return. … [In this situation,] I would describe myself as just a human being accepting gifts from someone that cares, that's expressing their gratitude. I don't think of myself as an employee, manager, anything, just one human being to another giving some thanks.

While fresh baked goods can be seen to have empowered Jordan in terms of his dietary needs and indulgences, affirmation that he is a good person is empowering to him as a person.

- Professional Thanks Leads to Personal Friendship and Trust
Roy owns a dollar store with two partners. While their original agreement was for Roy to manage the operation and the other partners to act as passive investors, one of the partners, Steve, took to helping out Roy from time to time. Roy has repeatedly extended his appreciation to Steve for taking over "probably 20%" of what Roy used to do. Roy noted one benefit:

> Individually the trust got even stronger, I think we're really tight right now, friends-wise, and I think, he counts on me a little bit more, too.

Roy's appreciation was part of a gratitude communication episode that empowers Steve in having a friend and being able to rely on a friend.

Empowerment: Sender and Receiver, Professional
- A Thank You That Empowers a Teacher

Gwen is the executive director of a private preschool from Chapter 3. As part of a performance review, she expressed appreciation to a teacher for what she was contributing to the organization and combined this with encouragement for the teacher to get credentialed. The credentialing would help both the preschool and the teacher but Gwen indicated the benefit she most valued:

> [F]or me it's more about empowerment and helping teachers see what they don't always see inside themselves.

- Thank You from Top Leadership Amounts to Freedom to Do My Work and Keep on Delivering Results, Including Financial Results

Jill is the research director at a leading pharmaceutical company. She and her team were tasked with closing down an entire facility, a potentially time-consuming and costly process. They made such incredible progress that they caught the attention of the president of Jill's division, and he sent messages of appreciation over the phone and by email. Jill shared these messages with her direct reports. She described the main benefit she experienced of receiving the thanks:

> [I]t's empowering. So if you've got good visibility, line of sight to your senior, senior leaders and they're giving you [the] endorsement that you're doing a good job, 'We don't have to micromanage this department, we don't have to send constant reminders because they're doing what they need to do.' I think, again, using the word empowering; it's empowering and it allows us to continue business as usual.

- Expression of Appreciation Motivates Me to Contribute More and Let's Me Know My Supervisor Is on the Same Page

Dwight, the head of a university library, found himself working under a new supervisor, an associate dean. In his yearly review meeting, his supervisor expressed her appreciation for a number of special projects that Dwight had advanced. It was motivating to have a supervisor acknowledge these extra efforts. Dwight described the benefit:

I got this positive feedback, it made me much more likely to want to continue to do this. The library has been, over the last couple of years, undergoing some changes with the new administration, reorganization and things like that. It made me think that the new person to whom I was now reporting actually understood what it was that I was doing, which wasn't necessarily always done before.

- Chairman Relays Empowering Client Gratitude to Manager, and Manager Relays It to Supervisors

Rodney, from Chapter 4, is the manager for an outsource staffing company of 5,000 employees that gets many contracts related to traffic and toll management. He was walking down the hall at his company's headquarters when the company chairman stopped him to share appreciation from a client on the good job he and his team were doing. Rodney explained,

[I]t was empowering. ... I try to relay that to my team all the time so that it empowers them, as well, to do a good job.

- Expressing Gratitude Creates Opportunity to Fix Problem Involving a Client

If you remember Rodney's story from Chapter 4, when one of the contract workers that Rodney oversees was in conflict with a salaried employee at the client's organization, and the client did not immediately dismiss the contract worker (as typically happens in this scenario), Rodney expressed his appreciation to the client. Not only was he able to express his gratitude face to face (as mentioned in Chapter 4), this also strengthened Rodney's ability to fix the situation and not lose the placement of a contract worker:

[W]hen you express gratitude ... they give you an opportunity to correct the problem.

- Appreciation Seen as a Sales Motivator

As a Housing and Urban Development manager tasked with selling foreclosed homes by overseeing contracted sales agents, Liz, introduced in Chapters 3 and 4, expressed her appreciation to her contracted sales agents for their part in reaching overall sales goals and for being exceptionally communicative about dealing with setbacks along the way. Liz described the benefit:

I think that the contractors are working harder to sell properties because they've realized that it's not just work; that they're being appreciated for what they've done. I have gotten the impression that they have felt that they've been kept in the dark a lot, and I try to be as open and communicative with them as I can be.

Empowerment: Wider Organization

• Recognizing a Good Job by One Sends a Message of Goodwill to All in the Organization

If you recall, Brendan from Chapter 4 works at a large grocery store and was thanked and awarded Associate of the Year for doing an exemplary job serving customers, particularly a woman who is blind and relies heavily on him to help her shop. The general manager who gave him the award spoke to a major benefit:

I think the benefit is bigger for the organization in general, so that way other associates see that we recognize associates for good deeds, good services to customers, and I think it actually spreads goodwill.

• Thanks, Promotes Knowledge of a Leader, Good Leadership Practices, and Inspiration For Making a Similar Difference

Jeff shared the good fortune and thanks he communicated when recognizing Kelly for 5 years of excellent work at their natural personal care products company. He described the benefits for the organization:

The benefits for some people that don't work with this individual day in and day out … were to get a clear understanding of what type of leader she is and the examples that she uses to motivate people. And also, to inspire others to take unique approaches to leading people and understand their impact they can have on people.

• Thank You Promotes Overall Retention

Angela, from Chapter 3, is a senior director of technology for a data services company. She called out a team of five people in a larger group meeting that included over 50 people. She expressed gratitude for the hard work they had done in completing a project that involved decreasing response time in the Philippines. She followed the large group recognition by taking the team and some colleagues who work closely with them out for lunch. Angela noted a couple of clear benefits around retention, even beyond those who were directly recognized. For instance, the lunch entourage included a couple of newer individuals who were not part of the Philippines project. Angela explained: "I think that both of these guys are fairly insecure with their position in the company. I think it made them feel better to realize that they were on a team that has a successful track record." More broadly, all those who took in the gratitude message hopefully were impacted in terms of wanting to stay with the organization, again as described by Angela:

> [R]etention is gonna be big for us in the next year. We have gone through, we're finishing a buyout, and we are changing technology platforms. These guys are groundbreakers in the newer technology, which is the technology of choice for our company going forward. And, frankly, I think any goodwill we can put forward in some of these new groups is going to attract other people into these groups, as well as retaining the talent we want to retain.

- Gratitude Expression From My Supervisor to Me and Top Leaders Shares Effective Ideas and Gave Me Confidence and Clarified Our Goal Direction and Alignment

Tonya is a regional manager for a temporary housing provider. Tonya and her company work closely with insurance adjusters and others to support individuals and families displaced because of emergencies such as natural disasters. Tonya's supervisor expressed gratitude to Tonya by email while also reaching out to the owners of the almost 200-person company. Tonya's supervisor included examples of Tonya's methods that "some of the other regional managers might benefit from knowing." Tonya also benefited from her rising confidence: "[I]t's given me a lot of confidence to be able to talk to people at different levels within the range that I should." And Tonya found this gratitude process had helped her get clear about the trajectory of the organization:

> Just having that exchange, we know that we're both headed in the right direction. ... I know who the owners are and I know their hearts so I know what's important to them ... the customer service, that's number one with this business. It also confirms that we're giving that constant message out to our customers. It's just knowing that those things are in alignment. That's a good feeling.

- Gratitude to a Vendor Done in a Way to Inspire Other Vendors

Brendan the general manager of a large chain grocery store showed appreciation to a snack food vendor. He gave the individual an award. Before presenting the award, Brendan photocopied it and later posted it in the stock receiving area of the store. He explained how what he did will probably help his own organization:

> I would say the benefit is probably better for the organization in general. The simple fact is if the vendors see that we're noticing the hard work they do, it might spread and continue through other vendors.

Recognition/Relationship

Recognition benefits were most common for sender and receiver as individual professionals, then the wider organization, and then for the sender and receiver individuals in a personal capacity.

Recognition: Sender and Receiver, Personal

• Listening to and Recognizing One Another's Feelings Brings About Closer Relationships After a Tragic Loss

Howard is the lead attorney in the law firm he owns. Howard, the other attorneys, and the staff were shocked when Neil, a senior attorney in the firm, was murdered. The months since have been difficult for everyone. To show his appreciation for everyone continuing their work, Howard organized a special dinner. Howard identified the main benefits, including listening to one another's feelings and generally strengthening relationships in the group:

> I think it made us all closer. I also brought a psychologist to the dinner, kind of unbeknownst to them. It was almost like a working therapy session, too, so that was a benefit, that everybody got to talk about what they were feeling. Instead of us just having a dinner and making a party of it, I wanted there to be some meaning behind it, too. So, everybody got to talk about Neil, their relationship with him, how they feel about things and maybe how it was gonna change their lives.

• Appreciating What They Do as Professionals by Appreciating Who They Are as People

Brad, from Chapter 4, is the parks and recreation director for a township. Each year, to show his appreciation to his full- and part-time staff, he hosts a lunch in their honor. At the event, he makes a point of asking about and listening carefully to learn about his employees' personal lives. Brad described,

I think it's just a good way to connect with employees I don't necessarily get to interact with [them] on a day-to-day basis. I'll ask about their families, it's not just work related. I'll ask, if they're doing anything, if they're traveling, just to learn a little bit more. And I think for them, I think they actually get a sense that I do appreciate what they do and that the township in general does appreciate what they do.

- Thank You With Cupcakes Because I Appreciate You, Our Friendship, and Our Ability to See Each Other's Point of View

Cal is a senior account executive at a marketing and communications company. He does not bake or even cook all that much but, when his account supervisor's birthday was coming up, he decided to bake some cupcakes. Cal knew it would be a hit because she was an avid baker. He wanted to show her:

[H]ey, you're appreciated. I know I give you a lot of shit sometimes. I don't necessarily turn in my time sheets on time, that sort of thing. But I wanted to let her know, you know, thank you for keeping me on track.

Cal spoke more about what he was trying to achieve with the gesture:

I wanted her to know that I appreciated her and that I appreciated our friendship and the ability for both of us to see where the other one was coming from and working together for something common.

- Appreciation for Running a First Marathon

Tracy is a recruiter at a rental car company from Chapter 4. One morning, soon after completing her first marathon, she was surprised when she walked into her office:

I came into work and walked into my office, opened the door and turned on the lights and just saw the decorations. And I saw a card on my desk so I opened it and the message was just very, [Me], you know, we're very proud of you and this is such a great accomplishment, and congratulations. And then [my colleagues] came in and hugged me and, you know, just like we're so proud of you. So that's really kind of, again, how it—it was small but again, it meant a lot.

This appreciation was recognition of Tracy's hard work and achievement in her personal life. It also demonstrated how the organization valued caring, supportiveness, and relationships beyond the workplace.

[I]t's just something that really showed me that they cared and again, that they thought it was important, personally, not just all from work. It was something small but it really did mean a lot. … I think it just goes to show that the company supports our employees no matter what they're doing—something important to them outside of work or inside of work, and that our relationships at work are very professional but also very supportive of each other, regardless of what we're doing.

Recognition: Sender and Receiver, Professional

- The President Let Me Know I Was Appreciated and My Good Work Recognized

Brittany is the development coordinator in a chapter office of a not-for-profit organization seeking to help those with a particular disease and cure the disease. She talked about receiving an award from the chapter president because her supervisor nominated her for work leading a team associated with a campaign. Among the benefits, Brittany noted how much it meant to receive appreciation and have her work noticed:

It made me feel really good because a lot of places that I've worked at I didn't really feel appreciated and I felt like whatever I was doing was not being recognized.

She emphasized how much she valued the recognition aspect of appreciation:

[W]hen the president is reading the names that have been nominated you want to hear your name.

- The Appreciation Itself Was Recognition and the Relationship Component Between Sender and Receivers Was Also Notable

Rick was introduced in Chapter 3 and is a social networking manager at marketing and communications company. When asked to give a year-end presentation to his firm on a highly successful client campaign, he included an appreciation shout-out to the media relations person and blogging person who worked with him on the campaign. There was recognition in terms of acknowledgement of the achievement to him and visibility in front of colleagues. It also benefited the relationships within the team, including among the sender and receivers. And it offered other benefits—obvious empowerment-related benefits—including productivity, service excellence, and profitability. Rick explained:

Everyone likes to be recognized. The benefits for them was the visibility into some of the work—it was a very successful campaign, hence that's why we were in front of the agency presenting it. So, to get their recognition and to be noticed in front of the agency and the executives for their work, yeah, I would assume was a benefit in and of itself. For the agency, the organization, I mean it's kind of a long tale but, you know, afterwards it only strengthened our working relationship, and with a strengthened working relationship then obviously we're more productive as a team and so that translates into better service for clients and then, you know, into higher retainers or things like that.

- Sending a Thank You Card After Interviewing Shows Respect and Caring

Ella is a community liaison for a hospital. When she was applying for the position and mainly dealing with the director of business development, she followed up her on-site interview by sending a hard copy thank you card. It communicated respect and caring to the director of business development and feedback from this person to Ella let her know that it made a difference in her getting the job. Ella explained:

I think the benefits to the organization were that they knew that I was appreciative of the opportunity, and it made it easier to make a decision in the hiring process for them. I think that the gratitude itself, people within any organization, respond well to people showing them thankfulness. That's something I do in my job a lot, communicating with others, and I think that when, it's just a respect thing if somebody does something that's a favor for you, it's nice to show gratitude and, you know, go a little bit above and beyond if it's appropriate to show them that you care about their efforts.

- Appreciation in This Instance Reinforced the Value of Caring Even Though Caring Wasn't Required Here

Kira is a vice president of human resources at a bank. She had to contact a colleague, Janet, on her day off because Janet was a conduit to the general counsel, and Kira needed to get something signed because it was time-sensitive. Kira described Janet and what Janet did:

Janet is, and always has been, a person that cares not only about just work but doing something for others, because she didn't have to do that.

She could have said I'm not in the office today, or she didn't even have to respond, actually, because she wasn't in the office. She checked her email and she didn't have to.

And by sending a thank you to Janet and letting her know she was "awesome," Kira reinforced the value of caring for each other and their work.

- Award for Fixing Problem Brought Recognition to Me and the Sender My Boss

Zara is a vice president of global sales in a very large financial services company. She had to put all of her regular work aside for 3 solid weeks to clean up a mess that others could not handle. Another group was charged with assessing the performance results associated with an educational seminar for sales representatives but the assessment had not taken place. Zara gathered and analyzed the data and created a report. Not only did she execute effectively but she delivered great news about the results of the program. Zara was awarded an in-house award. It was recognition for her and her recognition helped bring attention to the results she uncovered for the chain of command that provided her award. Zara explained:

The benefit for me was just being recognized and being called out to a number of people [showing them that] I had played this role. The benefit to my boss was that they finally got to put out results that were really positive.

Recognition: Wider Organization

- Gratitude May Be Expressed One Person at a Time but Over Time It Creates Camaraderie

Bill from Chapter 4 is president of a steel heat-treating company. He spoke about thanking a production manager who voluntarily stayed more than 2 hours past the end of his night shift to make sure everything was continuing to go smoothly. Bill talked about the benefit, given the context of regularly expressing this kind of gratitude to all his employees:

It generates a good positive camaraderie, it generates teamwork, which is what I desire of people working together.

- Recognition to Individual from Supervisor Brings Recognition to Whole Organization

Jeff is a customer team leader in a natural consumer products company owned by a parent company. His boss put him up for a major award that involved earning stock options. Approval had to come from both the immediate company and the parent company. Only a small number of awards were given each year. The award was a recognition for Jeff as he explained:

> *I was truly being recognized for making a contribution and being a valued member of the organization. There was an expressed feeling of gratitude that it was a two-way street. I thought, 'I enjoy working for the company, they enjoy having me as part of the company.'*

The award was also a recognition for his supervisor, his CEO, and his organization, again, as Jeff explained:

> *I'm sure for my manager, it probably benefitted him in the respect that he is now looked upon as somebody that's trying to bring recognition to his direct reports, and then we work for a small subsidiary of a larger parent company, so even for our CEO that somebody within the subsidiary is able to get this award. I think it shows the parent company that we do have quality people working in our organization. I would imagine that's a benefit that they would receive.*

- Respecting Each Other's Good Work Is Validating and Beneficial to the Organizational Leader-Sender and the Overall Organization

Helen is the executive director of a non-profit public health organization. She had an outside consultant manager working on a leadership activity with various constituents in a multi-organization network. Helen took the opportunity to catalog the achievements of this group and specifically pointed out the reason for the success had been the consultant-manager's leadership and her style of open communication and sharing credit and to thank her in front of that group. Helen saw the benefits for the consultant manager in getting recognized in front of those with whom she regularly works. She also saw other benefits, including organizational benefits:

> *I think that we get busy working together, even if there's a lot of goodwill, which there is in this instance, kind of universal agreement in this group that we're doing good work and that we enjoy doing it together. Respect each other's contributions to it and so forth. I think that it's not only good to be explicit about that from time to time, it makes everyone feel validated, but also in this case, since this is a multi-organizational, multi-system initiative, I think there's a benefit to me as the organizational leader to acknowledge*

one of my managers as being essential to this process. And it also affirms my organization's leadership in the network.

- Thank You From a Mentee Helped Wake Up an Organization About a Younger Generation's Perspective and Offerings

Monae is a vice president of foreign exchange at a major bank. She hosted an intern, and the intern sent a thank you to Monae and others she met. Monae's effort in bringing in the intern along with the intern's interactions and thank you led to a benefit for the organization. Monae described the outcome:

It was a benefit to the organization, certainly, because it woke up the managers on this side as to what we can be doing outside of the job, the everyday job, what we should be doing to help bring some folks along, to foster understanding of corporate culture to our youth. ... And it was beneficial, I think, in this small part of the organization because it awakened something in the management to say that, you know what, we should do more of this.

- Meaningfully Thanking Is Good for the Relationship and for What the Relationship Can Provide

Brittany is a development coordinator for a chapter of an organization dedicated to serving those affected by a particular disease. She talked about following up with one of her largest individual fundraisers for a bicycle event that she organizes. Brittany expressed her thanks to this gentleman by driving to his work and taking him out to lunch. She explained that benefits included building a relationship to benefit her organization in the future:

It was hard for me to connect with him during the [fundraising]campaign. I always said to him, 'Do you need anything, is there anything that I can do for you?' He was always fine. After the campaign I wanted him to know how thankful I was for everything that he did for us and for making these fundraising numbers so outrageous. I waited 'til after the campaign and then I asked him if he would go have lunch with me. That was my way of expressing gratitude towards him because when we sat at lunch we didn't talk about the bike ride the entire time; we also talked on a personal level and he asked me about my goals and my future and he introduced me to different things for young professionals. Now, if he does need something, he's not shy to ask me for it. He sends me an email and he'll say, 'Hey, Brittany, can you help me with this?' and I'm like yeah, sure, here you go, and I send it right to him. So, I think that helped our campaign next September.

Returning to the Opening Story: Benefits Beyond Those That First Meet the Eye

Gratitude communication can have many benefits, and the empowerment and recognition framework is a powerful tool for making sense of them. Of course, benefits can be understood differently by different people with different perspectives. Relatedly, sometimes even the gratitude act itself can exist for some and not exist for others in a certain circumstance. In once more considering the whale thank you story, it is interesting to note the possibility that the whale winking at Moskito while the diver cut the fishing line from around the whale's face could have been an additional thank you communication. Perhaps this winking was experienced as gratitude recognition by Moskito. If so, perhaps it also had an empowering effect by providing him feedback on the importance of his work and inspiring him to continue his efforts to free the whale.

Chapter Conclusion

This chapter considered the benefits of gratitude communication by understanding gratitude communication with the empowerment and recognition framework. In short, gratitude communication strengthens individuals in professional and personal capacities and it strengthens wider organizations. It also affirms and otherwise develops connections between and among individuals directly and indirectly involved in the sending and receiving of gratitude. The next chapter considers how gratitude communication is most positive and memorable.

Real World Recommendations

- The possible benefits of gratitude communication are many but can be summarized in terms of empowerment benefits (strengthening the self and entities such as organizations) and recognition benefits (strengthening concern for and connection to others).

- Any appropriate and effective act of gratitude is beneficial because it demonstrates recognition by the sender.

- Expressions of gratitude often entail two or more empowerment and/or recognition benefits.

- Gratitude communication empowerment and recognition benefits can be at the personal, professional, and/or at the organization levels.

- An awareness of the gratitude communication empowerment and recognition potentialities can be helpful for more fully realizing gratitude communication's benefits whether you are a past or future sender or receiver.

Your Opportunity to Work With Gratitude

- Reflect on a positive and memorable instance of gratitude communication in which you were directly involved as a sender or a receiver. Consider the ways that the expression of gratitude was beneficial in terms of empowerment and recognition for the various parties directly and indirectly involved.

- Brainstorm a genuine expression of gratitude you could direct toward a specific receiver in the days ahead. Tailor three different versions of the expression of gratitude with each version demonstrating some difference in the empowerment and/or recognition benefits. Finally, select and explain your selection of the optimal version for you to use.

Questions for Reflection and Discussion

- What are advantages and disadvantages to assessing gratitude communication benefits with each of the following methods: (a) accessing a transcript of the actual sending and receiving of gratitude communication; (b) accessing a video recording of the actual sending and receiving of gratitude communication; and (c) interviewing the sender(s) and/or receiver(s) after the expression of gratitude?

- How might insight into the organizational culture provide important information for assessing the benefits of a specific instance of gratitude communication? How could an outsider best come to learn about an organizational culture at it relates to a specific instance of gratitude communication?

Recommendations for Learning More

- *Fast Company Magazine* and its corresponding web site often address gratitude as a concept relevant to the cutting edge professional and workplace. Do an Internet search for "Fast Company gratitude" to see some article options. The following link takes you to an article on gratitude communication benefits. Notice how all the listed benefits are empowerment-related, and there is no mention of recognition.

- The empowerment and recognition framework (Bush & Folger, 1994, 2004) used in this chapter was originally developed for conflict interaction during which people are often feeling and acting their worst. Times of gratitude communication are often a time when people are feeling and acting their best. Read more about empowerment and recognition from a conflict interaction standpoint and consider how these concepts might need to be extended beyond what was covered in this chapter of the usually positive topic of gratitude communication. Possibly read *The Promise of Mediation: Responding to Conflict Through Empowerment and Recognition* (Bush & Folger, 1994) and *The Promise of Mediation: The Transformative Approach to Conflict* (Bush & Folger, 2004). Also visit the authors' Institute for the Study of Conflict Transformation, which can be accessed at this link:

6

What Makes Gratitude Communication Most Positive and Memorable?

"First learn the meaning of what you say, and then speak."

—Epictetus

Surprise! You're the Owners of a Lakefront View

Judee Burgoon (1993) shared a simple yet revealing story about the power of gratitude deriving from the degree of positive surprise in the overview of her work on expectancy violations theory and emotional communication. Every year growing up, she and her family summered at a cabin on a lake. Much to their anger and disappointment, they had a neighbor there who routinely parked his car and trailer in a location in his yard that blocked their view of the lake. This remained the case long after another neighbor diplomatically pointed out the situation to the offending neighbor! But then one year, seemingly out of the blue, the offending neighbor repositioned his vehicle and trailer and never again went back to parking it in its old spot. Judee's family got access to their view and felt immensely grateful, so much so they became friends with the neighbor.

The Deep Resonance of Positive Surprise

The theme of positive surprise is central to the impact of the lakefront view story. Both the surprise element and the positivity element were so great because Judee's family's impression of the neighbor and the situation were so strongly and seemingly permanently negative before suddenly and radically shifting into the positive. The theme of positive surprise provides an overall explanation for what often (but not always) made gratitude communication most positive and memorable for the individuals interviewed for this book. The theme of positive surprise sprang from not only participants' direct explanations for what made gratitude communication most positive and memorable in specific instances, but also implicitly in some of the interviewees' explanations that were better themed under a different primary category.

Although prior chapters mainly have focused on the gratitude communication expressed from one or more senders to one or more receivers, those interviewed routinely spoke about what might be termed the larger gratitude communication episode when asked to determine what was most positive and memorable. An episode encompasses the event or events that a given sender and/or receiver associated with initiating the gratitude communication response as well as the narrower gratitude messaging itself. Notice how the lakefront view story was vivid for Judee, not in the details of how she and her family expressed gratitude but what inspired it. The lakefront view story is emblematic of the need to recognize the episodic nature of gratitude communication. Nonetheless, for some interviewees, what was most positive and memorable for them was the act of gratitude itself.

In terms of direct explanations for specific instances of gratitude communication being particularly positive and memorable, interviewees' responses could be organized into 12 categories, which will be detailed in the Insights section. Before discussing the categories and providing examples of what made specific instances of gratitude communication episodes particularly positive and memorable, the Theoretically Speaking section will explore expectancy violations theory (Burgoon, 1993) to explain the strong connection between gratitude communication and positive surprise.

THEORETICALLY SPEAKING

A Robust Theory to Explain What Makes Many Gratitude Communication Episodes Stand Out

Expectancy violations theory (Burgoon, 1993) explains how behavioral expectations play an important role in interpersonal relationships and how negative or positive deviations from what is considered normal can act as turning points.

Expectancy violations theory helps us understand how people can violate our expectations in bad ways but also do so in good ways as well. The roots of expectancy violations theory are in research studies and theorizing around the use personal space (Burgoon, 1978; Burgoon & Jones, 1976). This was expanded to address emotional communication in general (Burgoon, 1993). Expectancy violations theory continues to be used in novel ways such as explaining how recent college graduates responded to unanticipated situations occurring as part of their job searches (Smith, 2017).

Burgoon's (1993) article titled "Interpersonal Expectations, Expectancy Violations, and Emotional Communication" is particularly applicable to gratitude communication and not only because it includes the gratitude anecdote shared at the outset of this chapter about a positive violation triggering feelings of gratitude and related behaviors. It provides a model often relevant to episodes of gratitude communication.

Two expectancy violations theory concepts are foundational. The first of these concepts is *expectancies* (Burgoon, 1993) or behaviors that are anticipated according to social norms and the past behaviors of a specific individual. Expectancies are shaped by the communicator, relationship, and context. Expectancies allow us to frame our interactions with others (Goffman, 1974, as cited in Burgoon, 1993). The second foundational concept is an expectancy violation. A *violation* occurs when a communicator is determined to have acted in any manner, to any degree, to any effect outside of expectations.

Other important aspects of expectancy violations theory include communicator reward valence, arousal potential, violation valence, evaluation, and interaction patterns and outcomes (Burgoon, 1993). *Communicator reward valence* is the net positive or net negative reward value of the sender as judged by the receiver. It gives context to the violation when the situation is ambiguous. *Arousal potential* means a violation is experienced as a triggered emotion or, more simply, a distraction to a certain degree, either positive or negative from a baseline of what is normal. This involves alertness and/or emotion. *Violation valence* is the degree to which the act is judged to be outside of normal. Putting all these aspects together, the receiver engages in *evaluation* or makes sense of the violation. Positive violations that are relatively stronger in violation valence are more likely to lead to positive interactions and other outcomes.

Expectancy violations theory offers many explanations for how gratitude communication episodes or, more narrowly, gratitude actions can be especially positive and memorable. Positive and memorable violations can lead to specific gratitude communications. Gratitude communications can themselves be or include positive and memorable violations. Gratitude communication can be enhanced with the involvement, especially the surprise involvement, of a high reward, possibly a high status, individual. A gratitude communicator can generate positive surprise by positively going beyond expectations based on past net negative or past net positive reward value. These are just some examples of how expectancy violations theory can apply to gratitude communication.

INSIGHTS BASED ON ORIGINAL RESEARCH

What Makes Gratitude Communication Episodes Most Positive and Memorable Is Largely an Element of Positive Surprise

The number of categories for responses to the question of what made specific gratitude communication episodes especially positive and memorable was quite high. But providing this level of detail was judged to be important for reflecting the breadth of responses and for indicating applied opportunities for others in the future. Participants' reports were categorized as follows: deep personal meaning; strong positive emotion (other than surprise); surprise; challenging overall situation; recognition of notable effort; the role of primacy; high status involvement; gratitude rarely happening in this particular organization; routine element; key financial element; previously unrecognized individuals; and shared aspect of gratitude reception. The categories are ordered according to overall frequency across all gratitude communication story types for all interview participants. These categories are demonstrated with examples below. Although some responses fit more than one category, other responses did not clearly fit even one of these categories. Some of these miscellaneous instances are shared below.

Surprise (as in positive surprise) was mentioned specifically by some participants and, therefore, it has its own category. However, surprise and, therefore, the relevance of expectancy violations theory is evident in most of the other categories. Here are some very brief descriptions of how this can be the case.

- Deep personal meaning: These episodes can at least occasionally be a violation from work events that typically do not have such a high degree of personal meaning.

- Strong positive emotion: These episodes may be violations of more typical mid-range or even lower than mid-range emotional states or moods.

- Challenging overall situation: These episodes can involve violations in terms of participants expecting events to go badly but at least the gratitude communication aspect is unexpectedly bright.

- Recognition of notable effort: The violation here may be effort beyond what is normal.

- The role of primacy: The first time a particular event occurs can be an instance of violating what is typical or expected.

- High status involvement: There may be a violation in the fact that high status individuals are not typically involved with this particular issue or these other individuals.

- Gratitude rarely happening in this particular organization: The violation is in terms of what is normal in this particular organization.

- Key financial element: A financial element may not be usual.

- Previously unrecognized individuals: The violation is in terms of what is normal for this individual.

- Shared aspect of gratitude reception: The violation may be that gratitude communication is not typically shared or shared so broadly.

The "routine element" category is an anticipated area to address by stakeholders in an organization; therefore, if it is missed, it is not consistent with expectancy violations theory.

Deep Personal Meaning

- Thank You for Providing an Opportunity That Positively Impacts My Whole Life

Hector is an office manager for a medical supplier. When the company flew him across the country for training and he met his manager in person for the first time, he expressed thanks to her for the opportunity and the financial investment the company was making in him. Hector spoke about how his expression of gratitude came as a result of the life changing nature of what the company had provided to him:

> That was my first time I ever met my potential supervisor and it might be drastic but it changed my life—a new job, new things to do, bringing income to my pocket, so I can do stuff. And I basically wanted her to know that I was thankful and it was because of her that I'm getting opportunities.

- My Colleagues Showed Appreciation for Me Completing My First Marathon

Remember Tracy, the recruiter for a major rental car company introduced in Chapter 5? She returned to work after running her first marathon earlier in the year. If you remember, her colleagues recognized her hard work and achievement with decorations, a card on her desk, hugs, and words of congratulations. It was most positive and memorable to Tracy that her co-workers appreciated her effort, achievement, and the personal meaning of what she accomplished,

[R]unning a marathon definitely takes up a lot of your personal time, as well as work time, and such a huge commitment that you're making. And, you know, I wanted to show them, hey, if I can commit to something, you know, a goal, I'm committed to it and I'm gonna work to achieve it and hopefully inspire them that they can do that, too. You know, so I just think that it's awesome to show them that, and to have their support was amazing.

- A Thank You of Pictures Closely Connecting Me With a High-Status Politician have Personal Meaning

Roger from Chapter 4 is a communications consultant specializing in work for politicians. When working with a particular politician client, this person's staff would take photos of the two of them. After the politician won a recent election, he had his staff print five or six of the photos in an 8 by 10-inch format. He wrote "personal detailed notes" on each photo, signed each photo, and sent them as a thank you to Roger. Despite the photos potentially being of significant financial value because "some people include this person on a list of potential presidents someday," Roger commented that he and his wife value the personal meaning of them the most.

You know, we would have been thrilled just to get one of these photos but as I recall there were five or six of them. And we framed them, my wife framed them for me, and now we display them on our wall.

- Volunteer Board Member Valued Appreciation That Was More Individualized

Mika is vice president of strategy for a physicians' services company. She is also active as a board member for a non-profit organization. When she took over a board committee leadership position, she was thanked by a fellow board committee member in the moment, by email, and in a phone call. This more senior board member expressed gratitude that she was on his team. He mentioned her skill set. He also invited her to join other board initiatives, which meant a lot to Mika. However, Mika spoke about how it was especially positive and memorable for her:

> It stood out over others because it was a higher concentration on me and not so much the group that I belonged to or the organization. It was more of a personal sense of gratitude and a personal dialogue about me. I was at the center of it.

Strong Positive Emotion

• I Did Not Expect People to Be So Moved by the Thank You

Angela is a senior director of technology at a data services company. She and some of her team members worked on a very complicated project to reduce response time at an office in the Philippines. To show her appreciation, she recognized a handful of key individuals in a group meeting of over 50 people. She also took the key individuals to lunch along with a few others. Angela mentioned a major reason the episode was particularly positive and memorable:

> [S]ometimes people can turn up their nose or just shrug their shoulders and walk off when you do something nice for them. But in this particular instance, because the parties involved seemed very moved by it, it was more memorable to me because of that; the reaction that they had.

• These Kinds of Situations Give Me an Extremely Good Feeling

Howard is an owner and leasing manager of four shopping centers. He was speaking with a potential tenant who was interested in setting up a dress store. The potential tenant envisioned spending a considerable amount of money renovating the space, including installing expensive floor tiles. Given his experience growing up in a family of dress shop owners, Howard helped the aspiring shop owner realize she could establish her business without such a large investment in interior design. He also made recommendations to her and her business partner about how best to layout the space and where to affordably purchase the basic display items they would need. The main business owner and her partner thanked Howard. He shared the reason this and other such episodes were positive and memorable:

It always makes me feel good to help any of the tenants and/or clients that we have in our shopping centers. And knowing the relationship that I have with most of them, this gives me an extremely good feeling.

- The Sender Was so Grateful to Me He Was Almost in Tears

Austin, a dentist, was out for a nice dinner with his wife on a Saturday evening. They had wonderful evening, in part, because the service they received from their waiter was excellent. He was friendly and decent looking but Austin could not help but notice that one of his front teeth was badly chipped. Austin gave the man his business card and said he wanted to fix his tooth. The waiter graciously accepted the card but explained that he was not in a position to pay for the work. When Austin said, "I won't even charge you, just come in, I'll fix it," the waiter was floored. After Austin did the work, the man immediately thanked him and followed up with a nice card. Austin described what made the episode most positive and memorable:

Well, it was memorable for me because when I finished working on him, he couldn't believe how good he looked. He couldn't believe he was walking around like that and he was literally almost in tears.

- I Had a Lot of Feeling and Those to Whom I Expressed My Thanks Shared That Feeling

Aaron is a sales and marketing coordinator for a sports licensing company. Prior to taking this position, he was an assistant equipment coordinator for a professional sports team. As Aaron was exiting his last organization, he expressed his appreciation in person to the HR manager and via email to the entire internal organization for being able to work there. Aaron characterized the response to his email:

I definitely got a ton of replies back; [they were] very excited for me, thanking me for the email, my professionalism; they said and how important I was to the organization and how I would be deeply missed. At the end, [this] really felt good for me, on the back end knowing that I did have significance in the organization—that was very big. And a lot of people were upset to see me go but very happy and excited for me.

Aaron described what made the episode most positive and memorable for him: "I was willing to express emotion and people were willing to join me in it in my future move to the organization I'm with now."

Surprise

• Surprise End of Year Thanks Visit From a Contractor With Gifts

Andy is a banquet manager at a golf club and catering venue. At the end of the year, the operators of a DJ business with which his venue frequently contracts brought in gift cards, cookies, and chocolate, and extended thanks for Andy's business and for being very easy to work with. Andy recalled what made the expression of appreciation most positive and memorable:

> It was out of the blue. I really wasn't expecting it. There are some things that you're used to getting and you kind of take it for granted at times, but this was something that was just out of the blue. So, it was nice to have that.

• Thanked by Another Wedding Guest Regarding My Professional Role Was Nice Surprise

Scott is a township manager. He attended the wedding for one of the township employees, and a township resident, whose name he knew but whom he never had met in person, approached him. Scott recalled the situation:

> [H]e wanted to meet me, wanted to introduce himself because he had heard I was doing a good job, which, coming from this person, he could have treated me like the busboy there at the wedding, but instead made a big deal of it and sought me out and acknowledged that he had heard I was doing a good job, which certainly for me, carried some weight.

Scott also commented on what made the interaction most positive and memorable: "I guess because I didn't expect it, I was taken by surprise, it was nice."

• Spontaneous Thanks From Multiple People at the Start of a Meeting Was Encouraging

Brad is a director of parks and recreation for a township. He was at a business development association meeting for the first time and was pleased and surprised when, during the round of self-introductions, numerous attendees thanked him for his work on a recent community triathlon he had organized. Brad commented on what made it most positive and memorable for him:

> I think just the kind of spontaneous nature of it was. It's encouraging. …
> I didn't know any of the individuals who spoke because I didn't directly
> oversee the volunteers; we had over 110, 120 volunteers last year so it's not

like I even got to personally thank each and every one of them. It was one of those things that I just didn't expect it and I have no idea why it kind of happened.

- Unexpected Appreciation From Industry Colleagues in the Airport

Tonya is a regional manager for a temporary housing organization whose direct clients are insurance companies. She was in an airport with three company colleagues after a tradeshow, and some individuals who worked for an insurance adjuster approached them. The insurance people could tell that Tonya and her colleagues were at the same tradeshow because they carried company bags and wore company-branded clothes. The insurance people expressed appreciation in person to Tonya and her colleagues for their professionalism in terms of their professional, branded image and how well they got along with one another. In other words, they genuinely liked each other. One person from the group even sent a follow-up email that Tonya shared with her company. Tonya noted what made the episode most positive and memorable:

Oh, the reason why it was so poignant was because it was in such an offbeat setting, unsolicited and just unexpected that we'd even be noticed.

Challenging Overall Situation

- Our Company Was Dying so a Buyout and New CEO Led to My Expression of Appreciation

Sharon's story from Chapter 4, functions for the purposes of this chapter. She is a senior director of legal affairs for an entertainment company. The company was not performing well, and it made Sharon and her colleagues uneasy. Fortunately, the tide turned. A private equity organization bought out the company. When the new CEO arrived, she met one-on-one with all those in the senior ranks. The buyout gave Sharon hope, especially because the new CEO seemed to have tremendous vision and energy. During Sharon's meeting with the CEO, Sharon conveyed her gratitude for what the CEO was bringing to the company:

She had one-on-one meetings with people of certain levels in management, and I was invited to have a one-on-one meeting with her. She asked me what she thought the best asset of the company was and what would be our best chance going forward of having success. I told her that she was. She was kind of taken aback by my comment. I just told her how much I appreciated her energy, her new ideas, her willingness to think outside the box and, was hoping that she would help us along to become a successful company again.

The fact that the company and Sharon personally had been through uneasy times made her expression of appreciation standout: "It sticks out because, as I mentioned before, our company had been through a lot."

- My Thank You to My Employees Stood Out Because It Was Such a Long Day

Jerry, as mentioned in Chapter 5, manages a golf course that serves out-of-town resort guests and local members. He and his team had a particularly demanding day. In the later evening, after they had completed all of the work and Jerry was home, he sent a group text conveying how "they were amazing and appreciated." Jerry explained what made it all so positive and memorable:

What made it stand out [was that] we were so tired; it was such a long day, it was like a 12, 15-hour day, and I remember thinking that we'll probably never have a busier day than we had that day. I mean there were so many things that went on, different little groups that went on. It wasn't like one big 150-person tournament. It was three or four 40-person tournaments that went on that day, outside of the normal golfers. And I just said to myself we can make it through this and still love each other afterwards and appreciate each other. And there is not gonna be a day this entire year that is going to be more difficult than this, and we came out of it perfectly fine, happier than clams. And it made me feel good about the rest of the year.

- I Thanked an Employee for Going Above and Beyond When I Faced a Personal Setback

Jayne is the owner of a women's clothing and accessories store. She injured herself last fall, and her employees helped keep the business going by taking on some of Jayne's responsibilities. In particular, she thanked one key employee face-to-face and took the person out to dinner. It was most positive and memorable to Jayne because,

I was just impressed with how, people pulled together in a time of need when you don't really expect it. It was nice to be pleasantly surprised that people are there for you.

- The Thank You From My Colleague Meant so Much Because We Came From Such a Bad Place

Angela is a senior director of technology at an information technology company. Her company assigned her to work with a colleague on a project in another country. Angela and her colleague struggled in the beginning in part because their units were set up to be competitive with one another. They had a difficult start to their relationship but Angela "very actively" worked on it, and they got through the project. Just before Thanksgiving, the colleague expressed appreciation to Angela in an email that also went to Angela's boss and her boss's boss. She thanked Angela for her work and remarked on their good relationship. Angela remembered what made the gratitude episode especially positive and memorable:

> I think because we had come from such a bad place. When we first started on this project, she had been pulled in from one of our other offices. She and I had not had a working relationship and her client group was very dysfunctional, they didn't have their act together. Her group and my group are set up as adversaries in our company. I think that she and I, building a partnership relationship this year, [and we've] become personal friends as well. She's actually moved on to a different project, and we still keep in touch when she's in town. So, I think that, that's a positive relationship and I would much rather a relationship with my client be collaborative rather than antagonistic.

- Mother's Day Baseball Tickets Thank You to a Client Was Special Because of How She Recently Sacrificed for a Family Member

Jay is a partner in an accounting firm. To thank the treasurer of one of his biggest clients for the company's business and for her being a great person, Jay surprised her with Mother's Day tickets to her beloved baseball team. Jay explained that what made the act of gratitude particularly positive and memorable was that she had recently been through a lot personally:

> What made this extra special was the fact that this past winter, she had actually just went through surgery. I think her husband needed her kidney or something; like one of those deals where she had to give up part of her kidney ... to a family member. So, she was through a surgery and all that, came out great and all. So, that made it extra special, I guess, to me, because it's kind of like a 'Glad you're feeling better, Happy Mother's Day,' kind of all wrapped up into one, you're a great client.

- Thank You Stood Out Because a Long Project Had Come to a Successful End

Jenny is an instructional designer for a company serving the pharmaceutical industry. She was part of a project team making an online training program for a large medical device manufacturer. Jenny's company anticipated that the project would take 6 months but it went a year beyond because the contracting organization kept changing its mind about key details. A project that was supposed to have two or three drafts ended up involving 12 or 13 iterations. When the project was indeed complete, the medical device organization sent an email of appreciation to Jenny and all those on her team. Jenny commented on what made the episode most positive and memorable:

> *It was just so nice to have the project finally end. When they drag on like that, you're so grateful when it's over that you think it makes it more memorable. And then you get a good story out of it because when you look back a few weeks later you can laugh about how terrible it was.*

Recognition of Notable Effort

- Thank You to a Prospective Hire for Going Out of Her Way to Interview

Matt is a corporate recruiter for a logistics and supply chain company. He was hiring for a high-level position for someone to work closely with the chief financial officer. He had a candidate who needed to meet individually with five top executives in his company, while juggling her then-current job and rush hour driving conditions for at least one of the interviews. Matt repeatedly expressed his appreciation to her over the phone and in person for her flexibility and understanding while also emphasizing what a good fit the position seemed to be for her. Matt remembered what made this instance of appreciation most positive and memorable for him:

> *[S]he had to go through hoops and kind of go out of her way. I wanted to make sure this was a special opportunity.*

- A Great and Worthwhile Effort Beyond Regular Job Duties that Benefitted Charity

Monae is a vice president for foreign exchange in a large bank. She also organizes the annual United Way campaign in her division. In running the campaign, she relies on other volunteers. One colleague in particular was extremely help-ful. Monae expressed appreciation to her by nominating her for a company recognition award. The woman was pleased Monae and the bank recognized her in this way. The recognition included a modest monetary gift. It was most memorable to Monae because the effort beyond ordinary work assignments:

> We all work together and, we've got our daily duties and deadlines and financial things and all those kinds of things that we do here at the bank. But this was outside of the day-to-day. And on top of that it was helping somebody else. When you look at the money that we raised just in our small division and then you contribute that to what the bank gave overall, and the many, many, many charities that were helped, it was just a very, very nice experience. And for people to show gratitude and to, you know, for me to give them something for them helping in such a great effort, it was just great, it was really great.

- Valued the Apparent Extra Effort in the Act of Gratitude Itself

Austin is a dentist who owns his own dental office. Around the holidays, his dental office manager, dental hygienist, and dental assistant showed their appreciation to him by giving him 20 lunches in the form of 20 cards each with $10 in it. They instructed him to bring, open, and read one card at lunch each day. Austin recalled what made it most positive and memorable for him:

> I liked it especially because there was a different little funny message in each card, and that made me feel like they actually worked a little bit and went out of their way rather than just stuffing cash in the envelopes.

- So Much Effort Into a Send-off Appreciation From My Clients

Jessica recently became the director of marketing for a medical laboratory. Prior to taking on this position, she owned a Pilates studio in another city. Around the time she closed the studio, 12 clients organized a dinner at a restaurant to express their appreciation and wish her well. They created a send-off bag of gifts, and one person in particular gave a speech honoring Jessica. One of the things that made it particularly positive and memorable for Jessica was the effort expended for her:

> It was just that I couldn't believe these people had gone to so much trouble just to kind of send me off.

The Role of Primacy

• A Thank You Professional Lunch and a First One-on-One Conversation

David is the head of communications for a large legal organization in a major U.S. city. He thanked his web manager for the amount and quality of work he was doing by inviting him out to lunch. David put considerable thought into the occasion. He purposely chose a restaurant that would give them time to leisurely walk together and chat and he chose a restaurant that had a good selection of vegan menu items given the web manager's diet. What made the occasion most positive and memorable for David, though, was this represented a first in their relationship. He described,

> Because this was my first time I was able to have a one-on-one with this individual outside of the office after several attempts that we had had to go out to lunch. It was hard to find a spot in his schedule, so I was glad that after several attempts we were able to do it.

• The Expression of Appreciation Was Connected to My First Time Being a Manager

Rodney, as introduced in Chapter 5, is the manager in an outsourcing staffing company. He moved from a straightforward supervisory role to this multisite managerial role when the former manager abruptly resigned. Rodney described his anxiety, the apparent anxiety of those he would be directly leading, and what he did about it:

> The employees were used to the previous manager; only a few knew me from being at certain sites but [there] was a lot of, uncertainty of how things were gonna go. So, I went to each facility and basically praised the employees for the job they were doing and showing that I do recognize their importance. And with that it kind of took the tension out of the change and fears in their mind.

Rodney also described what made his act of appreciation especially positive and memorable for him:

> Well, this was my first time being a manager and really it was nothing that I was prepared for. It was like okay, here you are, go and run with it ... I just wanted to eliminate their fears.

- It Was a Particularly Positive and Memorable Thank You Because It Came in Relation to a Kick-Off Event

Raquel is a director in the judicial branch of state government. As a manager, she does not receive overtime pay for extra work responsibilities. Because she was active in the implementation of a new program, she had to come to work on a Sunday. Even though her participation was essentially required, her supervisor thanked her in person that day for "the sacrifice." Raquel noted what made the episode especially positive and memorable:

> I guess because it was an historic event … and it was … a kickoff of something. And everybody was real excited about it. And the fact that the manager just didn't take it in stride, said okay, you're supposed to [do] this, but recognized that even with everything going on that I would give up personal time to help, to make sure that this went off without a hitch.

- Positive and Memorable Because We Never Thanked a Supplier This Way Before

Andy is the banquet manager at a country club. His organization works with a company that provides linens and sashes for chairs. A number of times, he has had to reach out at the last minute to get extra supplies for events such as weddings. To express their gratitude, Andy and his country club sent a card and a gift basket to their linen and sash supplier. Andy explained what made it a positive and memorable acknowledgement:

> It was memorable for me because we never have done that before for anybody in the past, [for] company. Most companies come to us and thank us for giving them business. But it was really the only company that I can remember that we've ever done that for, so it was memorable in that way.

High Status Involvement

- Big City Mayor Participates in Lifetime Achievement Award Presentation

David is the head of communications for a large legal organization in a major U.S. city. Although he is not yet 50 years old, the main professional association to which he belongs awarded him its lifetime achievement award. The award event was an act of appreciation that included David's supervisor, the head of the legal organization, thanking and congratulating David. What made it especially positive and memorable for David was that the mayor was among the people honoring him:

> *Well, the mayor spoke very kindly about me, and usually he'll come and read a proclamation from the city and maybe quote a sentence or two and then leave very fast. But he actually spent a good 10 minutes talking about me, and made my mom cry, so that made me happy.*

- Appreciation From the Head of My Organization and the U.S. President

Ben is head of security for a large organization. In the aftermath of a tragedy, he worked with a large team at his work and with the White House and Secret Service to plan a presidential visit to his organization with only 48 hours' notice. The event stood out in Ben's mind because of its size, the planning efforts to make it successful, and the thanks he received from top leaders of his organization. Ben commented,

> *And I guess the other part that made it most memorable is, about three weeks after this was all done, I got a letter from the president of the United States thanking me, so that was kind of nice.*

- My Supervisor Made a Difference by Expressing Appreciation About Me to the CEO

Ella is a community liaison at a hospital. She was part of a team that ran a banquet event for 500 staff at her facility. The event was challenging because the caterer made a mistake and fell short in the amount of food it prepared. Fortunately, though, Ella and two others were able to remedy the situation. Ella's supervisor, the director of development, followed up the event by sending an email to the CEO expressing appreciation for what Ella and the other members of the event team had accomplished. Ella explained what made it all most positive and memorable:

> *Because she took the time to write an email to our CEO about it. He is fairly high up within the organization and just that she would take the time to do that, to send a written email acknowledging the part that I had in making, making the holiday event a success for everybody, doing my part to do my job and go over and above what's required. She just made sure that we knew about it and that it was done in a very poignant manner. So I think that's the reason why maybe it sticks out to me. I never had a boss*

that did that before so, you know, I had situations where I've been told what I'm doing wrong but I never had someone go above and beyond; to take time to write a long email to one of the top leaders in the company about my superb performance.

- This Moment of Appreciation May Have Stood Out Because It Was in Front of a Higher Level of Leadership

Renée is the human resources director for the United States and Canada for a health products manufacturer based in Europe. She reports to the vice president for human resources. Renée was a key figure in planning and facilitating a session for the top 100 leaders across the Americas in which her regional president and global CEO participated. The event was different from previous years because they relied much more on in-house talent versus outside consultants. In a portion of the event that Renée directly led on positive leadership, she gave an example of her supervisor leading in an exemplary manner. Her supervisor and her president each approached her afterwards and thanked her for her comments. Renée reflected on why the episode was most positive and memorable for her:

I think the one reason why this may stand out is because people expressing gratitude and saying we did a good job when our global leadership team was there. So oftentimes we, just by the nature of our roles, have leaders in the organization. We do things in front of people but we don't always have the opportunity to do things like this under the eye of our global CEO and his direct reports. So people understanding that we put our best effort forward and appreciated what we did, knowing that it had global eyes on it also meant a lot.

Gratitude Rarely Happens in This Particular Organization

- A Sense That Others in the Office Don't Express Feelings This Way

Kristin is a vice president for a marketing and public relations firm. As part of her work-related community service, she organized an event to benefit the Cystic Fibrosis Foundation. Jean, the accountant in Kristin's firm, provided considerable volunteer support and gave a generous donation, the largest of all of Kristin's colleagues. Kristin prepared a handwritten card for Jean to thank her for her advice, volunteer effort, and personality.

The whole episode was especially positive for Kristin because of uniqueness of Jean's generosity and the uniqueness of the appreciation that Kristin shared with Jean, tying it to perceived gender norms. Kristin explained:

> *I think what stuck out for me about her act of kindness was that it was unexpected. It was over and above the call of duty. And I think it might be something to the fact that we're the only two females in the whole office so the men don't maybe express sentiment like we do. In that way it was different. And that's why it might be so singular of an experience among the other coworkers.*

- Owners/Senior Leaders Don't Often Get Thanked by Employees

Jay is a partner in an accounting firm. Ally, the firm's auditing manager, found a lead for a new client. When Jay invited Ally to be a part of the client proposal process, Ally was happily surprised and expressed her appreciation to Jay. It was positive and memorable because appreciation rarely got expressed to the company's owners. Jay described what made her thanks stand out for him:

> *Well, quite frankly because it probably doesn't happen a lot, in this strict work. The Happy Hour thing is one thing but like in this kind of situation I'm not so sure that we as owners get a lot of thanks. Do you know what I mean? Obviously we're paying their paycheck … but it felt good to actually get a verbal thanks for allowing somebody to do something extra.*

- We Just Seem to Be Too Busy to Say Thank You

Liz is a housing specialist for a government agency. Because of her degrees in finance and accounting and extensive private sector experience with appraisal work in the commercial and residential sectors, the Department of Justice (DOJ) asked her to be an expert witness in a fraud trial. Liz's support seemed to turn the tide in the case and a DOJ attorney thanked her with a letter that went to her as well as two levels of supervisors above her. Liz focused on how rarely gratitude is expressed in her work world when commenting about what made the situation most positive and memorable:

> *Just because I think we all get so busy on a day-to-day basis that we forget to say thank you to people.*

- Our Whole Industry Moves So Quickly We Forget to Say Thank You

Rick is a social networking manager at marketing and public relations firm. He had prepared a social media training program for a large group at a national conference, and the night before the event the organizer reached out to Rick to request that he create six customized sessions. Rick stayed up all night to make it happen. Rick's supervisor reached out to thank him face-to-face and also sent an email that notified others in their organization about Rick's hard work and results. Rick explained why the thank meant a lot to him:

> *I did work so hard on it and oftentimes not out of maliciousness or anything, but we're just so busy and we have so many different products, so many things that we're working on, and the turnover is so quickly. So, this is a what have you done for me lately industry. ... Yeah, because it's not an everyday event that you really get a sincere, personal thank you like that, nor recognized in front of your colleagues and superiors.*

Routine Element

- Thanks to an Employee Around the Birth of His Child Was Just Another Good Thing

Charles, the owner of a commercial and residential remodeling company, expressed appreciation to an employee when the employee and his wife had a baby. Charles sent a baby car seat along with a basket with diapers, other practical items, and gift cards. He also provided the employee with extra paid time off when his wife faced some complications after giving birth. Charles could not really explain why it was positive and memorable:

> *It's just nice to do good things, regardless of whether it's business or personal; it feels good to give when you can.*

- The Employee Thank You Dinner Is Just Another Nice Way to Show Appreciation

Andy is a banquet manager at a country club. He and his team were proud to show appreciation to all who worked in non-management positions at the club by hosting a holiday dinner. When asked about what made the event especially positive and memorable, he just responded:

Every year the holiday party is memorable. It's just always nice to be a part of something that shows appreciation.

- Thanking My Supervisor and My Supervisor Thanking Me Is Just What We Do

Madison is a junior recruiter in an engineering firm. Madison thanked her supervisor and senior recruiter in person and by text when her supervisor spent extra time with her to teach her new job applicant software. When asked about what made this instance of appreciation so positive and memorable, Jennifer shared,

I guess it's just normal. ... I thank her all the time and she always thanks me.

Key Financial Element

- A Customer Expressing Thanks Is Good for Business as Well as the Relationship

Mac owns a car dealership and, over the holidays, a customer brought in stromboli for him to show appreciation for a recent car purchase. Mac talked about why it was especially positive and memorable for him:

When you have a business and people form a relationship with you, and they like you, that's good for your business and that's good for everybody involved.

- A Restaurateur Thanked by a Famous Artist on a Top National TV Talk Show Drives Recognition and Business

Antonio is CEO of a regional restaurant franchise. He helped a world-renowned singer start a new business venture in Antonio's home city. As a thank you, the singer touted Antonio's restaurant on one of the leading national talk shows. The singer's talk show visit included video clips of him in Antonio's restaurant. Antonio explained what made it especially positive and memorable:

I got national recognition on the most popular show there is ... [L]ots of people came in, tons of people came in.

- Thanks Results in Visibility That Could Result in Financial Compensation

Zara, who works as a vice president in a large financial services company, received thanks in person and conference calls from her supervisors and from two individuals with an accreditation agency for her considerable work determining whether a sales training program had been successful. This expression of gratitude was positive and memorable for Zara because:

> [I]t gives some credibility to the ideas that I've helped develop with them, which in turn has created some nice positive effects with my manager and director. ... [I]t holds the potential of allowing me to engage in a project with them ... and might eventually lead to earning a promotion and/or an increase in financial compensation.

Previously Unrecognized Individuals

- Thank You Climate in Current Department Contrasts With That of Other Departments in the Same University

Peggy is the director of a university career development center. Recently, she gave an effusive review and the highest numeric assessment possible to one of her employees who joined her department from another department in the same university. This instance of sharing appreciation stood out because even though the employee has been under Peggy's supervision for quite a while now, it still stands out as a contrasting experience for the employee. Peggy described:

> It was especially positive because, as I said earlier, she's worked here for many years and she's done a great job for many years but she hasn't always gotten the attention to her work as she should have. And many times, she thought about leaving because of it. So, this change for her, was very positive. The change to our group was very positive for her in general, but then having her work lauded, was especially favorable to her.

- Extending Appreciation to a Direct Report Who Was Not Recognized Properly Before

When Jeff, a natural health consumer products manager, recognized one of his sales supervisors for her excellent work at a quarterly meeting, he found it positive and memorable because the sales supervisor unlikely had previously received the attention she deserved. Jeff explained:

> It was more positive because this is someone I feel has a lot of skills, and I wasn't always sure whether she was being recognized in the correct light, if she was really given the credit that she deserves. So, it gave me an

opportunity with senior people to show them what I have seen and the experience I've had from working with this person.

- Our Level of the Organization Is Often Overlooked so All We Have Is Each Other

Zara, who works as a vice president in a large financial services company, worked with two colleagues on designing and presenting a retirement symposium. After it was completed, she thanked both of them in person and reached out via email and in person to the manager of the person who was not formally assigned to Zara. The overall gratitude interaction was positive and memorable for Zara because the level at which they work is often overlooked in terms of accolades. Zara stated:

[W]e don't get a lot of the big credit for these things, even though we are right. We're the next layer underneath the directors who will get the biggest credit for it. We aren't the top dogs getting the credit. Sometimes all we have is each other, and considering that we got our bonuses yesterday, I would definitely say sometimes all we have is each other. I think gratitude and the relationships that we have at work are sometimes the only thing that gets us through.

- Thank You to a Person Early in Their Career Who May Have Felt Invisible

Bao is a data expert for a branch of the U.S. military. He communicated his appreciation to a new programmer in his organization for learning a new application quickly and having a great attitude. Bao explained what made the interaction especially positive and memorable for the two of them:

This person is really young, and he's new, and it's not his first job. He's about 29-years-old, but he's new to our organization, and I felt like it really made a difference. I think he felt somewhat invisible for a while, so it made a difference to him, that somebody noticed him in a positive way, his work.

Returning to the Opening Story: The Positive Surprise of Gratitude Communication Doesn't Depend on Things First Being Awful

One reading of the opening story can make it seem like Judee's neighbor did Judee and her family a favor by blocking their view for an extended period and only then giving them what they wanted. Another reading of the story, and another interpretation of these situations in general, is that all the benefits of the gratitude communication episode could have been delivered much sooner and, consequently, much more net benefit—calculated more broadly than expectancy violations theory suggests—could have been realized.

Judee and her family had their expectations negatively violated when their view was blocked by where the neighbor had parked his car and trailer. They might have reasonably thought, "Even a basic level of situational awareness would have meant he had to know he was obstructing our view." Continuing with this line of thought, their impressions could have been positively violated the first time the neighbor parked his car in the undesirable location if he had immediately moved his vehicle to a location not blocking the view for Judee and her family.

To elaborate and broaden this line of thinking, the power of positive violations does not license or otherwise justify ugly behavior toward others with the intention to stop the ugly behavior at some point later. The key takeaway from this research project is that positive surprise in some part of the gratitude communication episode gives the episode the best chance of being particularly positive and memorable. And the many stories in which the interviewees did not encounter a truly awful baseline experience shows that people should not be made to suffer on the tenuous justification that it will make them only more grateful when gratitude is more surprisingly shared down the road.

Chapter Conclusion

In this chapter, we explored what makes gratitude communication especially positive and memorable for those involved. Although some people focused on the specifics of gratitude communication messaging, others identified other parts of the larger gratitude communication episode as the key characteristics that made the situation stand out for them. A relatively large number of categories were found, and they represent focused options for crafting positive and memorable gratitude in the future. The paramount finding was that positive surprise is the single best explanation for especially positive and memorable gratitude.

This chapter and the previous three (on the why, the how, and the benefits of sending, respectively) complete the section of this book concerning the basics of gratitude communication. We will now shift to considering four boundary-related areas of gratitude communication, beginning with a chapter on reciprocation.

Real World Recommendations

- Gratitude communication can be particularly positive and memorable because of the gratitude expression itself or because of the larger episode of triggering gratitude, extending gratitude, and receiving gratitude.

- Gratitude communication is more likely to make an impact as positive and memorable when it positively violates expectations for those involved.

- An expression of thanks can follow an event that has deep personal meaning for the sender(s) and/or receiver(s) and/or when the gratitude communication message or message reception is felt to have deep personal meaning.

- Although appreciation itself is a positive emotion making thank you communications memorable, it is often the case that senders and receivers cite other positive and strongly felt emotions in relation to gratitude communication episodes.

- Surprise is important for making sense of what generally makes gratitude communication episodes positively standout. This finding points the way for those wanting to create powerful gratitude communication interactions in the future.

- Locating thank you opportunities in challenging situations can be especially positive and memorable for those involved.

- Recognition of notable efforts in relation to triggering events or in the act of thanking can make gratitude more positive and memorable.

- Primacy, or "the power of the first," in terms of triggering events and/or the expression of gratitude can make the episode particularly positive and memorable.

- Thank you triggering events and especially direct thank you communications that are extended by high-status people or have the awareness of high-status people stand out in people's memories.

- The rarity of certain thank you triggering events in certain organizations and, more commonly, the rarity of thank you expressions in certain organizations can make gratitude communication episodes stand out.

- In contrast to the theme of positive surprise in generally characterizing especially positive and memorable gratitude communication, thank you communications connected to routine events sometimes stand out as especially positive and memorable.

- The expression of thanks can indicate or create positive financial conditions for the sender and/or receiver and their respective organizations.

- Thank you episodes can be particularly positive and memorable when the gratitude recipient(s) have been overlooked in organizations that do not get generally characterized as lacking a gratitude communication culture.

- Gratitude communications were sometimes found to be experienced as especially positive and memorable for reasons beyond the more common ones listed here.

Your Opportunity to Work With Gratitude

- Relying on your own work experience or the work experience of someone close to you, identify a past instance of gratitude communication that was particularly positive and memorable for one or more people involved. Also, consider the features that made that past instance stand out and the degree to which they are the same as ones identified in this chapter.

- Choose an area of your life and design or redesign a gratitude communication episode that is likely to be highly positive and memorable while still realistically achievable to carry out. Make sure your plan incorporates at least three of the characteristics from this chapter. Explicitly state the chapter-related characteristics featured in your (re)design along with the individual(s) involved who would most likely experience the episode as especially positive and memorable and why.

Questions for Reflection and Discussion

- With reference to expectancy violations theory, consider actual or hypothetical episodes of gratitude communication that (could) function as positive for some individuals involved and as negative for others. Also, consider whether an attempt to positively violate expectations in sending gratitude communication is inherently risky versus using a routine means of sending gratitude. What are some possible unintended negative violations in sending gratitude communication, and how can these unintended negative violations be avoided?

- Again, referring to expectancy violations theory, to what extent is it theoretically and practically possible to positively violate expectations in all our gratitude communications? If a person or organization is limited, how should they best manage their limitations?

Recommendations for Learning More

- If you have access to an academic library, locate and read the following article by Burgoon (1993), as it is perhaps the single most relevant article concerning expectancy violations theory and gratitude. Although not focused specifically on gratitude, it includes a gratitude communication EVT example near the beginning: Burgoon, J. K. (1993). Interpersonal expectations, expectancy violations, and emotional communication. *Journal of Language and Social Psychology, 12*(1-2), 30–48. https://doi. org/10.1177/0261927X93121003

- Go to www.YouTube.com and search "expectancy violations theory" to locate and watch various clips demonstrating the theory and its concepts.

PART III

Charting the Boundaries
of Gratitude Communication

7

Reciprocation and Gratitude Communication

"I'll lift you and you'll lift me, and we'll both ascend together."

—John Greenleaf Whittier

Opening Story

Aesop gave us the story of *The Ant and the Dove*. A thirsty ant approached a spring to drink some water. The ant accidentally fell into the water and, having lost its grasp of the spring's edge, started to drown. Fortunately for the ant, a dove perched in a nearby tree saw what was taking place and decided to intervene. The dove broke off a small branch and positioned it in the water so the ant could climb aboard and safely return to solid ground.

Sometime later, the tables turned. A hunter managed to capture the dove in a net and the ant happened to witness this perilous threat. The ant bit the hunter's foot causing the hunter to abandon the dove and go away. The dove was unharmed and free (Keller & Keating, 1993).

The fable suggests that the ant's safeguarding of the dove was an obligatory act of gratitude.

Reciprocation refers to mutual giving and receiving. It is regarded as one of the most powerful forms of influence. Most basically, perhaps, all gratitude communication is positive reciprocation in that the act of sending implies a meaningful, even if only metaphorical, gift has already been received. Reciprocation is relevant to the topic of gratitude communication because many receivers immediately respond to acts of gratitude communication with a direct "thank you" of some kind. Most germane to the matter of gratitude expressions and reciprocity is how a gratitude escalatory cycle can develop. Several interviewees explicitly noted how gratitude communication and the positive benefits associated with it can gain terrific momentum in a relationship. The Theoretically Speaking section in this chapter explores compliance gaining theory (Cialdini, 2008) to give context to reciprocity as a strong and well-established form of influence.

THEORETICALLY SPEAKING

Reciprocity is two-way or circular giving and receiving between parties. Although it can function with both positive and negative behaviors, it has especially been studied in terms of positive behaviors from the point of view of one or both immediate parties and it is most often depicted as contributing to the broader social good. The importance of the concept of reciprocity is evidenced in part by the fact that those in various disciplines have studied it. These reciprocity-interested disciplines include anthropology, biology, economics, psychology, sociology, and communication.

A landmark work on reciprocity was Gouldner's (1960) article titled "The Norm of Reciprocity," which tied together a considerable amount of prior work on the topic across the disciplines of anthropology and sociology. Gouldner suggested that reciprocity was not just a pattern of social exchange but a moral norm across societies. Accordingly, he proposed that individuals self-monitored in terms of not wanting to over-benefit because of this moral force. Subsequent evidence has supported this line of thinking (Uehara, 1995). Basically, most people feel an obligation not to over-benefit in their relations with others.

Reciprocity has become recognized as a major category of social influence. Cialdini's (2008) research-based, best-selling book titled *Influence* includes it among six dominant types of influence: reciprocity; commitment and consistency; social proof; liking; authority; and scarcity. For Cialdini, reciprocity explains why marketers frequently provide a free sample before making a sale.

Gouldner's (1960) article seems to have provided the basis for, if not triggered, much other reciprocity research, and it highlighted a powerful general tool for marketers. Regardless, the subtleties of Gouldner's reciprocity work matter for the topic of gratitude and gratitude communication. Gouldner acknowledged that, while reciprocation can be motivated by obligation, it can also be motivated by gratitude, and, therefore, obligation and gratitude were at least theoretically different. Researchers have found that obligation is negative and uncomfortable while gratitude is a positive feeling experienced in response to receiving a benefit from another (Emmons & Crumpler, 2000; Fitzgerald, 1998, as cited in Goei & Boster, 2005) and it is connected to other positive emotions such as contentment, pride, and happiness (McCullough et al., 2001, as cited in Goei & Boster, 2005). Obligation is a state that one wants to avoid (Hendrickson & Goei, 2009) while gratitude is a state in which it is desirable to remain (Watkins et al., 2006). In earlier work, Goei and Boster (2005) carried out experiments that determined obligation and gratitude differently motivated compliance. Their research included an experiment in which research confederates did a favor for research participants by getting them a drink and, in one instance, diminishing any sense of obligation about the favor, and, in another instance, enhancing a sense of obligation. They measured self-reports of gratitude too.

INSIGHTS BASED ON ORIGINAL RESEARCH

Two main reciprocity findings are presented below and elaborated with several examples. First, gratitude communication frequently results in an immediate or otherwise closely temporally connected response of gratitude. Second, it was remarkable how gratitude expressions and associated positive behaviors could gain momentum in a dyadic or multiperson relational configuration and, thereby, escalate in a positive manner.

Gratitude Communication as Frequently and Immediately Triggering Reciprocity

This first category captures how expressions of gratitude were often immediately and/or with only a slight delay responded to reciprocally, commonly with an expression of gratitude by the original recipient of gratitude.

- Year End Thanks to a Most Valued Employee and Then Thanks Right Back
In this first example of instant or only slightly delayed gratitude communication reciprocity, Andy, the original sender, receives both an immediate reciprocal message of gratitude from the original receiver, Ed, and a slightly delayed reciprocal message of gratitude from Ed as well. Ed owns a pawn shop and check cashing business. Andy is the employee he relies on the most. Ed recalled how he said goodbye to Andy for the holiday season and gave Andy a large bonus check and a hug to thank him for his exceptional help over the previous year.

Ed explained how Andy reciprocated, including immediately:

Initially he thanked me and, I guess, he didn't open it in front of me, when he came in the day after Christmas he gave me a big squeeze.

- Thanks Even Though I Demur in Terms of Your Thanks for Me

In this second example, the original sender of a gratitude message has her message dismissed, seemingly because of modesty by the receivers, but, nonetheless, is a recipient of reciprocal gratitude messages, given the nature of the initiating message. Arguably, this demonstrates the strong force of reciprocity, even in instances of gratitude message rejection by the original gratitude message receiver(s).

Alana owns a store that sells women's clothing and accessories. Alana's shop is close to other vendors. Alana made a point of approaching and thanking these vendors when they helped take care of the needs of shoppers in Alana's store during a time when Alana was dealing with considerable pain because of health issues.

Alana recalled how these helpful individuals responded to her with both a dismissal of Alana's thank you and an expression of their own appreciation for her: "Their response was you don't need to thank me, and I appreciate it."

Alana helped by explaining the context:

I think it was just how we tend to look out for each other's businesses." Alana went on to explain how shoplifting can be a problem, other life and work issues can come up for vendors, and so generally there was an understanding that when necessary, they would "pick up the slack for somebody else ... and maybe just emotionally keeping our eyes out for each other and just being there when need be.

- Reciprocation of a Thank You as I Thank You for Righting an Inequity That I Discovered

Tracy is a senior manager in a museum who came to realize that two individuals in her sphere of influence were receiving grossly different amounts of compensation, even though they were carrying out similar work. She brought the matter to the attention of her supervisor, the chief financial officer, and the chief operating officer. These individuals acted and righted the injustice. Tracy thanked each individual in a phone call. She also thanked the COO face-to-face. She explained her gratitude message: "Thank you very much. It was very important to me, and I was happy to see some resolution."

Reciprocation then became a factor as she recalls:

They were thankful for my appreciation. They all expressed it verbally.

Gratitude Communication as Prompting Ongoing Reciprocity and Commitment

The valued reciprocal behaviors can include not only "thank you" for "thank you" but also more of the desired behaviors such as work effort and/or work results that were connected to the original gratitude message. This category demonstrates how gratitude reciprocation can continue beyond discrete and dyadic interactions involving relatively narrow instances of matching gratitude with gratitude.

In the first example, reciprocity took place in terms of expressions of gratitude for gratitude, and also reciprocity was evidenced in continuance of the cause of gratitude (e.g., intentional demonstration of more great work) from the original recipient of gratitude. This is a relatively expansive form of gratitude communication reciprocity.

Reciprocation can consist of gratitude in response to gratitude but also commitment to the originating trigger or cause for gratitude communication. There is joint commitment to a shared future.

The second example provides evidence for how a demonstrated work ethic can constitute gratitude messaging, along with typical verbal and non-verbal reactions to receiving a gratitude message, that themselves constitute gratitude messaging.

- Gratitude at Time of Employee's New Baby Results in Reciprocal Gratitude and a Commitment to Work

Ron owns a renovation business, and Grant is one of his best workers. When Grant and his wife welcomed a new baby, Ron along with others at the company sent Grant and his family a number of gifts and made sure his family was looked after in other ways:

We sent him a car seat and a gift basket, some gift cards and stuff like that for diapers and what have you. And his wife was really sick after the pregnancy so [we] gave him time, paid time off, as well, to help out with the situation.

Ron also commented on Grant's reaction: "Well, he received it well. ... Oh, you could just see it in his work ethic and, you know, his gratitude towards what we did for him."

- Reciprocating by Receiving Gratitude Humbly With a Nod to Reflecting and Strengthening the Organizational Culture

Kelly is a vice president in a financial services organization. She thanked two of her team members, Pam and Stacy, for organizing and leading an internal talent development event. She did so face-to-face and to each of their supervisors.

Kelly commented on the reactions to her expressions of appreciation:

I think they received the gratitude with gratitude. I think they were happy to be recognized, appreciated, happy to be part of the team that put it on and got the credit for it. So, I think it was received thankfully and received humbly, as well, which is a big part of our culture.

The mention of culture seems to be done in such a way to imply a joint commitment to building it further, building the bigger organization together.

- You Thank Me, I Thank You, and We Continue to Get Great Things Done Together

In this next example, a professional is the receiver of gratitude. However, the account is also notable for how the original receiver immediately reciprocates with a message of appreciation, and she and the overall event speaks to a strong commitment to doing good work in the future, possibly as a way to earn gratitude from the team. Again, reciprocal gratitude is a joint commitment that grows something larger.

Sara is vice president of recruiting at a regional center of a rental car company. She recently took Rachel, one of her team members, to lunch. Sara explained her rationale:

I really appreciated everything she had done for the department. ... [She] exceeds all the expectations and responsibilities that I give to her and, for those reasons, and going above and beyond and really helping to find and help me recruit the best people to the team.

Sara brought a number of Rachel's peers to the lunch along with Sara's own manager, in Sara's words "to recognize her in front of everybody."

Sara described Rachel's reaction, including her own expression of gratitude and her commitment to continuing to perform in such a positive way:

She was really excited. She was very, very excited. And I think she was also excited that everyone was there to see that happen, and very, very thankful and very committed to continuing her great performance.

Sara went on describe the reaction of others who attended the lunch:

I'm sure other people were like, wow, I want to be in that [and for]there to be a lunch for me some day. So, I think it kind of helps them see the recognition of others and kind of want that for themselves and maybe get inspired to do something good in their role, so they can earn that gratitude, too, or earn that recognition, too.

In the following example, we again see how messages of gratitude for good work may be reciprocated with similar gratitude messages and/or more good work facilitated by the "mutual admiration society," a relational entity with positive momentum and positive outcomes for those directly involved, including the organization.

• This Instance and the Pattern of You Thanking Me and Me Thanking You Make Us a Mutual Admiration Society

Cheryl is a contracting manager for a private sector organization that interfaces and supports the work of a federal agency. Cheryl has taken the approach that, even though she is technically hired to oversee and support other contracted workers, she also makes a point of supporting government workers too. More senior people on the government side of her work appreciate, in Cheryl's words:

I'm doing a good job ... and they have actually written to the contracting department and thanked me through contracting by saying they felt I was one of the easiest [individuals] in my role to work with and that I made it easier for them to do their job.

In terms of reciprocity, it is noteworthy that Cheryl added:

And I always thank them, too; I send letters to say please thank the staff or post this, you know, in your thing to say that I appreciate all their hard work. ... [F]or 14 months we have exceeded our sales goals. ... I mean it's unprecedented.

Cheryl described other ways she shows gratitude:

[I]n the evaluation of contracts which I have to do quarterly, I always make sure to mention how they've gone above and beyond. And I also mention the things that we screw up on, you know, so I think they see it as truthful.

Cheryl added, "I have to go out to visit the site two times a year. I go out to their contracting office, or to their office, and they all come up and say hello to me and shake my hand and say how easy it is to work with me and thank me, so it's like a mutual admiration society. I thank them, too, for all their hard work even when I'm there face-to-face, too."

• Receiving Thanks With Thanks and Looking Forward to Continuing the Journey Together

This final example shows how there can be a developmental flow of good work and gratitude communication among various parties, which can constitute a "journey" of reciprocity, in this case between two closely allied companies and key individuals.

Terry works for a company that prepares metal, which is then sold to other companies to make products. One of Terry's managers received an email from a major client that stated:

How helpful we are, and that our helping them create new products [expands] their reach and profitability. ... [The client communicated that he considers my company] one of two companies that he works with out of several hundred companies that are the best communicators, and the integrity of our work is very high.

Terry shared the email with the head of his organization who then spoke with the head of his client's company. In the words of Terry, the company head "reciprocated on the acknowledgement and gratitude sent to me and my company for what we do for them. So, it's a beautiful thing."

Returning to the Opening Story

Aesop's tale of *The Ant and the Dove* can be used to explore various issues related to reciprocation, gratitude communication, and related behavioral drivers, including feelings of obligation and gratitude. Analysis of the research interviews underpinning this book showed that a gratitude expression often immediately triggered a corresponding gratitude expression in the receiver of the first message. It seems noteworthy that the ant did not explicitly thank the dove. One interpretation of the story could be that gratitude communication per se did not take place. Yet it is an age-old story of gratitude because the ant literally saves the dove's life after the dove saves the ant's life. To most who learn the story, this probably seems like an expression of gratitude pure and simple. It is a perfectly reciprocal act and a life-saving act. We do not know, based on what Aesop wrote, whether the ant and dove went on to have a friendship, an ongoing working partnership of some kind, or a relationship in which they helped each other on an as needed basis.

A research finding was that gratitude communication and reciprocity could become the basis of a strong and mutually fulfilling relationship. Again, we as readers just do not know if this was the case with the ant and the dove. The situation and the meaning of the situation is further complicated for some, no doubt, because of the matter of motivation. If the ant helped the dove because of obligation, was the act gratitude-related, obligation-related, or both? Should the meaning of gratitude communication be determined in whole or in part by the participants' stated and/or attributed motivations and/or by what is strictly supported by actual behavior? Thoughtful scholars, professionals, and lay people may very well come to different conclusions. Nevertheless, The tale highlights the force of reciprocity in society along with the sometimes-related matters of expressing gratitude whether it is borne of obligation.

Chapter Conclusion

Reciprocity, the social force of responding to another as that person has behaved towards you, is a major form of influence. It is a social norm that may be impacted by gratitude and/or obligation. The research interviews forming the basis for this book resulted in the findings that an expression of gratitude is often met with an expression of gratitude either immediately and/or shortly afterwards, and gratitude reciprocation can continue with considerable stability in a two-person relationship or among a larger group of individuals. When reciprocity takes hold in this manner, it is not just about individuals thanking one another endlessly. Triggers of reciprocity and ongoing drivers include behaviors like good work performance, as understood by all parties to the intensified reciprocity relationship. The next chapter addresses the closely related topic of gratitude communication philosophies. Although reciprocity is typically present in all detailed accounts of gratitude communication, individuals hold and demonstrate in actual interaction different views about whether gratitude communication benefits and should benefit the sender, receiver, or both.

Real World Recommendations

- Reciprocity or giving and getting in equal measure has been established as a strong social norm. Expand your awareness of how this social programming is present for most people and whether it is strong in you.

- Reciprocity is one of the most powerful influence strategies with other influence strategies existing as alternative choices. Get comfortable developing different reciprocity scenarios as well as different scenarios for the use of other influence strategies.

- Positive reciprocity (reciprocity in the interests of all involved parties) can be motivated by obligation or gratitude. Clarify your basic stance on what tends to drive you.

- Recognize that a gratitude expression for a gratitude expression is common and whether it is important for you to do.

- Recognize that reciprocation, specifically gratitude-oriented and otherwise positive, can develop into powerful engines of well-being and performance at all levels of workplace interaction.

Your Opportunity to Work With Gratitude

- Describe a scenario in your near future (that is not necessarily gratitude related) when you might legitimately prime another person for reciprocity (i.e., use reciprocity as a primary influence strategy) so that you can reach one or more important goals. Describe the situation and your goal(s). Also, consider what might be most challenging about this influence attempt and how you can overcome one or two of your main challenges.

- Give someone a sincere compliment in person. You may or may not know the person well. The compliment may or may not be gratitude related. Take note of the receiver's response. Consider whether the person accepted and/or agreed with the compliment. Also, consider whether the person responded to you reciprocally. For instance, did the person compliment you in return in a manner identical to or different than the way you complimented them?

- Identify a person you know well and think of a reason to express your appreciation to them. Compose and send your gratitude message in some text-based format such as an email, text message, or hardcopy card. Take note of the receiver's response. Consider whether the person "accepted" the gratitude message. Also, consider whether the person responded to you reciprocally. For instance, did the person thank you in return in a manner and with content identical to or different from the way you shared your gratitude message with them?

Questions for Reflection and Discussion

- What is a new research study that could inform whether mutually beneficial actions in one or more workplace relationships are predominantly or wholly driven by obligation or gratitude?

- What evidence supports the argument that reciprocity exists as a strong social norm in current society? Locate some evidence that supports or refutes that reciprocity is a social norm. Also, try to locate evidence for conditions that support positive reciprocity, especially in workplaces.

- Given any of the theoretical and/or research finding content from this chapter or your own additional research, what can a manager do to foster reciprocal gratitude communication in their team?

Recommendations for Learning More

- Perhaps no individual has made reciprocity such an inviting topic in recent years as Adam Grant (2013). Read all or portions of his very accessible book, *Give and Take: Why Helping Others Drives Our Success*, to more fully grasp the history of the concept, its mechanisms and its possibilities in general. There is no question that Grant regards reciprocity as a major social force.

- While reciprocity can play a central or exclusive role in some social influence situations such as gratitude communication, there are other forms of influence that exist and can be used in addition to or instead of reciprocity. Read Cialdini's (2008) well-regarded book on the topic: *Influence: Science and Practice.*

- Reciprocity is a sometimes-simple idea about social exchange that can get complex in certain contexts. Read Gouldner's (1960) seminal article on the topic: "The Norm of Reciprocity: A Preliminary Statement."

- Mutually Assured Destruction (MAD) is a form of negative reciprocity that gained considerable attention during the Cold War, the nuclear arms proliferation and overall military and political standoff that developed between the former Soviet Union and the United States after World War II. The MAD rationale for both sides was to deter a first strike from the other side by having such massive nuclear capability virtually guaranteeing the ability to annihilate the other side. Reciprocity in this situation was based on each side communicating their ability and intention to win an all-out nuclear war initiated by the other. Read the transcript of a speech by then U.S. Secretary of Defense Robert McNamara (1967) that makes a case for MAD as U.S. policy. Try to place yourself in the context of the 1960s and consider whether the argument is convincing to you. Also, consider whether the argument is convincing to you in the current world.

8

Philosophies of Gratitude Communication

"This is my letter to the world,
[t]hat never wrote to me."

—Emily Dickinson

Clarifying Who Should be Served by Gratitude Communication

Ronald Reagan began his career as a sports announcer and actor and later became president of the Screen Actors Guild and governor of California. In 1979, he was elected president of the United States. In January 1980, at almost 70 years old, he was the oldest person (at that time) to become a U.S. President. A little more than a year later, he was nearly killed by an attempted assassin's bullet. Nonetheless, he went on to complete two terms as president (Spitz, 2018).

In 1994, approximately 5 years after leaving office, former President Reagan announced to the nation that he had been diagnosed with Alzheimer's disease (Crezo, 2012). He shared the news in a handwritten letter that opened with "My Fellow Americans" and used evocative language, including a description of him moving towards "the sunset" of his life. The letter was powerful not only for the tragic information it conveyed and its personal and poetic tone, but also because it directly communicated his gratitude. Reagan wrote, "In closing let me thank you, the American people for giving me the great honor of allowing me to serve as your President." And as he ended the letter, Reagan again expressed his appreciation, writing, "Thank you, my friends." ▬▬▬

A Philosophy of You, Me, or All of Us?

Philosophies of gratitude are closely tied to a consideration of reciprocation. While the link between reciprocation and gratitude communication was not challenged in the study on which this book is based, interviewees differed as far as whether gratitude communication should cycle back to the sender. Essentially, a spectrum emerged with some plainly using gratitude communication as an instrument for self-related gain, some asserting that all sending of gratitude communication was done without any expectation of even simple acknowledgement, and most others expressing views somewhere in between. It is important for individuals—and organizations—intentionally to choose their spot on the spectrum and embrace the limits and potentials connected with doing so. The Theoretically Speaking section in this chapter addresses several different ethical philosophies including self-oriented, other-oriented, and hybrid/self-and-other philosophies of sending gratitude, including encouraging predominantly instrumental concern for the interests of others.

THEORETICALLY SPEAKING

Notably Different Views on Who Gratitude Should Serve

The Philosophy of Selfishness

Selfishness, also known as rational selfishness and rational egoism, is the view that it only makes sense for us to act in our own benefit. One of its leading proponents was philosopher and writer Ayn Rand (1964/2005) who authored a book titled *The Virtue of Selfishness*. For Rand, selfishness was more than logical; it was a moral imperative. In making her argument, Rand railed against altruism (Campbell, 2006). One of her main claims was that attempts to justify or promote altruism were attacks on the concept of the inviolate individual. For Rand, we do not have to accommodate others to legitimize our own existence. We should only act to advance our own happiness.

The Philosophy of Enlightened Self-Interest

Enlightened self-interest is a justification for selfishness while recognizing that addressing shared needs and wants and the needs and wants of others can play an important role in advancing our own interests. Enlightened self-interest is associated with Alexis de Tocqueville (1835/2000), a French philosopher, writer and, later, politician who famously traveled throughout the United States in the early 1800s and documented his impressions in the book *Democracy in America* (Kimpell, 2015). In writing this book, Tocqueville was explaining the United States to his home country and unwittingly providing the United States with a glimpse of itself that remains impactful. Tocqueville observed that Americans acted out of enlightened self-interest in forming associations to address mutual concerns and that American democracy was a sight to behold in large part because self-interests were met by those who served as leaders (Kimpell, 2015).

The Philosophy of Relationalism

Relationalism is a term intended to capture the hybrid view that a strong self should be valued in ourselves and others along with the recognition that we live in relation to one another. Therefore, individual gain and non-instrumental support of others are simultaneously valued. This view has been advanced, in part, by psychologist and feminist Carol Gilligan (1977, 1982). Gilligan began her career working under Lawrence Kohlberg (1976) on his theory of moral development, which assumes those in higher stages of development see individuals as separate entities. While Kohlberg's work elevated the reasoning of boys and men who frequently take a justice orientation, as opposed to human caring orientation, Gilligan's (1977) work more closely looked at the reasoning of girls and women who frequently take a caring orientation towards others. Consequently, Gilligan (1982) called for a moral philosophy that prizes both individual autonomy and a concern for others.

The Philosophy of Altruism

Altruism is the view that others' happiness should be valued more highly than our own. Philosopher and founder of sociology Auguste Comte coined the term, and his motto is known to have been "Live for others" (Gane, 2006, p. 135). Comte was so committed to this view that he claimed that even self-interested acts as modest as positive self-assessments should be avoided (Campbell, 2006).

INSIGHTS BASED ON ORIGINAL RESEARCH

The Philosophy of Gratitude Communication for Self-Related Gain

- I Wanted to Express Gratitude Because He Was Helping Me Meet My Goals

Sean is a senior administrator at a university. The nature of his work means students do not typically approach him, and yet they are instrumental to his work. Sean explained one recent situation when a student approached him as head of his office:

> *I just really wanted to thank him for reaching out to me. It was as simple as that. And the reason why I wanted to do that was self-serving, in some respects, to be quite honest, because I appreciated his doing that because I needed to connect with students.*

Sean's expression of gratitude was very closely related to him completing his work responsibilities, helping him progress with his own work accomplishments.

- Thanks and a Related Bonus Mid-Year Can Cause Individuals to Expect More in the Future

Josh is a partner in a small investment firm. Josh's comments describe a gratitude philosophy based in individualism and self-interest that he sometimes encounters in others and rejects:

> *[Senior leaders and organizations] don't want to pay a midyear bonus … because then all of a sudden everybody's going to expect it. And I kind of found, you pay that midyear bonus or you make that compliment or you make a big deal of it and it works itself out. If the person comes back and says, 'But last year we got a midyear bonus, where's mine this year?' And you say, 'Sorry, there's not enough money for it,' they really respect that. They're irritated at first but it makes them realize oh, that was a special surprise last year; this year it isn't.*

The Philosophy of Gratitude Communication to Benefit Others

- Everyone Here Deserves to Receive Gratitude in This Organization

Janice manages a career center at a university. Her comments reflect the view that those who are often overlooked, the rank and file employees, should be engaged with gratitude communication:

> I think more gratitude needs to be shown, not only [in this organization] but especially in [this organization]. ... I've been here for a long time and, in my position, I get an opportunity to feel gratitude, but there are a lot of people who don't. And I think everybody needs to feel that. It is a long work life, a very long work life.

- People Need to Know They Are Appreciated for Helping

Roy is the co-owner of a dollar store and holds several other part-time positions. His comment here focuses on making sure employees in his main organization and elsewhere are the recipients of gratitude. His remarks suggest that regular workers may not be receiving the gratitude they are due:

> It's just the way you treat people ... you take that one second it takes to text them or email them and say, I appreciate you sent that over, you know, whatever, how benign it is people like to hear that people are grateful for things that they help with because people love to help. ... They just want to know you appreciate it.

The Philosophy of Gratitude Communication to Benefit Both Self And Other

- Our Customers Are Real People and Not Just Numbers

Stan, an independent grocer, exemplifies a philosophy that all can and should share in positive reciprocity. Stan explained,

> I guess the intended receiver would probably be the customers, but the end result is I'm shown appreciation also. ... So, it ends up being both of us. ... The message sent to the customers is that they're not just numbers, they're real people, and we appreciate them.

- It Was the Right Thing to Do for Someone and It Builds Client Loyalty; Sender and Receiver Benefit

Troy, an investment advisor, contemplates how both investment clients and their advisors should benefit from gratitude. He commented generally, "Gratitude is an attitude and if you have the confidence to express gratitude on a consistent basis, it says a lot about that individual." Troy continued:

> First of all, it feels good when you do something nice for someone, that there are benefits to the sender, as well as the recipient. ... And when you do something for someone when they're in trouble or ... when they suffer a setback, people don't forget this. You don't do something like that for self-serving reasons because if that encumbers what you do for people, usually it falls flat or it's transparent. Do something for someone because it's the right thing to do or it's a nice thing to do for them. And the side benefit, obviously, is it builds client loyalty in that particular instance because it's in all kinds of surveys why people deal with an investment person. Believe it or not the number one reason is because they like them. It isn't because they make them the most money; they like them and they trust them.

Returning to the Opening Story

The sum total of the Reagan details shared at the beginning of this chapter are not enough to establish his overall gratitude philosophy, but the particular account of him thanking the American people for the honor of serving as president seems very gracious. Arguably, it was a mutually meaningful communication for Reagan and those who read and/or who otherwise heard of his message. In tone and content, it seemed to reflect a high degree of sensitivity to self and other and, reflected a relational philosophy (although Reagan probably would have cringed at being connected to a view espoused by Carol Gilligan, an important 20th century feminist).

Chapter Conclusion

This chapter considered various philosophies of gratitude communication, including self-orientation, other orientation, and hybrid self-other orientation, the latter including relationalism. These philosophies are sometimes evidenced in interaction, sometimes evidenced in statements on the topic by individuals, and sometimes both. Just as Chapter 7 on reciprocation closely links to this chapter on philosophies, so too Chapter 8 on ethics connects, at least in part, to reciprocation and philosophies.

Real World Recommendations

- For others and for yourself, take time to consider the interests that are directly stated and/or implied in instances of gratitude communication.

- Consider whether you primarily ascribe to one gratitude communication philosophy (e.g., focus on advancing your own interests, the other's interests, or a combination, the latter possibly captured by the term relationalism) or whether it depends primarily or near solely on specific circumstances.

- Consider what it means to appropriately and effectively put your gratitude communication philosophy into practice in terms of particular verbal and nonverbal communication behaviors.

Your Opportunity to Work With Gratitude

- Take some time to reflect on and then make your own written statement of what your beliefs are about the purpose of gratitude communication. Include whether it should primarily be used to advance the interests of the sender, receiver, and/or both parties.

- Recall a recent gratitude communication episode in which you were the sender or receiver. Focus on the sender's verbal and/or nonverbal behaviors, and make a case for the gratitude communication philosophy on display.

- Identify an upcoming opportunity to express gratitude communication to one or more people regarding a particular issue. Craft your possible message, and then indicate how it follows or does not follow your predominant philosophy of gratitude communication.

- Think about movies, television shows, and similar content (e.g., YouTube® videos) you have seen recently, and identify an instance of gratitude communication. Now consider the philosophy of gratitude communication that was most evident in that instance. Finally, consider how that person might have communicated differently and, thereby, demonstrated another philosophy of gratitude communication.

Questions for Reflection and Discussion

- Can you find a reading on discourse and ideology (e.g., Lazar, 2005; Putz et al., 2004), and examine a gratitude communication message using a critical communication lens?

- Ideological discourse analysis often focuses on revealing a communicator's philosophy (used here as a synonym for ideology) as found in their interaction with others rather than privileging their stated philosophical position. This theoretical orientation is especially concerned with revealing power dynamics, particularly those based on privilege and/or exploitation such as racism and sexism. Can you step inside an ideological discourse perspective and locate two or more examples of notable people's "thank you" expressions and their implicit ideologies?

- Select a specific genre of "thank yous" such as expressions of gratitude by an author at the beginning of a book or in entertainment industry award acceptance speeches. What are two different gratitude messages by two different speakers? Make a case for the gratitude communication philosophy contained in each.

- Identify a thank you message from a major figure revered by many in the business community. It may be part of a larger speech and/or written statement or account. Quoting two or more specific passages, argue for the gratitude communication philosophy conveyed. Indicate how the message could even more strongly reflect this philosophy. Also suggest how it could be edited to reflect a different philosophy and whether this move would have strengthened or detracted from the business figure's likely goals.

Recommendations for Learning More

- The following book takes a comprehensive yet accessible approach to introducing the topic of how ideologies or philosophies of communication are contained in interaction: Simpson, P., Mayr, A., & Statham, S. (2018). *Language and power: A resource book for students*. Routledge.

- The following book is a foundational writing on the topic of how communicators express, often unwittingly, philosophies that empower or disempower: van Dijk, T. A. (1988). *Ideology: A multidisciplinary approach*. Sage.

- Oprah Winfrey and Ellen DeGeneres are two popular figures known for their expressions of gratitude. Find examples of gratitude communication on their web sites (www.oprah.com and ellentube.com). Compare the philosophies in two or more gratitude communications by one or both of these influencers.

- Douglas Conant was CEO of the Campbell Soup Company®. Read the following *Philadelphia Inquirer* article that describes Conant's incredible amount of gratitude communication sending while leading that organization. Then consider how you would develop an overall research study design to make a case for Conant's stated philosophy and the same or slightly different philosophy-in-practice. What data would you want to access for this study? Melamed, S. (2016, November 24). Gratitude tips from the author of 30,000 thank-you notes. *Philadelphia Inquirer*.

- If you are intrigued by Conant's gratitude communication activity, especially from an applied point of view, consider reading the following book: Conant, D., & Norgaard, M. (2011). *Touchpoints: Creating powerful leadership connections in the smallest of moments*. Jossey-Bass.

9

Ethics of Gratitude Communication

"As we express our gratitude, we must never forget that the highest appreciation is not to utter words, but to live by them."

—John F. Kennedy

Just Because It Is Gratitude, Doesn't Mean It Is Ethically Appropriate

Bonnie Elizabeth Parker and Clyde Barrow—better known as simply Bonnie and Clyde—were a legendary romantic and criminal duo from Texas. They first met and fell in love in 1930 when they were both around 20 years old. Clyde had endured a hardscrabble childhood and was already a hardened criminal who had been to prison and who had murdered. Bonnie and Clyde, who sometimes worked with associates, went on to carry out a rash of robberies and killings and earn a mythic, national reputation (Guinn, 2009).

Despite Clyde Barrow's tough upbringing and even tougher experiences as a criminal—variously terrorizing people, running from the law, and spending time in prison—he seemed to have a spark of consideration about him. On April 10, 1934, he allegedly penned a thank you letter to Henry Ford, founder and head of the Ford Motor Company® (Crezo, 2012; Guinn, 2009). The letter was received at the company in Detroit 3 days later. The letter read:

Dear Sir: -

While I still have got breath in my lungs I will tell you what a dandy car you make. I have drove Fords exclusivly when I could get away with one. For sustained speed and freedom from trouble the Ford has got ever other car skinned and even if my business hasen't been strickly legal it don't hurt enything to tell you what a fine car you got in the V8 -

Yours truly
Clyde Champion Barrow (Crezo, 2012)

Bonnie and Clyde met their demise in a shootout with law enforcement on May 23, 1934. They died inside a stolen Ford, less than 6 weeks after Clyde seems to have written and sent his thank you letter. Incidentally, records indicate Mr. Ford directed his secretary to reply with a thank you letter to Clyde. Clyde, though, was not around to pick it up (Guinn, 2009). ════

Different Ethics Guiding Gratitude

There is no question that gratitude communication can do tremendous good. However, there is the potential for gratitude communication to cross ethical and even legal lines. Many professions, organizations, and even whole economic sectors have rules about receiving certain kinds of gratitude, especially those involving money. This means a clear view of the law, terms of employment, and professional accreditation are important. General consideration is needed regarding the following: shared expectations between sender and receiver; any use of touch; acts that transcend the personal-professional boundary; and responsibility to your organization and those you serve in carrying out your overall job. It is not just about possibly breaking a hard and fast rule. It is about making sure that gratitude communication is enhancing rather than taking away from your individual reputation and the reputation of your organization. The Theoretically Speaking section in this chapter proposes stakeholder theory (Donaldson & Preston, 1995) as a way of respecting all of the interested parties in a gratitude situation, regardless of a sender's particular philosophy.

THEORETICALLY SPEAKING
────────────────

Gratitude Communication in Whose Interests?

A stakeholder approach to corporations (Freeman, 1984) emerged as nothing less than a fundamentally new way of conceptualizing those entities. It signaled a departure from the view that an organization's sole purpose was to serve stockholders (Friedman, 1970). Although some leading proponents have cautioned against applying it to organizations other than corporations because of the clear legal rights and obligations of the latter (Donaldson & Preston, 1995), it has often been extended in this way and will be in this chapter. Ethics concerns the matters of right and wrong in human affairs. Of course, the focus here is on using stakeholder theory as a guide to ethical considerations and ethical decision making of work-related gratitude communication for those in various kinds of organizations.

Donaldson and Preston (1995) provided a highly regarded overview of stakeholder theory: A *stakeholder* is an individual, group, or entity with one or more legitimate interests in the affairs of an organization. Stakeholder Theory assumes that all stakeholders anticipate benefits from their involvement with the organization. It has been characterized as descriptive, instrumental, and normative (Donaldson & Preston, 1995). The theory is descriptive in its potential to chart the past, present, and future states of affairs of an organization. It is instrumental in that it can be used to point the way to achieving valued objectives such as profitability. Finally, stakeholder theory is normative in that it can provide ethical guidance for an organization. Notably, the normative aspect of the theory has been described as most critical.

The application of stakeholder theory to the ethics of work-related gratitude communication is useful as it offers a reasonably straightforward yet comprehensive and adaptable framework. In this way, gratitude communication senders and receivers should see themselves as organizational stakeholders with a responsibility to one another and to other stakeholders. These additional stakeholders include those subsumed in the sender's and receiver's primary affiliated organizations (e.g., a relevant employing organization), including these individuals' relevant professional associations and any relevant jurisdictions. Further, this stakeholder approach to ethics should extend throughout the gratitude communication process from preparing to send, to sending, to immediate reception, and to the wider receiving context.

The development of stakeholder theory has led to the realizations that stakeholders are sometimes difficult to identify and balancing the interests of different stakeholders can be challenging (Dempsey, 2009). On the first point, some scholars limit stakeholders to individual humans or groups of humans while others include organizational systems themselves and other entirely non-human stakeholders such as non-human animals and forests (Dempsey, 2009). On the second point, some theorists suggest that stakeholders be prioritized according to their actual or potential influence on the organization, the legitimacy of their organizational claims, and the urgency of their claims (Mitchell et al., 1997, as cited in Dempsey, 2009).

INSIGHTS BASED ON ORIGINAL RESEARCH

Ethics are implicated in gratitude communication in a number of respects. Ethics categories are types of situations when matters of right and wrong become central to gratitude communication. Gratitude communication needs to be considered in the context of hard legal, professional, and other ethical boundaries. Carefully consider whether the use of touch is welcome and whether it is appropriate and effective, particularly from the standpoints of the possible receiver and the relevant organizational contexts. Consider how personal as well as professional interests may be involved in a gratitude communication situation. Professionals should remember they often have a fundamental ethical responsibility to their organization.

Gratitude Communication and Legal Limits and/or Strict Professional Limits

This ethics category captures instances or potential instances of gratitude communication that may very well violate laws and/or hard professional boundaries of what is allowed.

• Government Manager Aware of Limits on Expressions of Gratitude Communication, Specifically Use of Bonuses, in This Sector Versus the Private Sector

Renée is an administrator in the non-political side of state government. Her entire staff was involved with a major project and completed it successfully. Renée thanked the individuals on her team by speaking to them individually and face-to-face.

Renee was aware that, in working in government rather than the private sector, she was limited in how she could express her appreciation. Renee shared:

> It means when I worked in the private sector there were different ways that people could demonstrate gratitude and appreciation and there are things like bonuses and gifts and things that are not allowed in government. ... [W]e do things a little bit differently sometimes than people in corporate America.

In speaking about a situation in which her own supervisor expressed her thanks to Renee for her extraordinary effort to come in on weekends to finish a project, she noted how this person was limited in expressing gratitude. Renee described her own effort and achievement:

It was something that went into effect on a weekend and I came in on the weekend to assist in facilitating the implementation of this program. We are managers, there is no additional pay or anything in there, but the fact that I did without even blinking say, sure, I'll come in on Sunday, and we'll get this done.

Renee seemed keenly aware of forms of gratitude communication she did not and could not take:

If I were in the private sector it would have been bonuses, maybe time off, maybe a gift certificate to something to say just job well done and here's a little token of appreciation. But we're not allowed to do that here.

This next example also highlights the actual and potential friction between the government and the private sector concerning gratitude communication.

- Even Verbal Expression of Gratitude Inappropriate in Private Sector Business Involved in Government Contracts

Shane is a senior manager in an engineering company that has government contracts and, therefore, coordinates quite closely with government employees. While Shane has expressed thanks to his direct reports and sometimes given monetary rewards, he has also received appreciation in a similar manner from his own supervisor in his firm. Nonetheless, he is aware of not engaging in gratitude communication even, apparently, without monetary incentives or gifts with those government employees with whom he interacts, "The reason is that all the work that we do is government contracts and they don't want to show that there was any favoritism."

Use of Touch

The following example indicates how gratitude can be shown in a way that is accepted as appropriate and effective through touch (i.e., a handshake that is within reason) or, contrarily, inappropriate and ineffective through touch (i.e., a handshake that actually becomes physically uncomfortable).

• A Vigorous Thank You Handshake That Hurt My Shoulder

Dale is a college instructor who used to be a full-time church minister. In his role as a college instructor, he was asked by a teacher to give a presentation to middle school students. He did so, it went well, and he was thanked by the teacher. Dale explained:

> [T]he fellow who contacted me, he was just falling all over himself. Apparently, they've had some speakers before that didn't go very well and bored the kids out of their minds and things like that. And he was just falling over himself expressing his gratitude for me and the way I connected with the kids and stuff like that. In fact, I'm going back in February to give another talk. So that felt good to get that kind of affirmation from him.

Dale added, though, that a part of the thank you from the teacher was uncomfortable:

> Well, this was in person, and it was both verbal and non-verbal. He's grinning from ear to ear and shaking my hand 'til my shoulder just [about fell off]. Yeah, he was very effusive with this.

It was very frequently the case that a hug and/or a handshake was seen as appropriate and welcome by a recipient of gratitude communication.

It needs to be generally recognized that touch raises a multitude of ethical considerations, including potential intimidation, sexual assault and harassment, and general disrespect for personal boundaries and cultural and professional norms.

Navigating Personal and Professional Interests

The theme of the personal sphere and professional sphere overlapping in the realm of gratitude communication will be explored in Chapter 10 on the personal and professional. However, it is pertinent as a gratitude communication ethics issue and will be addressed as such here. Many ethical issues are involved with deciding to share or not share information about gratitude communication with others as well as possibly direct others to disseminate or not disseminate such information. Broadly, it is assumed that the circumstances for gratitude can be legitimately scrutinized from an ethical standpoint, even while the primary concern is with gratitude communication. In fact, perhaps that for which a sender is grateful cannot be entirely separated from any narrower consideration of the related gratitude communication itself. When does a gratitude communication gift or reward for one person violate fair access to others, either as a basic benefit or a possible earned benefit?

- Gratitude Communication and Hiding Another's Medical Status

Dale, from above, a former minister and now college instructor, shared an example of how he shifted from the assistant minister role to acting senior minister while the senior minister dealt with end of life health issues. He also discussed the way in which the senior minister and his wife thanked him. In the situation, Dale essentially was at least partially hiding the senior minister's health situation from the congregation. Dale described the situation in part:

> [I]t was about a 2,000-member church. The senior pastor was close to retire-ment and was in the early stages of Alzheimer's. And for the last year of his career I managed to hide the Alzheimer's. He would have been embarrassed, frankly, if people started finding out. And I was very diligent in shielding him from that. So up 'til the point, it wasn't until after he retired that people began to be aware that he was suffering from this. And I remember the last Sunday, when he gave his farewell sermon, and thanked me in the sermon in ways that I knew what he was saying but nobody else did. It was very coded. And his wife came up afterwards and she was crying her eyes out and gave me a big hug, because she knew what had been going on. And so, I guess I did what I did partly out of gratitude for who he was, I had a lot of respect for him. He's since died.

It seems fair to consider whose interests are met and unmet in this example of hiding health information, including the decreased abilities of the top leader, as an act of gratitude and, perhaps, speculatively, as a motivation to receive gratitude.

Dale remembers being thanked verbally "in code":

> [H]e's thanking me for being a good assistant. But if you were on the inside, you knew, the words that were chosen had a lot more meaning than, they had meaning to anybody, but if you were on the inside, there was a lot more being said than was realized. … And the fact that he did was an indication for me of how much it meant to him. Well, for the organization, that was that congregation, the transition from him as senior pastor to retiring went smoothly and helped them move on to the next chapter in that congregation's life. I think if it had come to knowledge, I think it would have been much rockier. He would have been probably pushed out earlier than he wanted to

go. And so I think for the organization it was helpful and it brought some closure, I guess, for us too. Any time you have a retirer like that, there's some grief that goes on. We'd gotten pretty close.

Notably, Dale was ethically satisfied with himself, proud even, to have hidden the senior minister's medical condition. Dale reflected, "I haven't told too many people about this, because the whole idea is that I didn't want anybody to know that he was struggling with this kind of mental health issue."

The power shifts during this time for Dale of communicating gratitude and earning gratitude were remarkable. Dale commented:

Yeah, there was a leadership dimension to this. He was the senior pastor, and I reported to him, but in the same way that I am now a parent to my parent, there was that kind of role reversal there as well. He was aware that he wasn't in a position to do the things that I was doing. And so, without it being discussed, we just kind of did that little dance, and I stepped out in front and led the way for that last year.

With this story, there is the dimension of concealing (i.e., not verbally communicating the purpose behind) Dale's actions. Did this save face for Dale and the senior minister? Did this best represent the interests of others such as the congregants? Who needs to be a part of deciding what is right and wrong in these kinds of circumstances?

Acts That Transcend the Personal-Professional Boundary

Another example of the sometimes-blurry line between personal and professional interests and gratitude communication concerns Paul who was thanked, in part, for his good performance, with a higher tier of medical benefits than his colleagues.

- Thanked With Enhanced Medical Benefits

Jeff is a regional sales manager for a natural personal care products company. Jeff was a top performer but struggled with looking out for his wife's health and health care spending given her serious medical condition. His supervisor expressed appreciation to Jeff by working with human resources to eliminate some health care debt for Jeff and his family and to provide Jeff and his family with better coverage going forward.

Jeff regards this act of gratitude as a private or personal matter that is not or perhaps should not be shared with others, even though they might, at least technically, be similarly deserving from a work accomplishment standpoint and would very much benefit from a similar act of gratitude (i.e., improved medical benefits). Further, Jeff does not feel the need to share with these people even with those who are friends because it is, in his words, "personal."

Jeff commented on the privacy surrounding what he was given, "[I]t was a private [gesture] ... I think this is the first time I'm sharing this story."

Jeff very much regarded his supervisor's act as good. Jeff emphasized the personal and private nature of the act. There is the sense from Jeff's point of view that his supervisor did the right thing not discussing the event and, likewise, his organization did the right thing by not bringing it up again. Jeff offered:

> I don't talk about it. None of my peers, and I still have friends that I worked at that company with, I never told any of them about it. It was just something that was just very personal, and I just kept it to myself. I don't think it was necessary, and they never held it over my head, even after I left the company a few years later, and it was never held over my head. And I spoke with him several years after that and it was never even, never brought up again. It was something they did, and that was just the type of organization, you know, they did it because it was the right thing to do.

Responsibility to Your Organization and All Those You Serve

A further category-level issue concerned ensuring that gratitude communication should not threaten the overall organization.

• Expressions of Gratitude Cannot Jeopardize the Organization's and/or Owner's Financial Standing

Jake, the owner of a small company, suggested that, in one instance, he could have given an employee more money as part of an overall thank you to him. However, Jake, worried this kind of action could be financially threatening to him and, presumably, the financial security and longevity of his organization. Jake offered his rationale:

> I always give each decision a lot of thought and I help out when we can. It's always that magic percent of what can you afford to give away without impacting your life and how much money do you need to live the rest of your life. You know, there are all those unknown factors that you don't wanna give it all away where you are now, not having enough to maintain your lifestyle. At the same time, how much is excess that you really can afford

to part with, without really causing yourself financial concerns? So yeah, there's always that magic line. The only way it could have improved was if the numbers were bigger, the amounts would have been bigger, I guess. But you know, I feel good about what we did and, you know, as I said, I sleep good at night.

Returning to the Opening Story: Can a Gratitude Exchange Work for Sender and Receiver, yet be Unethical?

The story of Bonnie and Clyde raises a lot of ethical issues. Their crimes and the way Barrow's thank you to Ford was premised on Ford unwittingly (up until the arrival of Barrow's letter) facilitating these crimes by making Ford vehicles appealing in eyes of Barrow. This triggers the issue of whether the expressions of crime-related/law-breaking-related gratitude are somehow null and, therefore, should be avoided by would-be senders and would-be receivers. We are reminded that the analysis of gratitude communication cannot be separated from the overall details of the acts acknowledged. A stakeholder approach could have been used to consider what was at stake not just for Barrow, Parker, and Ford, but Ford employees, customers, prospective customers, and the public at large. Although it might be flattering to receive an expression of gratitude from an outlaw in the case of Ford or the head of a major company in the case of Barrow, perhaps it is not always ethical.

Chapter Conclusion

Ethics refers to what is right and wrong. It is involved in all aspects of gratitude communication. It is a complex topic that goes beyond the scope of this chapter but can be supported by research findings that, for example, point to some hard boundaries. A stakeholder approach may be particularly helpful for identifying and managing the interests of all those involved. The next chapter builds on some of the topics raised here in considering the personal and professional aspects of gratitude communication.

Real World Recommendations

- Ethics refers to matters of right and wrong.

- Ethics are thoroughly involved with all aspects of gratitude communication

- Stakeholder theory and specifically a stakeholder analysis, or systematic consideration of likely ethical considerations for all involved parties, offers a way to proactively, transactively, or reactively get clearer about the ethics of a gratitude communication episode.

- Consider whether gratitude communication situations involve any strict boundaries related to applicable laws and to relevant policies and procedures of all organizations involved.

- Carefully consider whether the use of touch is welcome and whether it is appropriate and effective, particularly from the standpoints of the possible receiver and the relevant organizational contexts. (Consider how an act of touch can be unsafe, uncomfortable, construed as sexual in nature, or otherwise be threatening and/or disrespectful and/or non-consensual.)

- Consider how personal as well as professional interests may be involved in a gratitude communication situation. Act responsibly, particularly if personal interests are involved or could be involved for one or more parties. Pay close attention to whose interests are met when privacy is invoked by one or more parties.

- Professionals should remember they often have a fundamental ethical responsibility to their organization. This does not mean they should follow direct or implicit instructions to act unethically on the organization's behalf. Rather, professionals should advance the legitimate interests of their employer, including with their work-related gratitude communication.

Your Opportunity to Work with Gratitude

- Think back to a time when you were unsatisfied with how a gratitude communication situation involving you played out. List the parties involved and indicate interests that were met or unmet. Finally, discuss how the situation could have played out differently to better fulfill relevant interests.

- Think back to a time when you were very satisfied with how a gratitude communication situation involving you played out. List the parties involved and indicate interests that were met or unmet. Finally, discuss how, if at all, the situation could have played out differently to fulfill relevant interests even better.

- Plan and then deliver a gratitude communication message that reflects your efforts to primarily meet the interests of the receiver, yet still respects your basic interests, the organizational context, and the overall legal and societal context.

Policies on the Ethics of Giving, Receiving, and Declining Thank You Gifts

- Expressions of gratitude in workplace settings can involve gifts of considerable monetary value. To help ensure that influence is not being inappropriately bought and/or sold, organizations often have policies about the circumstances under which such gifts can be accepted or given. Research these policies at two or more organizations, and make an argument for their ethical soundness.

Questions for Reflection and Discussion

- What are the ethical dynamics of a popular gratitude example? Locate a workplace gratitude communication example documented in a major popular news source or professional publication. Write a summary of the gratitude communication situation, and then apply a stakeholder analysis to identify whose interests were met and how interests could have been more fully and/or fairly met.

- Can you create a schematic tool to brainstorm ethical gratitude communication possibilities? Using information from this chapter and possibly supplementing it with other material in this book and/or your own research, develop a graphic model (e.g., a flow chart) for sending gratitude communication ethically. The model should function for a range of specific workplace situations.

Recommendations for Learning More

Exploring and Developing Advice for Ethical Gift Giving and Receiving

Read the following *Huffington Post* article on gift giving in the workplace, including gifts that reflect a sender's gratitude. Identify two key points that seem most pertinent to you from an ethics point of view. Propose two additional points not found in the article that offer additional, complementary guidance on this topic: Gottsman, D. (2016, December 9). 9 office gift-giving dos and don'ts. *Huffington Post.*

The Ethical Standards of Professional Associations

For your chosen or intended professional area, identify and compare the ethical standards from two or more professional associations. For instance, a communication scholar and/or practitioner might look at the ethical statements of the National Communication Association (NCA) and the International Communication Association (ICA). Consider the two ethical points from your search that seem like they would be most helpful to your future decision making. Propose two additional points that offer additional, complementary guidance.

The ICA Code of Ethics

The NCA Credo for Ethical Communication

10

Personal and Professional Lives and Gratitude Communication

"Once we believe in ourselves we can risk curiosity, wonder, spontaneous delight or any experience that reveals the human spirit."

—e. e. cummings

Gratitude Communication and the Personal and Pro LeBron James

The basketball great LeBron James was born on December 30, 1984, in Akron, Ohio, less than a 45-minute drive from his hometown NBA city of Cleveland. James was an early standout player who led his high school team to various championships, becoming the first high school sophomore to be named to the *USA Today* All-USA First Team and the first high school junior to appear on the cover of *Sports Illustrated* (Graham, 2016).

James was the number one overall draft pick in 2003 and signed by his hometown Cleveland Cavaliers, a team that had never won an NBA championship. While James was a league standout from the start (earning rookie of the year recognition, all-star team recognition from 2005–2010, league MVP honors in 2009 and 2010, and more), the Cavaliers could not clinch the national title in the first 7 years of James's professional career. On July 1, 2010, James announced that he had signed with the Miami Heat.

James's overall decision to leave the Cavaliers sparked many controversies. One that got considerable attention was an open letter, written by Cavaliers's majority owner Dan Gilbert, addressed to "Cleveland, All of Northeast Ohio and Cleveland Cavaliers Supporters Wherever You May Be Tonight" (Lombardi, 2018, para. 4). Referring to James, Gilbert began, "As you now know, our former hero, who grew up in the very region that he deserted this evening, is no longer a Cleveland Cavalier" (Lombardi, 2018, para. 5). Gilbert's rant was an ugly attack on James that included a characterization of James's decision as a "cowardly betrayal" (D'Andrea, 2018, para. 8). The NBA judged the letter to be so out of line that it fined Gilbert $100,000 (Skowronski, 2010).

James moved to Miami, maintained his incredible level of athletic performance, and led the Heat to the NBA Championship titles in 2012 and 2013. In 2014, James returned to the Cavaliers and led them to their first NBA Championship in 2016. On July 1, 2018, James announced he was again leaving the Cavaliers, this time to play with the Los Angeles Lakers (O'Shaughnessy, 2018). How would Gilbert react this time?

With gratitude. Gilbert and the Cavaliers posted a statement of appreciation to James that opened with the memory of him playing the lead role in breaking a 52-year-long national championship drought for their city and region. It explicitly acknowledged that this would not have happened if James had not agreed to return home (D'Andrea, 2018). Gilbert spoke not just for himself: "The entire Cavaliers franchise thanks LeBron for that precious moment and for all of the excitement he delivered as he led our team to four straight NBA Finals appearances" (para. 5). The letter was personal in its overall tone and personal in recognizing James as first a family man (D'Andrea, 2018).

Well-intentioned work-related gratitude communication very often reflects and generally affects senders and receivers simply as human beings. It is a major finding of the research project underpinning this book. In addition, many times personal and professional lives significantly overlap in the sending and receiving of gratitude communication. In so many of these instances, there is plenty of upside and little or no downside, although there are actual and/or potential downsides. On the upside, frontline workers are more committed to an organization that aligns with their personal values, as is often showcased with the sending and/or receiving of gratitude messages. The relationship between a manager and a direct report can be fortified with an overall gratitude interaction that appropriately recognizes what matters to an individual beyond the workplace. The Theoretically Speaking section in this chapter highlights the theory of relational dialectics (Baxter & Montgomery, 1996) and communication privacy management (Petronio, 2002) as ways to explain the ongoing and not necessarily negative tension between the professional and personal when communicating gratitude.

There Is Often a Personal-Professional Tension Managed in Gratitude Communication

The theory of relational dialectics (Baxter & Montgomery, 1996), established that different tensions exist in interpersonal relationships and communications. Others, including Petronio (2002) have identified and elaborated some of these tensions. Communication privacy management theory (Petronio, 2002, 2007, 2009) was developed in relation to a long line of theory and research on disclosure. However, communication privacy management theory (CPMT) broke from earlier work by attempting to more effectively explain the breadth of findings that had been amassed. CPMT originator Sandra Petronio incorporated the theory of relational dialectics (Baxter & Montgomery, 1996) into her work, specifically the idea that disclosure and privacy comprised two poles in tension with one another. For instance, if whether addressing the purely personal, the purely professional and/or a fusion of the two, communicators tend to make decisions about what should be shared and what should remain private. Unsurprisingly, gratitude communication inevitably takes place in these circumstances. The issues of tension and/or balance may be implicitly and/or explicitly negotiated by one or more of the communicators in a given interaction.

CPMT (Petronio, 2002) proposes that five principles provide a basis for understanding how privacy and disclosure are handled in interpersonal and other kinds of social relationships.

1. Individuals own the private information about themselves and have the right to control access to it.

2. Access to private information is managed using privacy rules that can vary according to factors such as personal identity categories and culture.

3. When an individual discloses information to another party that party becomes a co-owner of the information and assumes a responsibility for appropriately and effectively handling the information.

4. The owner and co-owner(s) of information must have some level of coordination around further sharing of the information.

5. Deficits in coordination can cause violations and dilemmas.

A dialectic can be described as a tension between two poles, such as a desire to share and a desire to keep information to oneself. Dialectics can shift, for example, two individuals in a close relationship agree that it is okay for one person's private story to be shared with others beyond the dyad. Although the privacy-disclosure dialectic does not necessarily correspond to the divide between personal information and professional information, it can sometimes correspond quite closely and it can inform other dynamics, including so-called positive and/or negative information.

INSIGHTS BASED ON ORIGINAL RESEARCH

Gratitude communication can demarcate the line between the personal and professional and at other times transcend the line. Sometimes gratitude communication at work is valued more when the main message is relatively personal. Sometimes core work is thoroughly personal in terms of roles mixing and involving gratitude communication. Personal biographical overlaps with others in the workplace can involve gratitude communication and be meaningful in a positive way. Sometimes work-related gratitude communication is very personal in its core content. Sometimes work means interacting as a person/human being rather than a professional or worker. Some individuals are just deeply committed to using positive communication, including gratitude communication with all those they encounter in work and life.

Sometimes Gratitude Communication at Work Is Valued More When the Message Is Relatively Personal

Notwithstanding comments in Chapter 3 on the why of gratitude communication and the general recommendation to follow Dweck (2006) and reinforce specific behaviors, some prefer gratitude communication that is concentrated on an individual and/or an individual's behaviors, (the latter of which could be consistent with Dweck) rather than a larger configuration of people.

- Gratitude Felt Good Because It Was More About Me Personally

Sana is a communication strategist. Over the past year, she shifted from operating her own business to being hired as a salaried employee by one of her clients. The appropriateness and effectiveness for gratitude messages to sometimes be targeted at one person was evident for Sana in terms of an employee to whom she shared performance feedback as well as in Sana's own receipt of gratitude communication from her new full-time organization.

Sana arranged a conversation with an employee about that employee's performance, growth, and remuneration. She described these conversations as something "I do on a regular basis, personally and, then again, professionally." The employee here is Daliah, a marketing specialist.

Sana recounted the situation with Daliah:

I have an employee, and she's a stellar performer, she's just a great asset to the organization. And she had issues with her compensation levels. ... And after evaluating just her contributions to the organization, that means heard her say something once or twice, and helped her understand what the next step may need to be. And my desire came out of a gratitude for her contributions to the organization after doing the research. When I did the research and I saw how much she's contributed toward the organization, one of the last things she needed to be concerned about is her compensation. So I sought out the right steps in order to get her where she needed to be, and in that—oh, in that came just a great desire to share with her what I was able to accomplish for her and express my gratitude to have her on my team. So that's something very simple and I would say pretty standard, but not really. This was not during any promotional period or anything, it was just a great opportunity to show somebody that you care through the things that are of value to them, and that's her livelihood.

Notably, Sana included a very personal, "[Y]ou're valued," in her written and spoken message to Daliah. Sana's reference to Daliah's "livelihood" also seemed personal.

Daliah responded very positively. Sana explained what she observed:

Ecstatic, overjoyed—in addition to just those heightened temporary emotions, she began to exhibit, I would say, a different swagger about her job. As much as she was dedicated and she contributed before, she did so even though she was struggling on the financial side. She felt she deserved more and wasn't getting it. And after making the adjustment, in addition to the gratitude that was expressed and her joy, it was confidence that was exuding from her now, she's just on fire. In fact, this financial thing was really hindering her before and she was doing so well before. Her potential is far greater now that those things are no longer concerns for her. It turned into more of a confidence and, I don't know, a response that is definitely outwardly visible.

The personal meaning of the financial improvement for Daliah seemed striking for both Sana and Daliah.

Well, I'll say there was an underlying theme of her not pursuing the thing that she wanted, her being afraid to. So you're talking compensation, right, and she's being compensated. She walked into an agreement, she had a deal and she agreed to a certain compensation package. However, she is a strong performer, she works hard and after a while she felt like she should be ... and she wasn't acknowledged for her efforts. But she was also afraid to speak up because in her mind she was saying to herself, 'I did agree to this,' it's not like they didn't deliver on the expectation. They set the expectation and I agreed to it, it's just I really want more and I don't know how to say it and I don't want to be controversial or confrontational when I have a conversation. She absolutely refused to bring it up. In fact, it was not just the refusal, it was, 'I can't do this, I can't, I don't like confrontation.' I'm like there's no—confrontation is right now, it's all in your mind. I was like it doesn't exist, you have not spoken this to anyone. I was like until you speak it to somebody, and you justify the reasons why you think you might be eligible for more, it's just a conversation, it's not confrontation. And so, there was a lot of coaching that I had to do to get her, 'cause I told her I wasn't gonna do it all for her, I wasn't gonna do it all for her. I was like I'm gonna strengthen you through this process and I'm going to encourage you every step of the way. What you're gonna do is you're gonna write a petition requesting a change and you're gonna do this and you're gonna submit this and you're gonna do it by this date. You feel this way, you're gonna do it; you're not gonna complain to me anymore, you're gonna do it. And so I had to walk her through this process that was very difficult for her.

The women exchanged messages of thanks related to Daliah's growth and this exchange was personally meaningful for Sana: "My being the recipient of her personal note about her growth that had taken place during this process is something I'll probably keep in my little time capsule." To be clear, this is an example of Sana, a manager, expressing gratitude to and receiving gratitude back, in the form of a personal note, from a direct report.

- When I Felt Personally Valued in the Recruiting Process, It Made Me Want to Commit to the Organization Professionally

Sana had another story of the personal merging with the professional and involving gratitude communication in the position for which she was recruited:

> Let me take a step back—to my coming on board, this was a client of mine, and I guess I would say being the recipient of, being pursued, to me, is a great sense of gratitude. And so, having a previous business relationship with the group here that leads this organization, because I was a consultant through my own consulting firm, and they were a client, they pursued me and wanted me to assume this role as VP for their company. They didn't want anyone else and they invited me to join their company and be a part of the growth that they anticipated.

When Sana was getting recruited by her then-consulting clients to work as an employee, they made it clear they appreciated her and did not want anyone but her. They expressed their appreciation through wonderful food and accommodations, including at a Florida resort. Sana recalled:

> Yes, yes, that's the thing, [two senior executives] were like, if you won't take the role, that's fine, we're not gonna make you, we can't make you, but we want you to know it's only you we want but if you have to say no, then help us find somebody else.

Again, Sana continued about the gratitude gesture shown her: "[T]he greatest flattery for any consultant is to be brought in, no longer a third party, you'd be welcomed in, it's an ushering of you are welcome here and we want you to stay, you know." The executives with whom Sana met expressed recognition of her talents and she perceived their treatment of her as showing appreciation. Sana took a few days to make up her mind. She committed to the new position after considering how it would fit with her private life:

> I am a stay-at-home, or work-from-home mom, if you will, so I did not want to jeopardize my role and my presence with my kids in their lives. This is a way that they expressed gratitude, and also, my desire to take on this position is every time I came at them with a hindrance or a potential barrier for my being able to accept this role, they completely, they removed it. So when I said, you know, I'm not gonna relocate, I'm gonna stay here, my family's here—my husband just took a new job so it's not gonna be easy for me to relocate, and I don't want to. So, they said okay, well, if you decide

to accept this position, we won't make you relocate, we're just gonna ask that you come and be with your team for, you know, a period of time or a frequency that will add value to your team.

Sana negotiated so she could stay with her family and her immediate team in Houston. "So they just made it really easy, they made it really easy. They removed all barriers in order for me to say yes." Sana was emotional in a positive way about the way she was welcomed with gratitude: "I'm being recognized and crying because you guys think I really matter. So that's kind of the gift of it."

Sometimes Regular Work Is Thoroughly Personal in Terms of Roles Mixing and Involving Gratitude Communication

This category reflects instances when the personal and professional are one in the same and involve gratitude communication.

- My Boss Is My Wife, and She Expresses Gratitude to Me

This next example of personal and professional roles thoroughly overlapping is of a professional who works with his spouse and experienced a conflict with her. The conflict was at least partially resolved with an expression of gratitude towards him.

Ian is a graphic designer in a small firm owned by his wife, Michelle. In the past summer, Ian and Michelle had a conflict when Michelle expressed her concern about the sales function needing to be better addressed. In response, Ian voiced that he felt like his work was unappreciated and that their work relationship was affecting their marriage. This seemed to quickly trigger Michelle to express her appreciation to Ian. Ian explained:

I had reached a point with working with her that I thought maybe it was time for me to go and find something else to do. I just felt the relationship was not going as well as I had liked, the working relationship, and I thought it was impacting our marriage. And what was there for me was the sense that the work I was doing was not being appreciated. I was very frustrated with that because one of my primary reasons for being hired was sales, and what I've done while there is almost everything with the exception of sales because there were so many other things that needed to be done. And so for my wife, the fact that the sales aspect wasn't done was really all that kind of mattered to her, and the other things did not matter as much. And so I felt really like I wasn't being appreciated, so I brought it up with her. And the way in which I brought it up somehow I had kind of gotten through, so to speak, and I know that I had gotten through because shortly, after our conversation, I mean literally the same day, she had come into my office and we sat down and we talked and she had thanked me for all of the things that I had done. And she had done it in a way that left me definitely feeling appreciated and acknowledged. And that, at the time, meant all the difference in the world. You know, I was considering finding something else to do for a living and I now still work there, you know, so it was like that kind of transition.

Ian summarized his boss's/wife's message to him:

The message to me was 'I have noticed what you've done, it has made a huge difference and I'm grateful for it.' One, I interpreted it as genuine, there was an authenticity to it, which mattered because, you know, just empty thanks, which we all have had the experience, you know, it's just you can see it when you experience it. So, it was genuine, it was authentic. I interpreted it as real thanks for the work that had been done, a recognition that the work was important and that absent me the work would not have been done. That's how I interpreted it. I felt reinvigorated and empowered to do my job. I think it was especially positive because it was very real, like I was gonna probably hand in my resignation and the fact that it went in a different direction, an unanticipated direction.

For some, work relationships not based on family biology and/or marriage are metaphorically or literally treated like family relationships, another example of personal and professional roles mixing considerably. It is important to note some ethical issues and practical issues could conceivably arise in these relationship dynamics, which are not fully explored here.

- A Heartfelt Thank You to a Figurative Work Spouse

Possibly the most ethically controversial account of personal and professional roles blurring occurred with a dentist and his manager whom he described as his "work wife." Was she herself indeed comfortable with this description? Can present-day organizations be run in this manner, even if two individuals are consensual in using this sort of description for their interpersonal relationship?

Max is a dentist who owns his own practice. He recalled expressing his appreciation to his longtime manager, Irene, in a very personal way. Notably, it was an extremely personal message because he described their relationship as being like a married couple, even though, apparently, they were not romantically intimate with and/or committed to one another in a literal family bond. Max's message was also personal in that he mentioned how she bettered his life (i.e., his personal sphere) not just his work (i.e., his professional sphere). Max explained:

> *I called [my manager] and I thanked her for 45 wonderful years of making my life and job easier, for taking care of me, treating me just like I was her husband in business and not just 'she's punching an eight-hour clock.' For some people that watch the clock and other people don't even look at the clock, they're just trying to help the organization and the business, and Irene for 45 years is like a second wife.*

Max spoke to Irene over the phone and it was emotional for both of them. He expressed his love for what she had done and, according to Max, "[S]he was crying, couldn't believe what I said." Max spoke about his work wife with affection and obligation:

> *Because you can't say it often enough, and sometimes when I'm content you don't say things. Like you're married, and every day you don't say you love your wife. But she knows you're there, and you're taking care of her and providing and you love everything you do together, but yet every day you don't go and say you know what, I love you, you're the greatest thing that's ever happened to me. So, you have to express it verbally every once in a while, even though she knows it.*

Some might perceive that Max was sexist and/or had ulterior motives, yet the meaning was limited for him:

> *That was, to me, just saying, thank you. I expressed it as a friend in telling her how much she's meant to me. ... She's more than an employee, so I don't like the word.*

• My Work Group and the Gratitude Communication Expressed There Makes Up for the Family Experience I Lost

Nadia is a recent graduate with a part-time position at a large utility company. Family-related relationships came up for her in that setting and in a previous role she had as a student worker in a college career center.

In the utility company, Nadia became aware that her supervisor was having a tough time with her family. Nadia spoke with her supervisor, in part sharing her own family's difficulties. Nadia provided an overview of the situation: "[My supervisor] was going through a difficult time with her family and, we just sat down and talked. I told her about my experience with my family, and it made her feel better." Nadia provided more detail:

We talked about [how] her father is very sick and, they were in another state, and she was, obviously, close to her dad, so the distance thing bothered her. And I just expressed to her that, your parents will always love you and you do what you can to be there for them. And I told her about my past, and, when I was younger my mother passed ... I learned to pretty much accept the fact that, life happens to everyone, and you have to stay strong, stay positive, and do what you can.

Notably, Nadia listened and provided advice and combined these roles with an expression of thanks for her supervisor. Nadia's thank you to her supervisor was the following,

I really appreciate you taking me under your wing. Even though I'm not a fulltime employee here and pretty much a stranger, you took a chance and took me under your wing, and I really appreciate all that you have done for me.

Nadia explained her apparent main goal with the overall exchange:

[T]o just let her know, it doesn't have to be related to work, it could be on a personal level. We kept it business but she said if I needed her with anything just let her know, because I opened up to her, she opened up to me.

Interestingly, Nadia was aware of the melding of the personal and professional spheres and their differences, including her need to balance tensions between them.

Yes, it's good to always have a good relationship, especially with someone above you. But the benefit between our relationship was we knew how to separate that business and personal, and it grew into something a lot more.

- I'm Grateful We're Family Despite not Sharing Biology

Nadia remembered another situation at the nexus of the professional and the personal that invoked quasi-family and gratitude communication. Upon leaving her student worker role in her college career center, Nadia sent an email expressing "how I felt and ... I am blessed to have them a part of my life, and throughout everything that's happened I consider them family."

Nadia recalled what she wrote to Geraldine, a full-time administrative assistant with whom Nadia worked closely as a student:

'I'm blessed to have you in my life. Even though you're not my blood mother, I still consider you my mom.' I just wanted her to know that no matter what happened between us I love her and she is my mom. And her response to the email, she felt the same way, so she was very grateful for my honesty.

Nadia added, as if to emphasize her point, "You don't have to be a blood relative to be family."

When Nadia extended her appreciation to Geraldine, it reinforced the family connection between the two of them. The thank you addressing Nadia for being herself seems personal in another respect.

The face-to-face conversation in Geraldine's office made Nadia feel like she had a place in the world.

Nadia spoke of her relational progress, "It felt good because since I [moved away after college], you know, I was sort of isolated. … And I felt like I belonged again, you know, when she said that to me."

- Celebrating My Birthday Made Me Feel Valued by My Colleagues

A final gratitude communication episode in which Nadia participated and which took a strong personal bend was when a group of individuals working in the career center gave her a birthday celebration.

Nadia explained who was involved and why it was poignant for her: "It was my 18th birthday and everyone from the director to various counselors [were there]. They all took the time and celebrated my birthday. And that's something that my family hasn't done since my mom passed."

Notably, words of thanks were expressed not only in terms of Nadia's work-related strengths but who she was as a person, too. Nadia recollected,

I showed them my strengths, then how much of a good person I am and that they were happy to have me work for them.

- Able to Involve My Loved One in Workplace Gratitude Event

Steve is the police commander at a large university. Two years ago, the student government named a student award in Steve's honor, as an act of appreciation toward Steve. It was deeply meaningful to Steve that he was able to bring his father to the event that recognized Steve as the namesake and first recipient of the award.

As well as being a commander, Steve was also an ex-official member of the student senate, so he worked very closely with them in the student government.

Steve described the purpose of the award and how it was named: "And it's awarded to a student every year who exemplifies community service involvement and dedication to the university. And the award is actually called the Steve Johnson Student Award of Excellence."

Steve talked about the event:

It came as a surprise to me, actually. It was awarded to me as the first recipient at a banquet, and again, I didn't know this was going to occur, and then they said, we have a special award tonight and it's given out for the first time. And the student body president at the time went into kind of a spiel about the work that I had done with the student government and with students, etc. over the years. And he said from now on this award will be given out on an annual basis.

Steve talked about his reaction:

I'm very rarely without words but I was taken back that night. It meant the world to me 'cause working with these kids over the years is such a great joy, and just working with them is a lot of fun and everything but to get this was just really special, and to know that it's going to go on forever, so.

Steve mentioned that the event was especially positive and memorable for two reasons, including a strong personal connection:

[O]ne, because I was very surprised by it, and two, my dad was with me. And that was very special. … [I]t was my mom and dad's anniversary, that's what it was, and my mom had just recently died. And so I didn't want dad to be alone on his anniversary, and I wasn't going to go to the banquet, you know, we were just gonna go out and go to dinner or something. And they said no, no, no, don't do that, you know, we understand, bring your dad, you know, that would be great. So that's how he ended up being there.

Personal Biographical Overlaps With Others in the Workplace Can Involve Gratitude Communication and Be Meaningful in a Positive Way

Garret is a catering manager at an event venue and golf course. Several years ago, he was involved with showing appreciation to an employee who was living with the same cancer diagnosis as Garret's mother. Garret recalled:

A few years back, I had an employee, Jenna, who was working for me in a different business in a different setting, who found out she had cancer. And it was the same cancer that my mother had at the time. She was going through financial difficulties. She was going to have to stop working. She would have [had] medical bills. And I've kind of been through it with my family so I decided to get the [work] district together and without her knowing, we got a ton of people to walk for her for a cancer benefit and awareness walk. She was shocked to see us there. We all had t-shirts made with her name on it and a picture of her on the back. Her family was kind of in on it and knew that we were trying to get it together but had no idea that the outcome would be as good as it was. We had a ton of people there. We raised over $5,000 just from the employees, and then the company that I worked for at the time matched it. And then we also gave her about a thousand dollars in just random gift cards to like grocery stores, things that would help out with everyday life.

The message that I think that I was trying to relay to her would be that times are going to get tough, it is going to be difficult, but there's a lot of people that care for you that you might not realize and that are willing to be here to support you in any way that you need. And I love you.

Jenna was surprised in the middle of the charity walk. Garrett explained,

They actually turned a corner in the walk, and I had everybody in the organization ready to go. And I knew she would be coming through. I was contacting her children throughout the entire walk, through text messages. So we had an idea. And she came around the corner and had no idea and started crying, started bawling actually. And then we just explained why we're here and the message we were trying to relay to her. And that we really care about her.

Garrett put the whole situation in perspective and also seemed to draw out a bigger lesson:

Do not forget that you're dealing with people. And that you're dealing with people who have feelings and who deal with problems and who have things going on in their life. And although you try not to bring anything in to work, there are some things that are inevitably going to be brought in under some circumstances.

Garrett explained why this episode had such resonance for him:

It was very positive and memorable for me because my mother dealt with the same cancer that she had and when my mom had the cancer, they gave her, they told her she had four months to live. And it was hell getting my mom to go through treatment and stuff like that. She didn't want to and she fought it and she beat it.

Garrett continued wistfully,

So it was really memorable because I had been there before. Not personally but associated with someone who had it so it made it memorable to reach out. I wish we'd had that help that she received.

Sometimes Work-Related Gratitude Communication Is Very Personal in Its Core Content

Perhaps nothing symbolizes the personal as much as a home. Ray, an insurance broker, was quick to help out one of his clients when he learned they suffered a house fire. Ray was quick to show up in person and also secure the involvement of various insurance company representatives and contractors to take care of the clean-up and rebuild. He was thanked with a dinner out, which included his wife. The client's message as relayed by Ray, was, "Thank you for thinking about me, so this is just a little token of my appreciation, you know, not a payment, just a little token to express my thanks to you, you know, we really appreciate it."

Interestingly, Ray felt and shared gratitude in this situation, too, especially towards those other professionals that were able to help at his request. "You know you have the trust that they're gonna take care of that person and treat the person fairly."

The family was extremely inconvenienced by the fire and clean up. Ray shared:

Because this was a major fire, the family had to live in temporary housing for almost three to four months. It was the fall so they were actively there right away trying to restore the home as soon as possible so that they could, get the family back into the home. And I just think, that when I went over there to the home with the fire, you know, they were there and they just started trying to do whatever they could to mitigate the damages. And I told them, you know, everything is gonna be okay and, you know, everything was taken care of for them. So it took it off of, you know, what we do for them initially, putting them up right away and going in and being able to take care of their home because to see your home go up in flames—and it was an accident, you know, a cooking accident, but still.

Yes, that's an awful thing to have to think about because you stand a chance to lose everything. And it was contained in the kitchen, I mean the fire department has to be a part of the applause also because they got there expeditiously, and they contained it so it wouldn't spread all over, but you still have the smoke damage, you know, everywhere.

Sometimes Work Means Interacting as A Person/ Human Being Rather Than a Professional or Worker

• A Dentist Participating in Gratitude Communication at Work Is Just Being Human

Returning to the conversation with Max the dentist—he was adamant about participating in gratitude communication because of its humanity.

Referrals from employees are an instance, in his eyes, of receiving deep humanistic gratitude:

Well, to me the main thing is if my employees respect everything I've done and they see how I learn and study to be a better dentist, then the finest expression of that would be them sending their family, relatives, children, fathers, mothers, aunts and uncles to me, and they did. So that would be, to me, how they're expressing it to me.

• The Professional Charity Work I Do Is Because I Care About People

A way that Max feels like he and the office extend their fundamental human appreciation to others is with their charity dental work.

Max talked about performing charity dental work for a woman who, along with her husband, was dealing with life difficulties:

Okay, every year the charity we give in our office is, you know, in these times it's very rough, so people that have come here for decades, we know them more as teeth—no, we know them more as human beings, and if we know they lost a job, her husband lost his job, they're in trouble, we give tremendous courtesy to these people. That's my charity. I don't like charity but that's giving back for what people gave me when things were great for me.

Max continued with the details of this act of charity:

This last month a patient came in, needed probably close to $5,000 worth of work. She was crying, she's 80 something, her husband's dying, she needed this work, she had no money, they're on welfare and I did the fee for the low cost of like $1,800. That just happened probably three or four weeks ago.

Max described his basic message to this patient:

You're more than teeth, we understand your circumstances, and we care about you, and this is something we want to do as a gift for you.

Max was comfortable and happy to give and yet was aware of his limits:

I said I'm willing to lose money. Here's what I can do it for you. Below this I can't because I just would go out of business, but I can come down to this number for you because of who you are.

Max expressed that he hopes she knows "someone cares about her." Both Max and the patient were quite emotional:

Oh, she was crying, she received it well because I almost started crying.

Max listed the benefits he saw for the patient:

The benefits put her in a better state of health, better beauty, functionality and confidence, and helping her whole life, actually.

Max explained his motivation:

Well, personally for me it shows that I care about people, I'm not above a certain situation that I don't care and it's how I give back.

• My Gifts to Patients and Their Families Are to Show My Appreciation and Caring

Max will sometimes receive food, gifts, and words of appreciation from patients and families he has helped. In these instances, he also concentrates on the humanity.

See, in that one I would describe myself as just a human being accepting gifts from someone that cares, that's expressing their gratitude. I don't think of myself as an employee, manager, anything, just one human being to another giving some thanks.

Perhaps the most dramatic and longstanding act of humanity-inspired gratitude that Max showed over the years was acknowledging the significant wedding anniversaries of couples with a gift certificate for a sitting for a portrait with a professional photographer.

Max shared how meaningful it was and also why he chose to stop:

The people would come in crying, crying. One particular instance, I had done it for a couple married 60 years. Two weeks later her husband died. And she came over, she had made something for us. She said you know that picture, I said yeah, she says I can't tell you how much it meant, we hadn't had a picture taken in 30 years together, and that's right in my living room, and I know every time I look at it what you did for us.

Then finally [I was paying] $500, $700 and then I had to finally stop it, which I hated because the expression of gratitude from everybody over these pictures was just amazing. So that would have been the most positive thing I loved doing, but I had to stop it.

- Gratitude Communication in an Instance Where I Provided a Listening Ear to an Employee Dealing With Personal Emotional Issues and Career Decisions Sheila is the owner of a retail shop. One of the gratitude stories she shared was getting thanked by an employee, Dana, for being a sounding board during a difficult time in her personal life. Sheila explained:

One of my employees was going through some personal emotional issues as far as some changes in her life in another career that she had and in need of a listening ear and maybe some advice. And I was able to provide that for her on many occasions during the course of maybe a few weeks. … She needed some help kind of coming to some decisions, as well as just needed to be heard. And she expressed her gratitude to me face-to-face as well as through an email.

Sheila talked about what it seemed to mean to this person, including triggering gratitude toward Sheila: "[She] felt gratitude for me listening on multiple occasions and helping them with some other problems [she was] going through."

Sheila seemed to stress that while it seemed very positive for the employee, it was not a big imposition on Sheila:

I guess it being positive and memorable for me was to know that I was able to help somebody else, you know, to me it was something very little and minor in my life, but yet it seemed major to her at the time. So again, it was positive to me to know that by my just listening or saying a few kind words helped somebody else out through a rough time.

- Remembering My Team Members' Birthdays With a Card and a Gratitude Message

Carey works as a manager in the insurance industry. She explains her work arrangement and how she acknowledges her team members on a personal as well as professional level.

I work remote so all of my colleagues are across the United States, all right. I have home office people in one state and I have colleagues in random states across the U.S. Well, I think I take the time to remember their birthdays. Okay, now this is silly, this is my colleague, this is my peer, I take the time to mail them a happy birthday card. 'Cause many times, you bounce things off of your colleagues for direction or what would you do in this case. And I just handwrite that little thank you card, and you don't know how touched these people are when they get a thank you—I mean I handwrite the birthday card. They get a birthday card from me. You would think it's like a million dollars and it's just me taking my time out to thank them for their friendship, wishing them well, and wishing them another year of health and success in business.

Carey described the reaction she gets when she expressed gratitude to colleagues in her organization:

They were very pleased, they were, I think, touched, and flattered. And my biggest reward, we give something just because you want to give it because it's needed, but they say, Carey, it's always a pleasure working with you. Many times your peers are not as nice as you are. Your peers are just not very nice when they talk to us … you always treat us so respectfully and nice and kind, I really want to thank you for that, thank you, that really was very nice of you, thank you. So I think they really appreciate it because I think my colleagues treat everybody the way I treat them, but I learned, that we are just individuals, and some people just don't, some people don't have a nice approach when they need something. They have a demanding approach. I can't do that, that's not the way I was—that's not me. And I think that the people receive it, people who are nice when asking for things and people who are, do this, what did you do wrong, you need to do this, you need to get this paid versus hey, what do you think you could do to help me out here. We had a tragedy in the city. Seven people were killed by a guy who walked into a health spa. How can you help me, what can we do to get this claim expeditedly paid? You know what I mean? And that's the person, you treat people nicely, they treat you nicely. You treat people rude and mean, they treat you—they don't wanna work, they won't wanna help you.

Carey elaborated how work becomes personal and friendships develop:

I think because you get to know these people that you work with, you get to know about them. You know when their child is sick, you know when an illness happens and you know when they go on vacation, you know when they have a good vacation, a bad vacation and it kind of lends a little bit of a personal end of sharing, which is true. I mean it's not fake. You have a true personal end of sharing and you become that person's friend, as well as their colleague. And then when you have the friend and the colleague, it's much easier to kind of work through things.

Some Individuals Are Just Deeply Committed to Using Positive Communication, Including Gratitude Communication With All Those They Encounter in Work and Life

• It Is Really Okay to Deliver a Compliment in the Form of Gratitude Communication

Stewart is an entertainment professional (including producer and writer) who also works as a university instructor. Stewart discussed his overall view toward the topic of gratitude communication at work:

You know, I think I'm pretty aware of this type of interaction, and I've also gotten this philosophy, developed this philosophy of, even though it doesn't seem to be something that's done very frequently in my business of entertainment, I've always kept to the idea that it's nice to give people a compliment. You don't always have to, you know, tell people when there's a problem. I mean that's not the only time that you should be speaking with people that you work with is to tell them something's wrong. It's really quite okay to deliver a compliment. And a lot of times, ... but especially in New York City, when you would compliment someone, they would react with a, oh, what do you want, you know, type of reaction, like as if I was being disingenuous or manipulative by offering a compliment, 'cause those things were so rarely doled out. So, in the last year at the university where I teach, I expressed gratitude to my boss. It was an anniversary of something or other, not really exactly sure. It could have been the second-year anniversary of my employment there. But I made sure to let him know that I was very grateful for him having hired me and for having had the faith in me to, you know, allow me to do and develop my own job and to keep my own hours, and to continually be supportive. And I'm trying to think if I can elaborate in any way. He received it well, you know, he didn't go overboard, but he pretty much gave the same kind of reaction right back to me, like you know, what a great gift it was to have me on the staff and, you know, that I'm part of the family there now, and a nice exchange.

- Showing Caring for People Is Most Important

Frank is a soon-to-be retired financial planning professional, the founder of an investment group, who is very aware of extending and receiving caring in his professional life.

First, it feels good when you do something nice for someone, [and] there are benefits to the sender, as well as the recipient, as you very well know. And when you do something for someone when they are in trouble or when they suffer a setback, people don't forget this. You don't do it, you don't do something like that for self-serving reasons because if that encumbers what you do for people, it usually falls flat or it's transparent. Do something for someone because it's the right thing to do or it's a nice thing to do for them. And the side benefit, obviously, is it builds client loyalty in that instance because it's in all kinds of surveys that why people deal with an investment person. Believe it or not the number one reason is because they like them. It isn't because they make them the most money, they like them and they trust them. And there's been all kinds of studies in the investment industry about that. People think it's oh, you're dealing with someone because they make you more money than you think anyone else can make for you, make you. That's not, that has not been the survey that's been done of clients across the industry.

Well, also this woman being a widow, her husband died, actually it was in 1985 he died. He was actually a colleague at the firm and he suffered, he had a heart problem and passed away. And he told his wife that if anything should happen to him to come to us for advice, and which we did. So that relationship goes back a substantial amount of time. She, as I said, she and her family went through horrendous times in the Netherlands during the war.

It isn't the size of the present that you give to somebody; it isn't the quantity necessarily; it's the fact that you expressed the fact that you cared.

Well, I'll tell you one thing that makes me feel good, and fortunately I hear this with reasonable frequency, which makes me feel good. When I built a business that was based upon being honorable with people, trying to give them good advice and trying to take care of them and caring about them over a period of years—we had very low client turnover and a lot of client loyalty in a very competitive field. And when I was considering retirement I felt that I had to bring on other advisors and build the team so that some day when I retired that my clients would be taken care of with the same diligence that I had tried during the course of my career, and the people would echo, that I brought on would echo this culture that I had tried to build up. And what I'm getting to is that I have received many, many compliments about the fact that I left them in good hands with this team that I built up. I'm just telling you what people have said, right or wrong. This is very important, that I left these people in good hands and that they're really taking care of them, the same thing for many clients. And I really did a good job in selecting these people. and they're very happy. That is important to me because I've spent a career trying to build this culture, and the fact that it's continuing and that we had a textbook case of this succession agreement that really worked, not only worked for clients but it worked financially for me and for the participants and that the succession, which was very carefully done, worked very, very well, and the clients appreciate the fact as to what it meant to them. That is a major, that's one of the sweetest things that had occurred relative to business.

A gratitude message that Frank received, and which he holds close to his heart, came from a client of over 40 years. According to Frank, the individual introduced Frank to a friend and said, "This is Frank Wright. This is the person who takes care of me." Frank continued:

And I've never forgotten that. I thought that was one of the nicest things that somebody said because they looked—the way that I took it, and I think that that's the way he meant it, is that it was more comprehensive than just giving somebody financial advice here and there. I cared about their family, their kids, you know, asked questions about the family. We try to treat the whole person, not just making investment recommendations because that's out of context as to what people really need and want, and their goals in life and what they want for themselves and their kids and everything. And that's what we've tried to do for people, is to try to take care of them, to be their representative in the financial community. But it's amazing the amount, the number of questions that we get on a variety of subjects that have nothing to do with should I invest in this or invest in that. Because they come to you as you would hope that they would come to you, as a trusted family advisor. And this, and when this person said this to me it made me feel that at least this one person felt that I was a trusted family advisor.

Returning to the Opening Story

Returning to the opening LeBron James story and considering it through the lenses of the chapter's theoretical frames and research findings, it seems noteworthy how the personal and professional blurred for James. Although somewhat speculative, it is not unreasonable to suggest that Gilbert's description of James at one point as a "former hero" was almost certainly painful for James given, among other things, that this drama was largely set in James's hometown, well, his home NBA town. It was, therefore, extremely personal. It is interesting to further speculate whether this made Gilbert's later public message of appreciation to James more meaningful or less meaningful to him and Cavalier fans. The James story seemed to highlight how work was personal and the personal could be work and how an expression of appreciation got confusing in this context.

What is arguably most striking is how Gilbert missed opportunities to emphasize humanity for both himself and James. These aspects would have enhanced Gilbert's message of appreciation for James and enhanced Gilbert's and the Cavaliers' self-positioning. It certainly was notable that Gilbert did refer to LeBron as a family man because this was inherently respectful of LeBron and also indicates how CPM was demonstrated in bringing information across the personal professional divide.

Chapter Conclusion

Work-related gratitude communication can be personal in several different respects. This can be positive and/or problematic. It is best understood by not only reviewing the chapters on reciprocation, philosophies, and ethics, but also reading the next chapter on workplace gratitude communication and challenging situations, which includes those that amount to or include interpersonal conflict.

Real World Recommendations

- Remember that gratitude communication at work is more highly valued when it is relatively personal.

- Seize opportunities to recognize regular work as thoroughly personal in terms of roles mixing and involving gratitude communication. Some work with family or people who are like family and some involve family in work interactions, including gratitude communication.

- Take opportunities to acknowledge personal biographical connections to another's gratitude communication reception makes the whole episode more meaningful.

- See opportunities when the nature of the core work is more personal along with related gratitude communication.

- Recognize that sometimes work means predominantly interacting with others as a person/human being rather than a strictly defined professional or worker.

- Do acknowledge that some people are just broadly committed to using positive communication, including gratitude communication with all those they encounter in work and life.

Your Opportunity to Work With Gratitude

- With consideration to Petronio's (2006) work on communication privacy management theory (CPMT) and your own life experience, recall a situation in which a sender of gratitude communication disclosed inappropriately and caused the intended receiver to possibly feel like their privacy had been violated with an audience to the interaction. What was the violation and would you argue that it was an intentional or unintentional violation? How could the violation have been avoided and how could it have been remedied after the fact?

- For an expression of gratitude, ideally work-related, you could share in the coming days, determine how you could incorporate at least one personal aspect into your communication and how that could be beneficial to you and/or the receiver(s) and/or any wider audience.

- Reflect on one of your most cherished memories of sending and/or receiving a gratitude message, ideally in a work setting. How were issues of the personal and professional, and privacy and self-disclosure managed? Could they have been managed better?

Questions for Reflection and Discussion

- What are the conditions, if any, under which you would decline the opportunity to be honored with various statements of appreciation by your supervisors, colleagues, and some of those you serve at a workplace event?

- Is it acceptable for the recipient of a gratitude-related workplace recognition to request to bring a family member or friend to the event, if held during the workday?

- Is it ever acceptable for a supervisor expressing gratitude to a direct report to request that they keep their exchange private?

Recommendations for Learning More

Exploring a Comedy Central Roast as Professional and Personal Gratitude Communication

The Comedy Central Roast series consists of selecting a celebrity to simultaneously poke fun at and express appreciation to. The content is sometimes crude and tends to cross the target celebrity's personal and professional lives.

- Watch one entire roast and indicate the major ways it navigates personal-professional boundaries from the point of view of the target celebrity.

- Make an argument for whether the roast truly amounts to an expression of appreciation for the target or is just an attack.

- Explain whether you perceive if the target celebrity felt violated by the roast experience (in terms of the humor being too biting). Here is the Comedy Central Roast website:

Developing a Disclosure and Privacy Decision Tree for Crafting Gratitude Communication

Consult Petronio's (2006) work on CPMT, content from this chapter, and any other resources, and develop a decision tree for determining whether an intended goodwilled workplace gratitude communication is likely to be appropriate and effective from a disclosure and privacy standpoint, including information about the person's work life and personal life that may be shared. It may help to begin by drafting a hypothetical gratitude communication message.

Examining the Gratitude Communication Messages for Specific Business Leaders

Locate two or more written gratitude communication messages for business leaders or other public figures. These may be career or performance tributes published in magazines and/or at online new sites. Compare and contrast the degree to which the messages deal with the personal-professional divide and whether or not the subject was likely to feel violated to any extent.

Design a Survey to Determine Whether More Personal Gratitude Communication is Desired in Work Environments

Design a 10-item survey, the results of which would advance our understanding of whether more personal gratitude communication is wanted in workplaces.

PART IV

Becoming a Grand Architect of the Gratitude Communication Opportunity

11

Using Gratitude Communication to Transform Challenging Situations

"Life is mostly froth and bubble, [t]wo things stand like stone, [k]indness in another's troubles, [c]ourage in your own."

—Adam Lindsay Gordon

Gratitude and the Most Difficult Human Circumstances —

World War I extended from 1914 to 1918. The assassination of Archduke Franz Ferdinand of Austria by a Bosnian Serb triggered the war's start, which was immediately fueled by international alliances that were in place, and by the territorial ambitions of Germany. While the exact role of these and other causes of WWI are the subject of ongoing debate, the overall horror of the Great War is widely acknowledged. Over 16 million soldiers and civilians died. Over 20 million others were injured.

Though the United States did not enter the war until 1917 and its allies Great Britain and France suffered more casualties, many U.S. soldiers paid with their lives and U.S. involvement in the war was pivotal. The Germans launched into Belgium and France early in the war and the British and French suffered huge losses of soldiers defending and attempting to reclaim territory, most notably at Verdun and the Somme. The arrival of U.S. troops was a boon to their tired allies, and U.S. soldiers' efforts helped end the war.

The *New York Times* contributor Richard Rubin (2014) traveled to France on the 100th anniversary of the start of WWI to visit the French countryside where Americans had fought. Rubin found the visit remarkable for several reasons: how the passage of time had not led to faded memories and how the people of France were glad to make known their gratitude to present-day Americans for the courageous sacrifices of U.S. soldiers from so long ago. Rubin, a wry realist, explained, "True, the French don't speak much English, and they charge an outrageous amount for a small bottle of Coke; but they are grateful. Very grateful. They remember. Go to France and they'll remind you, too" (para. 3).

Gratitude Communication's Positive Functions in Tough Times

The good feelings of surprise and intense joy that are often associated with gratitude communication can blind us to the fact that we can use it effectively in some of the hardest moments we face at work. An expression of gratitude can be used to offer reassurance and boost confidence. It can offer an effective segue into making a request, including seeking client referrals. Gratitude can be paired with an apology and otherwise mitigate negative conflict. It can even be used to transition individuals during a necessary downsizing or a voluntary but unwelcomed retirement due to illness. Gratitude communication can also go a long way in working through the grief related to the death of a beloved leader or employee. The "Theoretically Speaking" section in this chapter offers an introduction to facework theory, and especially "mutual face" (Goffman, 1955), to shed light on an important common feature of effective gratitude communication in difficult times. Application of CCCM would suggest we find ways to acknowledge and tie empowering individual stories to the overall settled historical story.

THEORETICALLY SPEAKING

Faithfully Representing Our Own Story in a Milieu of Stories

Erving Goffman was a qualitative sociologist writing in the mid- to mid-late-20th century whose work remains influential not only in his home discipline but also in other disciplines, including communication (Shulman, 2017). Goffman broadly worked with and advanced a dramaturgical approach, which means he applied the metaphor of the theater to make sense of how individuals present themselves and otherwise manage social interaction. As Scott (2015) summarized, individuals are like actors who not only enact tactics and strategies to project desired identities (i.e., to carry out "impression management" in Goffman's view) but also frequently collaborate with other individuals/actors and with onlookers/audiences in accepting or rejecting these attempts.

Goffman's (1955) facework theory, explored in some detail here, represents one of his more focused contributions and one that is especially helpful to understanding the function of gratitude communication in difficult situations. *Face* is the positive social value that a person claims for themselves within an interaction. It is associated with a *line* or a coherent pattern of verbal and nonverbal behaviors. An individual's face claim and corresponding line has implications for the faces and lines of others involved. As succinctly delineated by Goffman (1955), *loss of face* can occur when someone is wrong-faced, out-of-face, or shame-faced. Further, *saving face* means acting to make it seem that one's face has been not lost. Additionally, *giving face* means acting to allow someone to take a better line than that person could have taken on their own. These dynamics amount to the rules of self-respect and considerateness guiding social interaction.

A theory of conflict transformation as positive narrative expansion, which incorporates Goffman's (1955) notion of positive face, is elaborated shortly to make additional sense of the potential value of gratitude communication in workplace conflict situations. Several research-based cases of gratitude communication as workplace conflict management are subsequently shared to demonstrate the transformative potential of gratitude communication. Consideration is then given to ways of increasing communication competency related to sending and receiving gratitude expressions in conflict situations, while acknowledging gratitude communication's dialogic quality. Finally, some limitations and future directions are noted.

Gratitude as Communication and Conflict Communication

Arguably, the most notable theoretical intersection already involving communication, gratitude, and conflict comes out of the symbolic interactionist tradition, a near relation to social construction. Facework theories, as Shimanoff (2009) noted, employ the metaphor of face for identity and are most closely associated with the work of Goffman (1955) and Brown and Levinson (1978). Gratitude and conflict do not seem to have been co-investigated within this broader theoretical arena, yet the fact they have both been considered as facework, again as noted by Shimanoff (2009) is indicative of their conceptual similarities, including the merits of recognizing each as very much co-constituted in social interaction. As noted in Chapter 2, communication theory addresses face work in several respects and therefore, conflict in several respects.

Conflict Transformation as Positive Narrative Expansion

Scholarly work in interpersonal conflict communication with the development (Brinkert, 2006) and elaboration (Jones & Brinkert, 2008) of the comprehensive conflict coaching model (CCCM), which draws heavily from the work of Kellett and Dalton (Kellett & Dalton, 2001), provides a way to conceptualize conflict transformation. The CCCM has been used or proposed for use in government (Brinkert, 2009), higher education (Giacomini, 2009), and nursing (Brinkert, 2011), as well as by ombuds (Brinkert, 2010) and facilitators (Brinkert, 2013) across sectors. In part, the CCCM involves a conflict coach (i.e., a knowledgeable and skilled conflict intervener) supporting a client (i.e., individual person in conflict) in understanding their conflict situation in terms of three themes: identity, emotion, and power. These themes, which come from the CCCM authors, were selected because of their well-documented centrality in conflict interactions and their interrelated nature. Notably, the theme of identity within the CCCM is closely aligned with facework theories and, therefore, reinforces and builds upon the connections among facework, emotion, and power within the conflict area.

Within the CCCM, the client is encouraged to consider both their own current condition and the other party's current condition in terms of the identity, emotion, and power themes. Then the client is encouraged to consider the themes in terms of ideal conditions for all relevant parties. These positive visions of identity, emotion, and power are then crafted into a story that is co-constructed in ongoing interaction with others in the client's professional and/or personal life.

This shift from a negative and oftentimes stuck conflict narrative to a positive and fluidly developing conflict narrative (and employing the themes of identity, emotion, and power) can be captured in the phrase *positive narrative expansion.* Transition to positive narrative expansion or the enhancement of positive narrative expansion can be considered forms of conflict transformation. Positive narrative expansion as conflict transformation is most obvious in its "transition" form because communication activity during a stuck conflict can relatively immediately and positively shift the conflict-related narrative(s) for all parties. However, conflict transformation also takes place when communication proactively averts a negative conflict narrative and/or proactively enhances a positive conflict narrative. Further, it may be reasonable to refer to conflict transformation as occurring even after the negative conflict narrative has been destabilized but before a positive conflict narrative is well-established. Conflict transformation as a transition to positive narrative expansion or an enhancement of positive narrative expansion can, therefore, happen before (pre), during, and after (post) high intensity negative conflict communication between parties. While explained here primarily in the interpersonal area, this kind of conflict transformation can apply to other areas as well, including small groups (or teams) and organizations. Accordingly, transformation as positive narrative expansion is widely applicable for descriptive and prescriptive purposes when considering various kinds of gratitude communication as conflict management, as demonstrated and explored in the following section.

Research-Based Cases of Gratitude Communication as Conflict Transformation

The following cases, which show the transformative potential of gratitude communication in workplace conflict, come from a larger study on gratitude communication in the workplace forming the basis of this overall book. Notably, the gratitude communication study design and preset questions did not directly address "conflict." The relevance of conflict to gratitude communication became clear only in the data analysis process.

Thirty-five gratitude communication cases were explicitly related to conflict. These cases were organized according to the temporal stages of conflict transformation introduced previously. Three cases involved the expression of gratitude in the *pre-conflict* period or prior to potential conflict interaction. Eighteen cases involved the expression of gratitude *during* conflict interaction, including as a way of transitioning from a phase of highly charged interaction (i.e., period of immediate damage to one or more parties in terms of identity, emotion, and power). Fourteen cases involved the expression of gratitude in the *post-conflict* period or after highly charged interaction or the potential thereof had subsided. Because of space limitations, only two pre-conflict cases, four during cases, and three post-conflict cases are shared in detail below. The number of detailed cases is intended to demonstrate some diversity within each category while also loosely reflecting the frequency of the different categories. Basic analysis of conflict transformation in terms of positive narrative expansion regarding identity, emotion, and power themes are offered for each case.

Pre-Conflict Phase

• Expressed Gratitude in Private to Avoid Potential Conflict

Chip, a sales and marketing team leader for a subsidiary of a Fortune 500 consumer products company received a stock option award as an act of appreciation from his boss. There was an extensive nomination process that involved the preparation of considerable documentation as well as vetting from the parent company. Only a few people get the award each year. The team leader got a letter about his nomination. He received the actual award by getting called to his boss's office and instructed to bring his briefcase. Following company tradition, his boss presented him with a specially colored envelope that contained the award. The purpose of the secrecy was to avoid potential conflict with others in the team and overall organization.

The team leader described how he received the award:

You know, the NFL, if they tell you to bring your playbook, you're getting cut. So, I said, 'What's up with that?' And he just put the [special] envelope in my briefcase and then explained it to me. He said, 'You know, there's a lot of other people who have been with the parent company that know what the [special] envelope means, and I don't want anybody to feel slighted, but I also wanted you to feel that, you've been valued.'

The boss and team leader agreed that the use of the private mode of gratitude communication here avoided negative emotions and loss of face for other people reporting to the boss. The potential communication of bad feelings, should others become aware of this gratitude communication episode, were also assumed to potentially take away from the good feelings and positive face that the team leader was able to experience. Communication efforts were intended to protect and enhance the narratives of the good boss, the good team leader, and the larger work group.

• Delaying a Thank You Because of a Potential Conflict With a New Supervisor
Shakira was offered the position of director of marketing at a medical laboratory company by the chief executive officer of the organization. She expressed her hesitance about accepting the position before the new chief marketing officer (her new direct supervisor) was in place. The new CMO arrived and supported the CEO's choice for the director position.

The new director explained the logic behind her hesitancy and delayed thank you:

I didn't accept the position when it was extended by the CEO because I felt like it wouldn't be a very intelligent thing to do given the likelihood of the new chief marketing officer possibly wanting to put his own people in. With that in mind, I thought, oh, I better not just accept this. So when I talk about expressing gratitude ... I went back to the CEO and made sure that he knew how much I valued them, honoring and continuing on trying to get me into the organization before they had even hired the chief marketing officer. I went into his office and I also sent him a thank you note on actual paper.

The delayed expression of gratitude by the incoming marketing director to the CEO was done to respect the face and related assumed power of the incoming CMO to make hiring decisions in the marketing area. From the point of view of the incoming marketing director, this avoided threatening the incoming CMO and causing potential conflict with the CMO wanting to force out the assumed incoming marketing director. Notably, the incoming marketing director was also aware of the potential face threat in delaying her thank you to the CEO. She seemed to be very deliberate in her effusive language and in her modes of expression to make it clear that she indeed was appreciative. This reinforced the CEO's status and power as well as his feelings about his status and power. The incoming marketing director therefore avoided conflicts with both her new immediate boss and the overall head of the company by how she managed her gratitude communication in this situation. Positive individual narratives were protected for all parties involved. In addition, positive relational narratives were likely established as a result of the sophisticated gratitude communication scenario.

During Conflict Phase

• Using Gratitude as a Strategy for Leading Through Team Conflict

Jasper, the communications director for a regional site of a large organization was working on a project amidst considerable staff frustration. There were feelings of resentment about the division of the workload and the nature of some of the tasks. Knowing the project had to get done quickly and needing a breakthrough in the group process, the director adopted a "thank you" strategy: "[W]hen people were engaging on the [tasks] that they thought were valuable, that I had assigned them to, and when they did good work, I was recognizing them in front of everyone."

Jasper was very articulate about his approach in this situation and in general:

> I'm really quite sincere when I use it. I really am. I'm very grateful for the work that people are doing or whatever they've done. And I always appreciate when I receive it. But for me personally in a business setting, it is an opportunity to motivate. I think people appreciate recognition and thanks. And so I use it as a tool. And in this particular case, I was definitely using it as a tool. It was very important that I just really acknowledged them and thanked them, because I was hoping that that would spur them on to further action.

Jasper saw a profound shift in the involvement with one individual in particular:

> I would say that, at least with one employee, there was almost a wall of tension that had been set up … got lifted. In other words, that was no longer an issue. I can let that go and now I can just move on.

The director characterized the overall benefits of this approach on the project: "So it was almost infectious, the level of gratitude that came out of the project. And we got it done."

In this situation, various specific expressions of gratitude comprised a larger gratitude strategy by the director. Individuals received recognition for their respective contributions by the director in front of their peers. The director seemed to be strongly seeking action as a result of the "thank you" strategy and he made it clear this was achieved. Employees demonstrated more commitment to completing the project; they felt more empowered and acted in an empowered way. Also, feelings of frustration, resentment, and tension lifted. Positive narratives promoted here included the successful director, successful individual employees, the successful team, and successful relations between the director and each employee.

• Expressing Gratitude to Handle Layoffs in a Principled Way

Ashley, a director of a research and development (R&D) department in a major pharmaceutical company was handling the downsizing of her department. This involved transitioning toward the elimination of her own position as well as the positions of her entire 20-person staff. It was "somber" and "sometimes downright sad" taking care of work commitments in the final months. To make the situation more bearable and as a way of expressing her own thanks to staff, she reached out to the global president of R&D and asked him to share words of appreciation with her team. He welcomed the opportunity to do so.

Ashley shared her staff's initial reaction:

They were dumbfounded and then just so impressed. You could see the smiles on their faces. A couple of them had tears in their eyes. And that to me just made all the difference.

The director went on to speak more directly about the benefits:

When they exited they were able to hold their heads up. They knew that they made a difference, they knew that they, you know, again, received a nod, you done good, you're able to now go on to, you know, the next chapter.

Ashley's effort at getting a senior executive to thank the departing staff was a face-saving act for the staff that mitigated the face-loss of getting laid off. It positioned their past efforts as important, something that was called into question with their entire area getting phased out. It also shifted the emotional climate toward the positive. Although not directly addressed in the director's remarks, the overall action was also face-positive for the director and senior executive. Finally, the overall act of gratitude communication supported narratives of professional dignity and self-worth for each of the individuals involved.

- Using a Formal Gratitude Channel to Help Transform a Promotion-Related Conflict

Aubrey, a new manager in a government department, had an employee assigned to work closely with her on an out-of-town project. The situation started out very badly. The employee would not sit in the front seat of the car with the manager because the employee had missed out on the promotion that the other person had recently received. The relationship improved somewhat with a conversation initiated by the manager over a drink. The relationship shifted most noticeably when the manager demonstrated appreciation for the employee and her work by nominating her for a formal recognition within department. The recognition included a day off from the project. Aubrey commented on a couple different benefits:

> And she really said that nobody there ever, nobody before this had ever gone out of their way to tell her that she had done a good job. And she was grateful for me just even mentioning to her supervisor that she had done a good job. … [The employee] had a union gripe against some of the officials for the jobs that hadn't gone to her. She removed that and … there was less of a chip on her shoulder in terms of working with other people who had been chosen for jobs and ended up jumping her, or whatever, if you want to put it that way. So, I think that it just, it eased communications all across the board for a lot of us. And instead of there being tension with coworkers, all of a sudden it was easier now for us to work together.

The formal expression of appreciation and its visibility to others in the organization seemed immediately affirming to the employee. The employee seemed to interpret it as face-saving and face-enhancing for her in the eyes of her supervisor and other higher status people in the organization. It led her to remove formal grievances against others thereby making others feel less constrained and defensive. All those involved felt more comfortable and better able to work in a positive manner. Each individual and various groupings of individuals involving the employee had more freedom to pursue their positive professional narratives, in part because fewer resources were used for threat-making and/or threat-responding.

Post-Conflict Phase

• Thank You to a Staff Member for Resolving a Conflict Faced by a Client

Rachel, the owner of a travel agency, thanked one of her travel agents for helping the owner's direct client who was having difficulties coordinating with the airline to return from Cancun. The owner was especially appreciative because she herself was away at the time. The owner expressed gratitude to the agent by sending a handwritten note and by mentioning her gratitude to the agent on the phone multiple times.

Rachel emphasized both her own initial lack of empowerment at the beginning of the incident and the agent's newfound confidence that resulted from the overall situation:

I was unable to take care of my client, which I think for her, it was a positive experience for her because she usually doesn't stand up and take control of a situation and it made her realize that she can.

Gratitude communication in this situation reinforced the staff member's empowerment and encouraged her development of a narrative of professional growth through greater assertiveness. This involved a shift in professional identity for the staff member. It could have reasonably been linked to reinforcing positive feelings of acting more boldly and supporting a transition away from feelings of wanting to seek comfort in a less assertive role. The owner's positive professional identity, record of accomplishment, and good feelings about being professionally successful are furthered by the staff member's own growth in each of these areas.

• Expressing Gratitude for Not Framing a Situation in Terms of Conflict of Interest

Jackson, a political communication consultant, has an existing client who is a well-known elected official. The consultant called him to see if he would be upset with the consultant taking on a new client given that it potentially created a conflict of interest. The existing client immediately said he would not consider it a conflict. The consultant wrote a detailed handwritten thank you note and sent it to his home, thanking him for his professional approach to the issue. Jackson described how the sharing of gratitude was a benefit to both parties:

Well, the first benefit is I always feel better when I act in a grateful way to people. I want people to know when I'm grateful and so I felt better because of it. And being an elected official this person gets a lot of criticism, the way most elected officials do, and a lot of the positive feedback he gets from people who don't know him very well ... so I think that him knowing of my personal support and appreciation was of a different character than the normal positive feedback he might get as an elected official.

The client's more personal identity is affirmed in this gratitude communication situation. In the context of a conflict-laden professional life in which a much more limited identity is displayed and co-constructed, the feeling is no doubt refreshing for the politician. Sending gratitude here expands the consultant's narrative of being a good person. Likewise, receiving such personalized gratitude expands the client's narrative of being a good person. This gratitude communication arguably builds trust via supporting face in a mutual fashion and also makes it more likely that both parties will be empowered by their relationship in the future.

- Thank You for Handling a Potentially Negative Leadership Conflict in a Quick and Tactful Way

Robert, the director of sales at a winery, was in a planning meeting with the winery owner and the owner's son about the winery's involvement at a major wine festival, their largest direct sales event of the year. The owner's son was taking on a much larger role and had some strong opinions on the event. The director explained that the son's proposal about which wines to highlight was not in the long-term benefit of the winery. The director described the owner's reaction:

And he pulled me aside, the owner, and said you handled him well because sometimes he can be hard to handle.

The director pointed out the benefits of the owner expressing gratitude in this situation:

I was allowed to do my job and obviously he trusts my decision making and the tactfulness of how I said it, or was able to implement it so it wouldn't be questioned.

The director also noted that their festival sales were up almost 40% because of the decision that was made in the planning meeting. He recognized that the event is frequented by novice wine consumers who prefer sweet wines and, therefore, they sold sweet wines in both of their festival areas.

The gratitude expressed by the owner toward the director is important for reassuring the director about the director's status and power in relation to the son's status and power. It would be reasonable for someone in the director's situation to feel uncertainty about whether to speak up and whether to share insights given a possible stronger loyalty on all levels between the owner and his son. Fortunately for the director, the owner appears convinced that the director's relatively high status is warranted given that the director's ability to be empowered supports the owner's professional success. This dance of gratitude communication as a follow-up to a calm but delicate and potentially highly consequential conflict situation demonstrates that a positive professional narrative is possible for the director in this family company. In fact, the director's narrative is very much tied to the narratives of the owner and the company itself. A challenge going forward may very well be finding ways to join the owner's son's positive narrative with those of the other individuals leading the winery and the overall narrative of the winery itself.

Summary Discussion of the Narrative Data

What might be termed a kind of "win-win-win" potential of gratitude communication in conflict and conflict related situations is striking. Each of the cases shared in this section involves neutral or positive impact on narratives as they relate to identity, emotion, and power issues, not only for the sender(s) and the receiver(s) but also for the third parties that were considered. One or more positive identities are narratively protected, enhanced, and/or developed for each agent category. One or more negative identities tend not to be mentioned or diminished. In general, positive narrative expansion is made possible, if not immediately realized. Therefore, gratitude communication is shown to have transformative effects in these instances of conflict or possible conflict.

Perhaps the foremost caveat to these findings is that, while the decision to send or not send gratitude seems to be important, more is involved here. Expressing gratitude does not secure benefits. The "how" or process of gratitude communication (including expression, reception, and context) seems to be a central and subtle issue in each case presented. This leads to a consideration of conflict competencies that support individuals, dyads, and larger social configurations in increasing the likelihood of success in instances of gratitude communication. Please consult Chapter 4 on the "how" of sending gratitude communication.

Identifying and Developing Gratitude Communication Conflict Competencies

Although a lay understanding of gratitude communication may be that it is straightforward (i.e., as simple as saying, "thank you"), an examination of actual cases demonstrates that it is a complex topic. This is particularly true when considering the use of gratitude communication in conflict or conflict-related situations. Because gratitude communication has been shown, at least in select instances, to play a transformative role in conflict, the issues of what constitutes gratitude communication competency and how it can be advanced in relation to conflict become pertinent.

Competence is generally defined as a function of knowledge, motivation, and skill, and involves managing issues of appropriateness and effectiveness (Cupach et al., 2010). Clarifying each of these concepts and their interrelationships for the topic of workplace gratitude communication and its intersection with conflict communication would be valuable not only for theory and research but also for practice. Whether considering gratitude communication in general or gratitude communication specific to the workplace, we would do well to understand, value, and have the ability to navigate key components of interpersonal and organizational conflict, including distal context, proximal context, conflict interaction, proximal outcomes, and distal outcomes (Cupach et al., 2010) Broadly, the skills (Hargie, 2011) necessary for an accomplished gratitude conflict practitioner would include the following: reinforcing (including recognizing and rewarding), reflecting, listening, explaining, self-disclosing, inducting and closing, asserting, persuading, negotiating, and participating with and leading others. This is a lengthy and challenging list to master.

As the cases presented in this section illustrate, communicators can sometimes demonstrate a high degree of competency based on varied backgrounds, including varying amounts of exposure to communication study and training. It is likely that many other interactants (and, theoretically, even the same interactants as studied here but placed in different situations) would need support of one type or another to achieve such remarkable transformations. Conflict coaching is one option to support higher gratitude communication competency, whether individuals are seeking competency in a relatively narrow context (i.e., contemplating strategy and tactics in a situation) or seeking to more broadly develop competency. Whether concentrating on developing such competencies with individuals, dyads, groups, or organizations, emphasis needs to be on the negotiated quality of gratitude communication and the sometimes shared and sometimes varied nature of the larger narratives at play, even in instances of conflict transformation.

Conclusion: Limitations and Future Directions

This study has a number of limitations that can be understood in the context of future possibilities. Particularly as research in this overall area progresses, sharper distinctions should be made in both mapping the transformational characteristics of "naturally occurring" gratitude conflict communication and translating these findings into specific and measurable means for deliberately boosting gratitude communication conflict competencies. Finally, the limits and pitfalls of gratitude communication and gratitude communication as conflict management also need to be studied, and further explored in terms of applied dimensions.

An examination of the literature reveals that gratitude communication as workplace conflict management has an important history. Gratitude communication as conflict management has value in facilitating conflict transformation. Gratitude communication can play a positive role pre, during, and post-conflict by facilitating positive narrative expansion by parties to a given conflict. Used as a tactic or a strategy, gratitude communication has the potential to expand cherished identities, generate positive feelings, and open avenues of action and impact. It therefore makes sense to further study the area to support a deeper theoretical understanding and better assist those in conflict situations that require transformation.

Returning to the Opening Story: Human Pain Can Open the Door to the Possibility of Gratitude Communication

Fortunately, unlike war, workplaces, for the most part, are not violent. The matter of the French honoring the U.S. war dead from WWI does involve various face issues and related issues (in terms of emotion and power) that are common to workplace conflicts, even those with a strong gratitude communication theme. The cemetery with its grave markers is presented with dignity—arguably effectively honoring those who sacrificed their lives and reflecting, as well, the dignity of French. A war that silenced so many individuals' narratives, here especially Americans, has now given way to a situation in which U.S. visitors, French hosts and visitors, and other visitors can hopefully honor and relate to a story of brave sacrifice and gratitude from one leading democracy to another. ━━━━━━━━━━━━━━

Chapter Conclusion

Just as gratitude communication can be used to convey acknowledgement of war time sacrifice, so can it play an important role in other kinds of challenging situations such as various types of workplace conflict. It is clear that any party to workplace conflict can, though challenged, consider dynamics of emotion, identity, and power to more appropriately and effectively position themselves and others as a way to identify and create conflict breakthroughs.

Real World Recommendations

- Recognize that gratitude communication can play a role in the pre-conflict phase.

- Recognize that gratitude communication can play a role during an active conflict.

- Recognize that gratitude communication can play a role in the post-conflict phase.

- Issues of identity (i.e., face), emotion, and power are almost always factors to consider for all parties to a conflict gratitude communication situation.

- Appropriate and effective development of identity, emotion, and power concerns for all stakeholders can amount to transformative change in conflict and gratitude communication situations.

Your Opportunity to Get to Work With Gratitude

- Incorporate gratitude communication in an interpersonal conflict taking shape. Identify an interpersonal conflict that may be taking shape in your work and/or in the work of someone you know well. Develop two ideas for how one or more parties in this situation could use gratitude communication to potentially transform the situation prior to the conflict becoming highly active.

- Find a past example of gratitude communication that made a difference in terms of conflict dynamics. Identify a past challenging situation in your work or personal life that benefitted from at least one party's expression of gratitude during the active conflict or the post-conflict phase.

- Explore a difficult case of conflict, gratitude, and transformation. Review the various conflict cases in this chapter and select the one in which it was likely most challenging to achieve transformation (i.e., the advancement of identity, emotion, and power concerns) of the two or three main parties. Make an argument for why it was the most challenging.

- Design and then deliver a gratitude communication in your current work life that is especially face-sensitive for all likely to be involved in the interaction.

Questions for Reflection and Discussion

- Using ideas shared in this chapter and/or your own research on one or more listed sources, what are at least three scenarios in which the expression of gratitude communication might be avoided or delayed to eliminate or temporarily avoid a face threat to one or more stakeholders?

- Locate a face-threatening gratitude communication from the past. Have you ever been involved in a gratitude communication interaction in which a party, possibly yourself, felt face threatened? What happened and how could it have gone better?

- What is an example of someone using gratitude in conflict, even hypothetically, to support not only a work team's identity about itself but also the prized individual stories of one or more participants? You may want to do a search of popular and/or trade sources to locate an example of a leader doing a good job with gratitude communication and, essentially, facilitating positive narrative expansion (i.e., transformation involving identity, emotion, and power) for one or more parties.

Recommendations for Learning More

The following book is considered a classic: Goffman, E. (1974). *The presentation of self in everyday life*. Anchor.

If you are intrigued by the concept of conflict transformation, read Kellett and Matyok's (2016) book. It offers different perspectives on the topic: Kellett, P., & Matyok, T. G. (2016). *Transforming conflict through communication in personal, family, and working relationships*. Peace and Conflict Studies.

12

Gratitude Communication as a Career-Spanning Commitment

"No one has ever become poor by giving."

—Anne Frank

Deeply Committing to Gratitude

The ancient storyteller Aesop left us the tale of *Androcles and the Lion*. Androcles was a man who escaped slavery and stumbled across a lion in the forest. At first, Androcles was frightened and backed away. But then he realized the lion was badly hurt. Rather than continue to walk away, Androcles tended to the great cat's injured paw, which included removing a painful thorn. The lion's injury eventually healed, and the cat actually looked after Androcles by sharing a cave with him and bringing him food.

A while later, both Androcles and the lion were captured. Androcles was sentenced to death. He was tossed into an arena with a starved lion. The famished lion approached Androcles but, instead of killing and eating him, the lion licked him affectionately. It was the same lion he had known in the forest.

The emperor, astonished by what was happening, called Androcles over to explain the situation. Androcles gave a full account. The emperor responded by freeing both Androcles and the lion. And the two went on to have good and full lives.

Walking Alongside the Masters

The story of *Androcles and the Lion* can be read as a grand story of gratitude, a story of two characters moving through a series of terrifying and joyful circumstances, with ongoing expressions of appreciation and thanks. The notion of gratitude as a journey forms the basis for this chapter, as does the related concept of gratitude masters.

While earlier chapters illuminated finer aspects of gratitude communication at work, here we pull back to consider gratitude communication more broadly, revealing interconnections among some of those grainier details. In the course of reviewing the 100 in-depth interviews that underpin this book, it became clear that some individuals stood out in their level of awareness associated with sending and receiving gratitude, their commitment to participating in gratitude communication, and the sheer dramatic power of their gratitude communication stories. These characteristics define these persons as *gratitude masters*.

The individuals profiled in this chapter were certainly not the only gratitude masters among those interviewed. However, the collection of individuals and stories highlighted here conveys some diversity in the circumstances of the senders and receivers, the sectors represented, the nature of the gratitude interactions themselves, and the lessons to be learned by those who want to use gratitude communication more effectively.

Before diving into the section that presents these captivating stories, the Theoretically Speaking section for this chapter offers more penetrating understanding of what is at work here. We will consider the concept of *human agency*—or one person's ability to have an impact on the world—as a way to generally make sense of what sets gratitude communication masters apart from those uninvolved with gratitude communication or those involved but not to the same extent.

THEORETICALLY SPEAKING

We Can Shape, Even While We Are Shaped By the World

Masters of Gratitude Communication: Agents of Possibility in the Face of Constraints

Do we have free will? Can we do anything that is not dictated by circumstance? Do we at work have the power to make a difference? Or is it simply the organization itself that programs our activities and is who we should look to for our every instruction?

These fundamental questions have been debated endlessly and will continue to be argued into the future. Nonetheless, considerable consensus exists among thought leaders involved with these questions that the individual is both empowered and constrained. The sociologist Anthony Giddens is arguably the most important modern writer on this topic, especially as it concerns the relationship between the individual and the organization. Giddens's (1984) theory of structuration suggests that there is both agency (i.e., an ability of an individual or other entity to act with volition) and structure (i.e., cultural rules, patterns, and/or other social realities that limit and/or empower individual action). In other words, there exists both restrictions and the possibility for some degree of individual action in our personal lives. From Giddens's point of view, neither agency nor structure can be explained without the other; and neither concept is more important than the other. From a workplace standpoint, any given organization necessarily limits some individual action yet also opens the possibility for other kinds of individual action. While organizations may sometimes feel confining to individuals, ironically, an organization cannot be sustained without individual actions.

Another important thinker on this topic is the philosopher Charles Taylor. Taylor (1985) takes an optimistic view of the individual's ability to assess their circumstances and act on that assessment. It is not simply a case of individuals acting like automatons and calculating assessments of the world in some blandly common manner. For Taylor, each person has control over their identities, and these self-identities can uniquely affect the person's read on situations and possible related actions. Situational factors certainly play a part from this viewpoint, but there is a lot of room for the individual to make a difference. However, an important caveat from communication scholars McPhee, Poole, and Iverson (2014) is that different individuals face different limits when trying to affect their work worlds, including access to resources and actions by those with whom they interact.

The ideas of human agency and, especially, strongly positive human agency, matter to an exploration of gratitude communication masters because these are people who consistently act like they are able to make a positive difference—and that others are able to do the same as well. I experienced these individuals as hopeful but not misguided about how gratitude communication could be carried out and what it could accomplish. Certain limits needed to be recognized, such as laws and strong social norms, but there were still amazing opportunities to act, whether expressing appreciation or thanks or graciously receiving such gestures from others. What is more, reading the accounts of the gratitude communication masters gives the distinct impression that these people see themselves as organizational leaders, not that they necessarily hold the top title (although some do). Rather, gratitude communication masters are not passively executing their organizations' agendas. Yes, they are advancing those agendas, but they are also adding to and transforming them for the better. Gratitude communication masters are enthusiastic builders of the organization itself. The gratitude master has a control and responsibility orientation that positively advances the master's own career, supports others, and generally develops the organizations with which the master is associated.

Gratitude Communication Master Cases

Gratitude communication masters exercise their capacity for making a positive difference and welcome when others do the same. Also, as noted in the chapter introduction, the masters convey a sense that their entire career path is a gratitude journey. Other commonalities occur among them, too.

Masters of gratitude communication can be more broadly understood as masters of engagement. Not only are they energized in their work, but they play a vital role in energizing others at all status levels. Further, they certainly have strong gratitude vocabularies—a range of ways to express appreciation and thanks. All are proactive and creative in doing so, and many have fun with it, when appropriate. Also, regardless of their philosophies in sending and receiving gratitude (i.e., whether more self-interested or more interested in what is in it for others), gratitude masters never give the impression of keeping a tight balance sheet about the process. If they are keeping score, they seem to operate with a long-time horizon and, therefore, with a sense of delayed gratification.

While these shared markers are evident across those who stand out as masters of gratitude communication and can act as lessons for all of us, other lessons are exemplified by particular masters, each with their specific collection of stories.

Each of the next four sections highlights a master and provides two lessons visible in their gratitude communication stories.

Restaurateur—Gratitude Communication as a Thrill and as a Major Currency of Business

As noted in Chapter 3, David owns a chain of sports bar restaurants, employing over 500 people. He is a well-known restaurateur in his home city, one of the 10 largest cities in the United States. Recently, the representative from David's cable

TV and Internet provider gave him an all-expense paid trip to a 5-star resort in the Cayman Islands. While David would have loved to take it himself, he gave it to the general manager of one of his facilities as an expression of thanks.

David remembered his delivery to the recipient:

> ... [W]hat do you think of the Cayman Islands? Do you think you and your wife would really enjoy this? You've been really good to me, and I think it's time for you to enjoy some of the wealth of [the business]. ... Here, go away with your wife for the week—private jet, everything.

David recalls that the recipient was "a little bit teary eyed" when first hearing his words. David's hope was that the individual would know that they were on the same page. He wants all of his employees to have that feeling. David explained, "I want my employees to know that I want to take care of them as much as I can."

The general manager returned with a sunburn but loved the trip.

In another instance, David received the Restaurateur of the State Award and, later in the evening, after the awards ceremony, he dropped by one of his restaurants. To David's surprise, his employees had hired a string band to perform in his honor.

To him, the employees were sending a pretty clear message: "We appreciate you. We think you're as great as [our state] does." David went on,

> [T]he employees were proud to work for me—not as much as I was proud to have them as employees—but they were proud to work for me and they were proud that their restaurant owner was recognized as the best by his peers in the state.

It was an extra special night for David. He spoke about the benefits of the gratitude he experienced that evening: "I guess it's twofold because you're getting an award by your peers, that's gratifying, and, more important than that, is your employees celebrating your achievement."

The added touch was that the band playing was the band that David himself performs in every New Year's Day. "[S]o it was great because they were all people I already knew."

In another account, David started a neighborhood grocery store prior to starting his restaurants and has had some very longstanding customers from that operation. A couple of times a year, former customers die. When this happens, David makes a point of reaching out to their households. He explained,

[W]hat we like to do is when people pass on, we like to take care of their houses and bring food over and make sure the house has soda and bottles of water and beer, whatever they might need. ... These are people that were customers for years. Without asking we just do that.

David described the act of kindness as enough, but he said the message was, "We appreciate your loyalty as a customer over the years."

David found that the gesture was always welcomed. He described how recipients were moved by the act: "Oh, very teary eyed, in most cases it was crying, when you come over, when you show up at their door with all the food." David added, "It's just saying 'thank you' to somebody who has passed on or their children or wife or significant other. The nicest time to say 'thank you' is when somebody is having a bad time."

He noted the benefits of these actions: "The organization benefitted before the act of kindness and we were just saying 'thank you.' But the individuals involved have been brought comfort at a trying time."

What makes it best for David is when he does the delivery himself.

As discussed in Chapter 3, when a Grammy Award winning singer was getting established with a non-music venture in David's city, David helped the singer establish connections to get his business off of the ground. When the singer was asked to be on *The Oprah Winfrey Show*, the singer agreed on one condition: The show had to include a segment with David's restaurant, the singer's favorite restaurant in the world. As David described, "So he was saying 'thank you' to me for all I had done for his [business] when he came to [this city]. ... Thanks for going over and above anything we could have expected."

Various benefits were associated with this thank you. David explained:

I got national recognition on the most popular show there is ... to a different consumer base. I'm usually a sports consumer. It was great. ... [L]ots of people came in; tons of people came in. He said he liked the white lobster pizza. It became the most popular pizza in [our restaurant].

David noted that the recognition was better than the financial benefit: "[I]t was great to be recognized by a world-renowned star. And it was major ... for my company to have national and international recognition."

Incidentally, the white lobster pizza is still the most popular pizza at David's restaurant. "White lobster pizza is off the charts, off the charts."

As the owner of a restaurant chain, David sells a lot of beer. The representative of one his major beer brands expressed his appreciation to David in a rather unique and spectacular way.

> So [he] said, 'David, you sell a lot of [our product]. Would you be all right if we asked you to open up for Kenny Chesney?' And I said, 'Well, what do you mean by that?' I said, 'I don't even know … one of his songs.' And he said, 'We want you to go out and get the crowd excited. It'll only be 70,000 people in [your city's major concert stadium].'

David got to go on stage prior to the main act to fire up the crowd. David spoke to the crowd and was paired with a man with a shirt gun. David pointed to a place in the audience, the audience roared, and the man launched a shirt in that direction.

David talked about the personal thrill of what he experienced:

> Well, I've never been in front of 70,000 people before, so it was exceptionally memorable to point at them, and they scream at you. So, it was like instant gratification, and I've never had that in that large of a scale before.

David summarized the benefits of this gratitude event:

> Well, … they got one of their great customers branded to [their beer]. You won't forget it, and they know you won't forget it. And they benefited by making me a more loyal customer. … I benefited by getting [my restaurant's] word out to the 70,000 people.

David even got to meet Kenny Chesney one-on-one.

One valuable lesson that arises out of David's interview is the truly thrilling potential of gratitude communication. Even his story about sharing at times of loss illustrates how gratitude can be a keenly positive emotional experience for those involved. In addition, as a businessperson, it is easy to see how vendors rewarding him with vacation and publicity opportunities is a return on investment for him. In this way, the reception of gratitude is like "money in the bank" for him. Likewise, when he shares perquisites with others such as valued employees, he is spending not just money but social currency to structure relationships that empower those individuals it also further empower David. This is very consistent with structuration.

Another instructive theme is the way gratitude communication can function as a major currency in business. David demonstrates that gratitude communication has value as it flows rather than if it is locked down. For instance, a vendor thanks him with a luxury vacation, and he passes the gift on to one of his managers as a thank you. When David receives a state-level award, stands in front of a large stadium audience, gets publicly aligned with a major celebrity, and is profiled on the top talk show at the time, he is receiving gratitude communication currency than is arguably far better for his business than the hard money someone might spend on advertising and promotions to attain the same effect.

Senior Functional Manager in the Pharmaceutical Industry—Connecting the Dots on Gratitude Communication in Large Organizations and Helping Leaders Lead with Gratitude

Maria works as a senior director of compliance for a top five global pharmaceutical company. The first three of her stories relate to the same major project, an effort to develop and execute a web-based compliance module for all company employees. Her final story comes from when she worked for another top five global pharmaceutical company.

Maria's organization operates in 25 languages and often needs training content translated—not just into different languages but different languages that reflect the local cultures of the company. She first must work with a vendor to translate material. Then she works with individuals inside the company to polish the translations. Maria made arrangements with her senior vice president (SVP) to send each of these individuals a thank you email from the SVP. In addition, the SVP's email was copied to each recipient's manager. She also arranged for each person to receive a monetary allotment through the company's internal award system.

Maria described the email that was sent out from the SVP:

I've known that we've called upon you numerous times to really help us with translations, in particular we re-launched our code of conduct and I know that there was a lot of effort in a short period of time, and we would not have been able to launch successfully globally without your help. Thanks for your continued support and help. We're going to call upon you in the future, and please know that I appreciate any effort that you give us.

Maria described the process of informing the would-be recipients' managers prior to notifying them:

I actually wrote the managers and said, 'We're preparing to provide a 'thank you' and a monetary award to your team member. ...' At that point in the communications a lot of the managers came back and said, 'Wow, thank you for acknowledging my team member. I'll make sure that I reinforce this with them. I'll make sure that I provide other splash and excitement about the thank you.' So, we actually heard a lot from the managers acknowledging the process as well.

Maria noted that her gratitude communication effort was valuable for giving awareness to the senior leader, assisting in getting commitment to future work, and giving high status feedback to the contributors. She went into detail about some of the most profound aspects of this gratitude effort:

[T]hese people are very far removed from the senior leader, so just for him to have that connection. ... And then for the folks deeper in the organization to understand that their senior leader kind of knows. So, for me it's making that skipped level connection.

In a nightmare moment in Maria's professional life, the effort to complete a customized e-learning module and the related vendor relationship fell apart 8 days before a global rollout. This forced her to scramble over the next 3 or 4 months to work with other vendors and fix the situation before encountering a government-imposed compliance deadline.

Her SVP, with a direct line to the president of the company, wrote her a very meaningful email of acknowledgement and appreciation. Maria talked about her emotions when first reading the message of gratitude:

I was like, 'Oh, God. Here's a message from my boss. Oh, no, my boss's boss.' I opened it up, and it really took me by surprise because it was short and sweet but very heartfelt. 'No one should have to endure what you've endured and you've led the team to be able to still deliver.' I'm quick to cry but it really hit me. ... My senior leader knows that this has been really rough.

Maria forwarded this email to her internal colleagues on the project.

Notably, the direct impetus for the SVP's email did not matter to Maria: "I know my boss prompted him to send it but it actually doesn't matter because he still had to be willing to send it."

Maria addressed the significance of the email:

Again, it was the acknowledgement that he was aware of what I was doing and how I was leading the team and sort of leading through a stressful time.

Because we were taking a lot of flak in the organization for possibly not making deadlines and not engaging stakeholders in the right way. And people didn't have visibility that we were under situations that we just couldn't have even described. So, my corporate executive team member, my boss's boss ... who is a direct line to the head of the company, understands what we went through. [laughter] ... [H]e's the only person that I needed to know got it.

Maria offered additional reflections on the benefits in this situation: "Well, I think it certainly means that he had our backs in this situation and sort of trusted what we were doing to resolve it for the company."

Upon completing the compliance-related global rollout, Maria was grateful to the small vendor team that helped, and she processed a monetary award for each of the five team members who were from two vendor organizations. She approached the would-be recipients' managers and made sure they were okay with the recognition. Maria sent personal emails with the dollar amounts. Some individuals contributed more than others to the project. Accordingly, the dollar amounts varied from $700–$1,200.

Maria addressed the benefit of expressing gratitude in this situation:

So they functioned like they cared and were acting like [company] employees and they don't have to do that. So I think for me it was the benefit of acknowledging that they cared about it, and they treated it like their name was on it because their name was on it, despite I was the one who would take the heat if we didn't make it.

Maria was previously an organizational development consultant and coach in the research and development division of another top five pharmaceutical company. She had about 2 years' worth of coaching time invested in a senior leader. In a large gathering of 8,000 leaders from across the organization, someone commented to the person she was coaching that he was a visibly different leader and asked what he was doing to change.

Maria recollected the observation and question from the member of the audience: "'I've really noticed that you're actually different than you were a couple of years ago. ... [H]ow have you done that?' The executive mentioned that he got a lot of coaching and was thinking about what he could do differently." Maria added that she thought, "Wow, this guy and his organization have noticed that he's different. I had my own little pride moment. ... I did that, I coached him, I helped him." Even better, the senior leader came up to Maria during the cocktail hour that followed the open session and said, "Did you hear the question asked me today? … I want to thank you. That was all you."

Maria mentioned the impact on her: "I was very emotional because he acknowledged that two-year commitment of coaching him and helping him be a different leader and that made a difference."

Maria recognized the pattern of gratitude in a person standing up in a large forum and positively commenting on how the senior leader had changed and then the senior leader extending thanks to Maria:

I mean this gentleman had to choose to stand up in front of 8,000 of his peers and get up and actually say something quite personal about the change journey that he's seen a very senior person go on. … [H]e was actually expressing gratitude to that senior leader, right? And then the senior leader saying, 'I didn't do it alone and I'm suggesting that you don't do it alone.' [laughter] … [T]here really is kind of a circle there.

Maria talked about the major benefit of this situation:

[H]e's a hard guy to get along with so to soften him a little bit is a huge. There's a huge benefit to the organization for him to see his shadow, to have a different shadow, and own that publicly.

Also, Maria noted that senior leader's ability to express gratitude was a sign of his larger transformation.

Maria's collection of stories is impressive, in part, because it demonstrates her success at facilitating gratitude across levels inside and outside huge companies. As with David's behaviors, exemplifying agency and structure, so too do Maria's actions reflect how she and those she represents are bound within an organization yet also help create new possibilities for themselves and others. Not only does she face bureaucratic challenges simply because of the size and global nature of the organizations with which she has been associated, but she must follow her industry's considerable regulations when sending and receiving gifts of any financial value. However, Maria sees opportunities to express gratitude and works hard to make it happen.

Another lesson that Maria imparts is the need to work together in crafting and distributing gratitude—and that senior leaders very often need such support. As she herself attested as a gratitude recipient, gratitude sent from a senior leader is not diminished if the receiver knows the sender had a nudge or more active support in expressing the appreciation or thanks.

Technology Industry Entrepreneur—Always Looking Through the Lens of Gratitude Communication and Making It Happen Even in Times of Resistance

Regis is the former owner of a medium-size technology company that he started himself. He remains active as a consultant to the organization after he merged his company with a competitor and then sold it to other investors. By all accounts, Regis is exceptional in terms of sending and receiving gratitude over the span of a career. His gratitude stories are best presented as one continuing narrative.

Regis graduated at the top of his class from a technical high school and felt that appreciation was extended toward him when the school awarded him a $50 savings bond. After finishing college, Regis started a technology company. When he saw that his industry was fundamentally changing and he needed to join forces with others to survive, he merged his company with a peer company and major competitor.

At the point of this merger, Regis surprised three key individuals who were particularly instrumental in contributing to his success. He voluntarily took 25% of his stock in the new company and divided it among the individuals— leaders whom Regis had relied on over the years. The act of sharing stock was a message of thanks, but it was also meant as an incentive to increase company value. Regis explained,

> I was giving them an opportunity to become a stockholder and to reap the gains and benefits of making this merger work, because our five-year plan was, in fact, already established to build this business up to become a profitable entity.

Regis also gave his office manager a large bonus. As he described,

> I gave her quite a nice retirement bonus to keep her happy and to let her know I appreciated her efforts.

Regis and his colleagues worked hard for the next 5 years to prepare to sell the merged, private company to a much larger, public company. After the sale was complete, Regis was able to withdraw equity. Rather than just retreat and enjoy the good life himself, he expressed thanks and shared some of the financial windfall by sponsoring a cruise for 200 people who had helped him succeed over the years.

Even though Regis was in the financial position to retire and did not control the new company, he chose to stay engaged in his longstanding professional relationships and continue to work with the company as a consultant.

Because Regis's original employees do not receive a holiday dinner party from the new company, he regularly puts one on himself. Regis provided his thinking:

> *I've always [put on a holiday party] since [the company became public], on my own, because the company never really wanted ... to go to that extra expense or that extra yard. And I think it was important that the employees know that we appreciate their efforts.*

When Regis heard that the new company was not willing to do anything to recognize a couple of longstanding employees who were retiring, Regis and his wife hosted a retirement dinner for approximately 20 people at their home. Regis explained,

> *I did this on my own and I wasn't doing it to get reimbursed. I did it because I felt we owed something to those two employees that gave us, you know, 15 years of their life. ... And they did a lot for me personally. ... I always felt ... if you treat the employees right, they'll go through walls for you and the payback will be there for you.*

Regis's expressions of gratitude toward regular employees extend across the years. When he was owner of his original company, he heard that his managers wanted to let go of an employee who was burdened by personal financial difficulties and was late for work on a couple of occasions because he did not have access to transportation. Regis, in appreciation for the worker's record of handling the late-night shift and doing a good job, paid off a car loan for him and gave him an interest free loan across an extended amount of time. Regis described the situation: "I said, 'Wait a second. This guy is a good employee. I think it's our responsibility to help him out all we can.'"

In later years, when prospective clients were walking through the facility, the person whom Regis had helped spoke highly about Regis on his own initiative. The prospective clients reported to Regis: "That guy in the back said he would go through a cinderblock wall for you." Regis reflected:

> *That kind of feedback is where my gratitude always came from. ... 'See that wall right there? I'll go through that wall for that man.' That's the payback. All of my other key people were like, 'Get rid of this guy. ... It's his responsibility to keep a car so he can come to work. ...' He's got a family. He can't*

afford to be out of a job. That's the gratitude. That to me was a message that ... he would go through walls for you.

More recently, a longtime employee with a sales quota was feeling a great deal of stress. She was managing to help her son survive an extended battle with cancer, but she wasn't able to hit her numbers at work and was about to be forced out. Regis helped by connecting her with the owner of a smaller, private company. Regis provided an update:

And I've talked to her since, and she's doing great and she's happy and she doesn't have the stress ... so I think it was a good move for her and for [the owner].

Regis's gratitude stretches beyond his direct business interests. He donates to his college and is on the board. The college president invited him to join a delegation to receive a national award in Washington, D.C. Regis's involvement in remarkable gratitude communication activities goes on.

Regis heads a foundation for student scholarships at the school where he got started all those years ago. He challenged all his employees and the faculty and staff at the school to give to the foundation for student awards and opportunities. He proposed matching their donations up to $5,000 if there was 100 percent support. The school gave him a distinguished service award. Incidentally, Regis, inspired by that $50 savings bond the school had given him 30 years earlier, gave the school a $30,000 gift to start the foundation.

Regis has certainly been boldly generous on repeated occasions but, arguably, stands out most in the way he always seems to lead through the lens of gratitude. For example, he was incredibly generous giving shares to major contributors and a major lump sum gift to his office manager. He did this as a "thank you" and as a motivator at a very key juncture in his company's history. There was a lot of awareness on his part and it not always self-serving, as in the case of the cruise he sponsored. Regis shows us that gratitude communication can help us take notice of what's most important in our world. Arguably, the breadth and depth of Regis's gratitude expressions seem remarkable, not only in the context of this study but of most people's workplace experiences, and this reasonably positions him as a gratitude communication master.

A strong theme emerges in some of Regis's stories about being unrelenting in expressing gratitude even when faced with considerable resistance from others, such as when others wanted to bump the low-level employee who others out of the organization, and yet Regis resisted. Regis actually considered the situation in terms of gratitude towards the employee when others were simply angry. Regis also shows his independent thinking and generosity around gratitude communication when recognizing people at the holidays and when they retire. The specific stories indicate that he was not just considerate but, basically, acting rebelliously (but not in a mean-spirited fashion) in sending gratitude.

Early Career Pharmaceutical Sales Representative— Gratitude Communication from the Get-Go and When Others (Even Recipients) are Indifferent

Marco is a senior sales representative with a pharmaceutical company. Even though he has been out of college only a couple of years and his career is very young, Marco deeply values gratitude communication. His high regard for the expression of gratitude is closely tied to his high regard for his organization and for people in general.

Marco shared gratitude to his regional director for offering him a promotion and a move to a more prominent region for the company. Marco explained:

> [I]t was based on an opportunity to meet the regional director down here last year, and we kind of hit it off. ... And he was like, 'I want to offer you a spot when I have an opening on my team.' And there were a lot of other candidates that were probably more qualified and had more tenure than I did at the time, but it was based on his word that he would offer it to me when it was available. I was really grateful for this opportunity and thanked him and thanked his own director and thanked everybody that had some level of impact in this decision and this opportunity. And I think a lot of people were like, 'You don't have to be thankful. You've earned this. This is something you deserve.' But it didn't stop me from being appreciative.

In his prior job, Marco not only expressed gratitude to his manager but nominated him for a company award. Marco explained,

> I think most people just kind of didn't really respect him or respect the position or whatever, but I did. And when he got recognition nationally for his efforts with me, I think it struck a chord with him. And it struck a chord with other people throughout the company that these are the people that he's creating. ... And he deserved a lot of appreciation for that and he got it. And he was given [our company's excellence award]. And, to this day, we speak regularly. I think he thinks about me a little bit differently that I did that for him. In turn, he ended up recognizing some of the things that

I had done. … It was almost like a little competition where I was giving him praise and then he ended up giving me praise in return. It almost got to be like a love story at the end. [laughter] It was cool. I think it definitely improved … our relationship professionally.

Marco talked about the resistance he could have faced transitioning into a role that the previous representative had held for 11 years:

I think it would have been easy for these offices to be a little tentative and not so welcoming, but to the contrary they've all been great. They've all welcomed me. I've been able to get in to see the providers and I've been able to have great conversations with the doctors and the nurses and everything. So, I'm always grateful to them, and I actually make it a point every time I walk out to say, "Thank you for your time. Thank you for welcoming me into your office. Thanks for sharing your experiences with me." And I think most of the time they kind of look at me like, "It's no big deal, dude. You're welcome."

Marco is especially aware of communicating appreciation to the physician, especially given this individual's history:

I was told by the previous rep that he doesn't spend a lot of time with reps. … But he sees me, he spends time, he asks questions, he's involved in the presentations, and I make it a point to thank him for that. And a lot of the other people in the office are "[This physician] really never spends as much time with reps, you should feel really lucky." So I definitely make it a point to thank him, and I think his numbers show it. I mean I think we've impacted what he's doing, and I definitely appreciate it.

Marco has a habit of being quite detailed in his thanks:

I always say, "Thank you very much for welcoming me to your office. Thanks for taking time in between patients to see me and speak to me. Thanks for taking time during your lunch, where I know you probably just want to relax, to see a drug rep and talk medicine while you're on your break. Thanks for allowing me to be your advocate and to provide resources and materials for your patients and for your staff."

Marco explains the importance of the access he has established with the physician:

At the end of the day, if the doctor won't do a lunch or let you in there, it doesn't matter if the nurses want to see you or anybody else, they can pretty much close the door.

Marco spoke about a particularly powerful example of engendering gratitude by helping a nurse practitioner who tended to get overlooked because other health care providers saw a lot more patients and wrote a lot more prescriptions.

And she would always just say, 'Oh, you should see so and so, go see somebody else.' But I said, 'Look, let's talk about the disease state. Let's get you comfortable with the disease state and then maybe down the road we'll talk medication.' And I know that she was kind of taken aback and really appreciates it. And she'll call me if she has any questions.

The overall situation has various benefits:

It's beneficial because now she's more knowledgeable to handle a disease state that she wasn't particularly comfortable with in the past. It's beneficial for my company, obviously, because we're getting our products out there to more people. It's beneficial for me because now I have another contact within the office, another person providing information to her patients. And it's just another advocate for the disease state. It's another advocate for the need for help. It's another advocate for our company and for our products.

One of the lessons to be learned from Marco is you can be a gratitude communication master from the outset of your career. You do not need to be 20 years in or at the end of your career to claim the mantle. You do not need to be in a high position or have access to extraordinary financial resources to express gratitude. Marco's awareness, depth and range of his gestures, and overall gratitude experience mean that he can be credibly described as such at the present time. Despite being early in his career, gratitude communication is already paying dividends—for him, for those with whom he works, for those he serves, and for his organization as a whole.

Another lesson to be learned from Marco is that gratitude communication does not necessarily decrease in value just because others, whether onlookers or recipients, do not claim to see the need for it. Arguably, Marco's enthusiasm around gratitude communication is linked to the energy he feels and communicates around his work more generally and why people choose to work with him inside and outside his organization.

Returning to the Opening Story: Being a Gratitude Communication Master Can Be Amazing but It Also Takes Effort

This chapter opened with *Androcles and the Lion*. The high points in that story are deeply memorable, including the act of kindness when Androcles pulled the thorn out of the lion's injured paw and the act of gratitude when the lion, though starved, warmly greeted Androcles in front of the emperor. Of course, the short tale has a lot of points when things could have gone a different way.

Given the philosophy of the masters of gratitude communication and focusing on what was in the protagonist's control, it is notable what the man and the lion *did not do* at different points along the way. Although injured, a lion was still fear-inducing. Androcles could have walked away in the beginning of the story but didn't. Although well-acquainted with Androcles but feeling starved, the lion could have pounced on the man, torn him to shreds, and devoured him, but it didn't.

In Maslow's (1943) hierarchy of human needs, food and safety are nearer the bottom while relationships and self-actualization are nearer the top, and it has generally been suggested that lower needs must be fulfilled before higher needs. Aesop's gratitude communication story is a tale of discipline to overcome gut reactions and commit to what is higher and better. That move to higher and better is tough, though. The long journey of gratitude communication requires dedication and personal discipline in the face of adversity.

Chapter Conclusion

We have explored the stories of four individuals who are gratitude masters. Hopefully, their tales are inspiring to you. Yet their stories also might strike you as overwhelming when you consider how you might come to achieve such successes. Whether you are already a master of gratitude communication, an aspirant, or simply an observer of the phenomenon, the Epilogue that follows helps make sense of how we might handle tomorrow and the next day, when we have such high expectations of ourselves.

Real World Recommendations

- View your entire career path as a gratitude journey.

- Develop a high level of awareness with sending and receiving gratitude, actively participate in gratitude communication, and share gratitude communication stories that have dramatic power.

- Think and speak as if you and others can make a positive difference.

- Be energized about your work, and energize others at all status levels.

- Find a range of ways to express appreciation and thanks.

- Do not keep a tight balance sheet about the process.

- Make gratitude communication truly thrilling for all involved.

- When possible, use gratitude communication as a major currency in business.

- Strive to be effective across levels inside and outside your company, even if it is a large company.

- Acknowledge the need to work with others in sending gratitude, and recognize that senior leaders may need such support.

- Consider making gratitude one of (if not your main) leadership lens.

- Find ways to appropriately and effectively send gratitude even when facing resistance from others.

- Realize you can be a gratitude master early in your career or even when you do not have access to financial resources.

- Stay committed even if others do not claim to see the need for expressions of gratitude.

Your Opportunity to Get to Work With Gratitude

- Identify an admired leader whom you have personally encountered or about whom you know quite a bit. To what extent, if at all, would you say this person is a master of gratitude communication?

- Is it desirable to you to consider yourself a master of gratitude communication or commit to becoming one?

- What behaviors might you adopt on a weekly, monthly, and/or yearly basis if you were to strongly devote yourself to being or becoming a master of gratitude communication?

Questions for Reflection and Discussion

- Assume you wanted to further study the concept of a master of gratitude communication. How might you go about more precisely defining this concept either prior to or at the end of your research?

- Research two or more theories of leadership and argue for or against the master of gratitude communication concept as relevant to embodying a valued form of leadership.

Recommendations for Learning More

- Read Chapman and White's (2012) *The 5 Languages of Appreciation in the Workplace*. Consider whether different individuals with different languages of appreciation in that framework could become masters of gratitude communication or whether there is an ideal type under that framework.

- Read Conant and Norgaard's (2011) *Touchpoints: Creating Powerful Leadership Connections in the Smallest of Moments*. Determine the degree to which the authors' book is a good practical manual for those who self-identify as or who seek to be masters of gratitude communication.

Epilogue

Closing Discussion of Gratitude Communication at Work

Gratitude communication is a complex phenomenon. The study established that work-related gratitude communication involves sending and receiving by and among various internal and external senders and receivers, using a variety media, in varied contexts, and with nuanced intended and received meanings.

Gratitude communication is often strategic for those sending it and often perceived as strategic when received and otherwise viewed by others. When recollecting instances of sending gratitude, study participants frequently spoke of purposely crafting their message for one or more specific receivers to achieve one or more desired outcomes. Likewise, study participants frequently assumed a highly deliberate approach from those who had sent gratitude communication to them. An assumption of gratitude communication as strategic places a high burden on senders to be appropriate and effective.

Gratitude communication often corresponds to and/or is, in and of itself, a highly important occurrence in individuals' work lives. Its potential centrality to work life justifies the need for continued study and the need to develop related competencies in the present and future workforce.

Gratitude communication has many links to the concept of engagement both inside and outside the organization. The study showed that gratitude communication can be an outcome of engagement, an act of engagement, and a trigger for engagement.

Given the sometimes complex, strategic, and important nature of gratitude communication, it makes sense to further study its effectiveness and appropriateness by and among different actors, using different means, finding themselves in and shaping various immediate contexts, and living and working in a variety of broader environments. Gratitude communication also needs to be explored as it exists within different cultures and as it occurs cross- and interculturally.

Particularly given the early stage of inquiry into this concept, advancement could occur with various qualitative and quantitative methodologies.

In terms of an appreciative approach to the study of gratitude communication, it would be particularly valuable to identify and study gratitude masters within or across sectors and also consider the phenomenon of highly competent gratitude communication within particular relationships, teams, and organizations.

It is important to point out that one of the main limitations of the study reported here is that the negative potentials of gratitude communication were certainly underrecognized given the study's appreciative frame.

Finally, the strategic nature of gratitude communication necessitates clarification of how it is learned and mastered both generally and as it relates to work life.

Putting Work-Related Gratitude Communication Into Practice

If you are a workplace talent development professional, a formal leader, or simply an individual committed to the concept of gratitude communication, I hope this book gives you additional knowledge, skills, and motivation to put gratitude communication into action in your own life and your work world.

Furthering Scholarly Understanding of Work-Related Gratitude Communication

If you are an academic, I sincerely hope this book helps you in your pursuits, possibly in carrying out your own qualitative and/or quantitative research and/or theoretical writing related to gratitude communication.

Thank You for Reading This Book

I very much planned and wrote this book as both a scholar and practitioner. As a scholar, I greatly value the responsibility and satisfaction of carrying out my research in accordance with academic norms, which includes explaining how my research findings and related theoretical insights relate to those of authors who have contributed before me. As someone with a career-long commitment to developing human talent in the work world, I prize practical tools that are supported by peer-reviewed theory and research and have face validity for the individuals and organizations supported in learning about them and applying them.

No matter your own background or interests, I appreciate you reading this book and considering its possible relevance to you.

References

Adler M. G., & Fagley, N. S. (2005). Appreciation: individual differences in finding value and meaning as a unique predictor of subjective well-being. *Journal of Personality, 73*(1), 79–114. https://doi.org/10.1111/j.1467-6494.2004.00305.x

Albrecht, S. L. (2010). Employee engagement: 10 key questions for research and practice. In S. L. Albrecht (Ed.), *Handbook of employee engagement: Perspectives, issues, research and practice,* 3–19. In C. L. Cooper (Ed.), *New horizons in management series.* Edward Elgar.

Algoe, S. B., Gable, S. L., & Maisel, N. C. (2010). It's the little things: Everyday gratitude as a booster shot for romantic relationships. *Personal Relationships, 17,* 217–233. https://doi.org/10.1111/j.1475-6811.2010.01273.x

Androcles and the lion and other Aesop's fables (1991). Kirkus Media LLC

Anthony-McMann, P. E., Ellinger, A. D., Astakhova, M., & Halbesleben, J. R. B. (2017). Exploring different operationalizations of employee engagement and their relationships with workplace stress and burnout. *Human Resource Development Quarterly, 28*(2), 163–195. https://doi.org/10.1002/hrdq.21276

Arnold, K. A., Turner, N., Barling, J., Kelloway, E. K., & McKee, M. C. (2007). Transformational leadership and psychological well-being: The mediating role of meaningful work. *Journal of Occupational Health Psychology, 12*(3), 193–203. https://doi.org/10.1037/1076-8998.12.3.193

Aronsson, G., Theorell, T., Grape, T., Hammarstrom, A., Hogstedt, C., Marteinsdottir, I. (2017). A systematic review including meta-analysis of work environment and burnout symptoms. *BMC Public Health, 17*(1), 1–13. https://doi.org/10.1186/s12889-017-4153-7

Bakker, A. B. & Xanthopoulou, D. (2009). The crossover of daily work engagement: Test of an actor-partner interdependence model. *Journal of Applied Psychology, 94,* 1562–1571.

Bakker, A. B., Demerouti, E., & Verbeke, W. (2004). Using the job demands-resources model to predict burnout and performance. *Human Resource Management, 43*(1), 83–104. https://doi.org/10.1002/hrm.20004

Baxter, L.A., & Montgomery, B. M. (1996). *Relating: Dialogues and dialectics.* Guilford Press.

Beck, C. W. (2016). Perceptions of thanks in the workplace: Use, effectiveness, and dark sides of managerial gratitude. *Corporate Communications: An International Journal, 21* (3), 333–351. https://doi.org/10.1108/CCIJ-07-2014-0048

Billikopf, G. (2009). *Party-directed mediation.* University of California Press.

Birkner, C. (2012). Give—and give again. *Marketing News, May 31, 2012,* 8–9.

Blau, G., & Andersson, L. (2005). Testing a measure of instigated workplace incivility. *Journal of Occupational and Organizational Psychology, 78*(4), 595–614. https://doi.org/10.1348/096317905X26822

Branch, S., & Murray, J. (2015). Workplace bullying: Is the lack of understanding the reason for inaction? *Organizational Dynamics 44*(4), 287–295. https://doi.org/10.1016/j.orgdyn.2015.09.006

Braten, D. O., Cody, M. J., & DeTienne, K. B. (1993). Account episodes in organizations: remedial work and impression management. *Management Communication Quarterly 6,* 219–250.

Brinkert, R. (2006). Conflict coaching: Advancing the conflict resolution field by developing an individual disputant process. *Conflict Resolution Quarterly 23,* 517–28.

Brinkert, R. (2009). The roots of the public policy process: Using conflict coaching to initiate and sustain public manager commitment to citizen engagement. *International Journal of Public Participation 3,* 63–79.

Brinkert, R. (2010). Conflict coaching and the organizational ombuds field. *Journal of the International Ombudsman Association 3,* 47–53.

Brinkert, R. (2011). Conflict coaching training for nurse managers: A case study of a two-hospital health system, *Journal of Nursing Management 19,* 80–91.

Brinkert, R. (2013). The ways of one and many: Exploring the integration of conflict coaching and dialogue facilitation. *Group Facilitation: A Research and Applications Journal 12,* 45–52.

Brinkert, R. S. (2016). Gratitude communication as workplace conflict management: Advancing a strategy and tactic for positive narrative expansion. In Kellet, P. M. & Matyok, T. G. (Eds.), *Transforming conflict through communication: Personal to working relationships,* 313–329.

Brock, D. C., & Moore, G. E. (2006). *Understanding Moore's law: Four decades of innovation.* Chemical Heritage Foundation.

Brodie, R. J., Ilic, A., Juric, B., & Hollebeek, L. (2013). Consumer engagement in a virtual brand community: An exploratory analysis. *Journal of Business Research, 66,* 105–114. https://doi.org/10.1016/j.jbusres.2011.07.029

Brown, P. & Levinson, S. (1978). Universals in language use: Politeness phenomena. In *Questions and politeness: Strategies in social interaction,* E. N. Goody (Ed.) Cambridge University Press.

Burgoon, J. K. (1978). A communication model of personal space violations: Explications and an initial test. *Human Communication Research, 4,* 129–142. https://doi.org/10.1111/j.1468-2958.1978.tb00603.x

Burgoon, J. K. (1993). Interpersonal expectations, expectancy violations, and emotional communication. *Journal of Language and Social Psychology, 12*(1–2), 30–48. https://doi.org/10.1177/0261927X93121003

Burgoon, J. K., & Jones, S. B. (1976). Toward a theory of personal space expectations and their violations. *Human Communication Research, 2,* 131–146. https://doi.org/10.1111/j.1468-2958.1976.tb00706.x

Bush, R. A. B., & Folger, J. P. (1994). *The promise of mediation: Responding to conflict through empowerment and recognition.* Jossey-Bass.

Bush, R. A. B., Folger, J. P. (2004). *The promise of mediation: The transformative approach to conflict.* Jossey-Bass.

Byrd, S. (2012). Hi fans! Tell us your story!: Incorporating a stewardship-based social media strategy to maintain brand reputation during a crisis. *Corporate Communications: An International Journal 17 (3),* 241–254 (14). https://doi.org/10.1108/13563281211253502

Cacioppo, J. T., Hawkley, L. C., & Thisted, R. A. (2010). Perceived social isolation makes me sad: 5-year cross-lagged analyses of loneliness and depressive symptomatology in the Chicago health, aging, and social relations study. *Psychology and Aging, 25*(2), 453–463. https://doi.org/10.1037/a0017216

Campbell, R. (2006). Reply to Robert H. Bass, "Egoism versus rights" (Spring 2006): Altruism in Auguste Comte and Ayn Rand. *The Journal of Ayn Rand Studies, 7*(2), 357–369.

Chalofsky, N., & Cavallaro, L. (2013). A good living versus A good life: Meaning, purpose, and HRD. *Advances in Developing Human Resources, 15*(4), 331–340. https://doi.org/10.1177/1523422313498560

Chapman, G., & White, P. (2012). *The 5 languages of appreciation in the workplace: Empowering organizations by encouraging people.* Northfield.

Chapman, G. D. (2010). *The 5 love languages: The secret to love that lasts.* Northfield.

Cialdini, R. B. (2009). *Influence: Science and practice (5th ed.).* Pearson.

Claro, S., Paunesku, D., & Dweck, C. S. (2016). Growth mindset tempers the effects of poverty on academic achievement. *Proceedings of the National Academy of Sciences of the United States of America, 113*(31), 8664–8668. https://doi.org/10.1073/pnas.1608207113

Conant, D., & Norgaard, M. (2011). *Touchpoints: Creating powerful leadership connections in the smallest of moments.* Jossey-Bass.

Cooperrider, D., & Whitney, D. (2005). *Appreciative inquiry: A positive revolution in change.* Berrett-Koehler.

Cooperrider, D. L. (1986). Appreciative inquiry: Toward a methodology for under-standing and enhancing organizational innovation. Unpublished Ph.D., Case Western Reserve University, Cleveland.

Cooperrider, D. L., & Whitney, D. (2005). *Appreciative Inquiry: A Positive Revolution in Change.* Berrett-Koehler.

Crezo, A. (2012, February 10). *11 amazing thank you notes from famous people.* https://www.mentalfloss.com/article/29959/11-amazing-thank-you-notes-famous-people

Cupach, W. R., Canary, D. J. & Spitzberg, B. H. (2010). *Competence in Interpersonal Conflict, 2nd ed.* Waveland.

Daft, R., & Lengel, R. (1986). Organizational information requirements, media rich-ness and structural design. *Management Science, 32*(5), 554–571.

Daft, R. L., & Lengel, H. (1986). Organizational Information Requirements, Media Richness and Structural Design. *Management Science 32*, 554–71. https://doi.org/10.1287/mnsc.32.5.554

Daft, R. L., & Lengel, R. H., (1986). Organizational information requirements, media richness and structural design. *Management Science 32*, 554–571. https://doi.org/10.1287/mnsc.32.5.554

Dasgupta, S., Suar, D. & Singh, S. (2014). Managerial communication practices and employees' attitudes and behaviours: *A qualitative study. Corporate Communications: An International Journal, 19*(3), 287–302. https://doi.org/10.1108/CCIJ-04-2013-0023

Dempsey, S. E. (2009) Stakeholder theory. In S. W. Littlejohn & K. A. Foss (Eds.), *Encyclopedia of communication theory* (pp. 929–931). Sage. http://dx.doi.org/10.4135/9781412959384

DeRosa, D. M., Hantula, D. A., Kock, N., & D'Arcy, J. (Summer–Fall 2004). Trust and leadership in teamwork: A media naturalness perspective. *Human Resource Management, 43*(2&3), 219–232. https://doi.org/10.1002/hrm.20016

De Tocqueville, A. (2000). *Democracy in America.* (H. C. Mansfield & D. Winthrop, Trans.) University of Chicago. (Original work published 1835).

Dobbs, M. (2009). *One minute to midnight: Kennedy, Khrushchev, and Castro on the brink of nuclear war.* Random House.

Donaldson, T. & Preston, L. E. (1995). The Stakeholder Theory of the Corporation: Concepts, Evidence, and Implications. *Academy of Management Review, 20*(1), 65–91. https://doi.org10.3138/9781442673496-011

Donaldson, T., & Preston, L. E. (1995). The stakeholder theory of the corporation: Concepts, evidence, and implicaitons. *The Academy of Management Review, 20*(1), 65–91. https://www.jstor.org/stable/258887

Dweck, C. (2006). *Mindset: The new psychology of success.* Random House.

Dweck, C. S. (2016). *Mindset: The new psychology of success.* Ballantine.

Dweck, C. S. (2017). The journey to children's mindsets—and beyond. *Child Development Perspectives, 11*(2), 139–144. https://doi.org/10.1111/cdep.12225

D'Andrea, C. (2018, July 2). Dan Gilbert's latest LeBron farewell letter came without comic sans or pettiness. SBNation. https://www.sbnation.com/nba/2018/7/2/17525560/dan-gilbert-lebron-james-letter-cavaliers-lakers

Emmons, R. A. (2004). Gratitude. In C. Peterson & M. E. P. Seligman (Eds.), *Character strengths and virtues: A handbook and classification*, 553–568. Oxford University Press.

Emmons, R. A., & Crumpler, C. A. (2000). Gratitude as human strength: Appraising the evidence. *Journal of Social and Clinical Psychology 19*, 56–69. https://doi.org/10.1521/jscp.2000.19.1.56

Fagley, N. S. (2012). Appreciation uniquely predicts life satisfaction above demographics, the Big Five personality factors, and gratitude. *Personality and Individual Differences, 53*, 59–63. https://doi.org/10.1016/j.paid.2012.02.019

Fagley, N. S., & Adler, M. G. (2012). Appreciation: A spiritual path to finding value and meaning in the workplace. *Journal of Management, Spirituality, and Religion, 9*, 167–187.

Fairhurst, G. (2011). *The Power of Framing: Creating the Language of Leadership.* Jossey-Bass.

Fairhurst, G. (2011). *The power of framing: Creating the language of leadership.* Jossey-Bass.

Fimrite, P. (2005, December 14). Daring rescue of whale off Farallones. *San Francisco Chronicle.* https://www.sfgate.com/bayarea/article/Daring-rescue-of-whale-off-Farallones-Humpback-2557146.php

Fredrickson, B. L. (2001). The role of positive emotions in positive psychology: The broaden-and-build theory of positive emotions. *American Psychologist, 56*, 218–226. https://doi.org/10.1037//0003-066X.56.3.218

Freeman, R. E. (1984). *Strategic management: A stakeholder approach.* Pitman.

Friedman, M. (1970, September 13). The social responsibility of business is to increase its profits. *The New York Times Magazine.* https://www.nytimes.com/1970/09/13/archives/a-friedman-doctrine-the-social-responsibility-of-business-is-to.html

Friedman, T. L. (2016). *Thank you for being late: An optimist's guide to thriving in the age of accelerations (First ed.).* Straus and Giroux.

Froman, L. (2010). Positive psychology in the workplace. *Journal of Adult Development, 17*(2), 59–69. https://doi.org/10.1007/s10804-009-9080-0

Fuller, R. B. (1981). *Critical path.* St. Martin's Press.

Fuller, S. H., Millett, I., (eds). (2011). The future of computing performance: Game over or next level? *Committee on Sustaining Growth in Computing*. National Research. https://doi.org/10.17226/12980

Gane, M. (2006). *Auguste Comte*. Routledge.

Gergen, K. (2015). *An invitation to social construction*. Sage.

Giacomini, N. G. (2009). The art of conflict coaching. In J. M. Schrage and N. G. Giacomini (Eds.). *Reframing Campus Conflict: Student Conduct Practice through a Social Justice Lens*, 100–111. Stylus.

Giddens, A. (1984). *The constitution of society: Introduction of the theory of structuration*. University of California Press.

Giddens, A. (1984). *The constitution of society: Outline of the theory of structuration*. Polity Press.

Gilligan, C. (1982). *In a Different Voice*. Harvard University Press.

Gilligan, C. (1982). In a different voice: Psychological theory and women's development, Harvard University Press.

Gilligan, C. (1977). In a different voice: women's conception of the self and morality. *Harvard Educational Review, 47*(4), 481–517. https://doi.org/10.17763/haer.47.4.g6167429416hg5l0

Giumetti, G. W., McKibben, E. S., Hatfield, A. L., Schroeder, A. N., & Kowalski, R. M. (2012). Cyber incivility at work: The new age of interpersonal deviance. *Cyberpsychology, Behavior, and Social Networking, 15*(3), 148–154. https://doi.org/10.1089/cyber.2011.0336

Goei, R., & Boster, F. J. (2005). The roles of obligation and gratitude in explaining the effect of favors on compliance. *Communication Monographs, 72*(3), 284–300. https://doi.org/10.1080/03637750500206524

Goei, R., & Boster, F.J. (2005). The roles of obligation and gratitude in explaining the effect of favors on compliance. *Communication Monographs, 72*, 284–300. https://doi.org/10.1080/03637750500206524

Goffman, E. (1955). On face-work: an analysis of ritual elements in social interaction. *Psychiatry: Journal for the Study of Interpersonal Processes, 18*, 213–231. https://doi.org/10.1080/00332747.1955.11023008

Gouldner, A. W. (1960). The norm of reciprocity: A preliminary statement. *American Sociological Review, 25*(2), 161–178.

Graham, B. A. (2016, June 20). It's time to call LeBron James what he is: the NBA's greatest ever player. *The Guardian*. https://www.theguardian.com/sport/blog/2016/jun/20/lebron-james-cleveland-cavaliers-nba-title-goat

Grant, A. & Gino, F. (2010). A little thanks goes a long way: Explaining why gratitude expressions motivate prosocial behavior. *Journal of Personality and Social Psychology, 98*, 946–955. https://doi.org/10.1037/a0017935

Grant, A. (2014). *Give and take: Why helping others drives our success*. Penguin.

Guinn, J. (2009). *Going down together: The true untold story of Bonnie and Clyde*. Simon & Schuster.

Haimovitz, K., & Dweck, C. S. (2016). Parents' views of failure predict children's fixed and growth intelligence mind-sets. *Psychological Science, 27*(6), 859–869. https://doi.org/10.1177/0956797616639727

Haimovitz, K., & Dweck, C. S. (2017). The origins of children's growth and fixed mindsets: New research and a new proposal. *Child Development, 88*(6), 1849–1859. https://doi.org/10.1111/cdev.12955

Hallberg, U. E. & Schaufeli, W. B. (2006). 'Same same' but different? Can work engagement be discriminated from job involvement and organizational commitment? *European Psychologist 11*, 119–127. https://doi.org/10.1027/1016-9040.11.2.119

Hargie, O. (2011). *Skilled interpersonal communication: Research, theory and practice, 5th ed*. Routledge.

Hauge, L. J., Skogstad, A., & Einarsen, S. (2010). The relative impact of workplace bullying as a social stressor at work. *Scandinavian Journal of Psychology, 51*(5), 426. https://doi.org/10.1111/j.1467-9450.2010.00813.x

Hawkley, L. C., & Cacioppo, J. T. (2010). Loneliness matters: A theoretical and empirical review of consequences and mechanisms. *Annals of Behavioral Medicine, 40*(2), 218–227. https://doi.org/10.1007/s12160-010-9210-8

Hendrickson, B., & Goei, R. (2009). Reciprocity and dating: Explaining the effects of favor and status on compliance with a date request. *Communication Research, 36*(4), 585–608. https://doi.org/10.1177/0093650209333036

Herbert, K. (1986). Say "thank you" or something. *American Speech, 61*(1), 76–88. https://doi.org10.2307/454710

Hill, P., Allemand, M., & Roberts, B. W. (2012). Examining the pathways between gratitude and self-rated physical health across adulthood. *Personality and Individual Differences, 54*, 92–96. https://doi.org/10.1016/j.paid.2012.08.011

History of Germany during World War I. (2020, June 15). In *Wikipedia*. https://en.wikipedia.org/wiki/History_of_Germany_during_World_War_I

Hodgins, M., MacCurtain, S., & Mannix-McNamara, P. (2014). Workplace bullying and incivility: A systematic review of interventions. *International Journal of Workplace Health Management, 7*(1), 54–72.

Hyland, K. (2004) Graduate's gratitude: The generic structure of dissertation acknowledgements. *English for specific purposes 23*, 303–24. https://doi.org/10.1016/S0889-4906(03)00051-6

Jaremka, L. M., Fagundes, C. P., Peng, J., Bennett, J. M., Glaser, R., Malarkey, W. B., & Kiecolt-Glaser, J. K. (2013). Loneliness promotes inflammation during acute stress. *Psychological Science, 24*(7), 1089–1097. https://doi.org/10.1177/0956797612464059

John F. Kennedy Presidential Library and Museum (n.d.). *Cuban missile crisis mementos.* https://www.jfklibrary.org/asset-viewer/archives/JFKPOF/098/JFKPOF-098-007

Jones, T. S., & Brinkert, R. (2008). *Conflict Coaching: Conflict Management Strategies and Skills for the Individual.* Sage.

Kahn, W. A. (1990). Psychological Conditions of Personal Engagement and Disengagement at Work. *Academy of Management Journal, 33*(4) 692–724. https://doi.org/10.2307/256287

Kahn, W. A. (1990). Psychological conditions of personal engagement and disengagement at work. *The Academy of Management Journal, 33*(4), 692–724. https://doi.org/10.2307/256287

Kashdan, T. B., Mishra, A., Breen, W. E., & Froh, J. J. (2009). Gender differences in gratitude: Examining appraisals, narratives, the willingness to express emotions, and changes in psychological needs. *Journal of Personality, 77*(3), 691–730. https://doi.org/10.1111/j.1467-6494.2009.00562.x

Katz, A. N., Lenhardt, M., & Mitchell, K. (2007). On acknowledging thanks for performing a favor. *Metaphor and Symbol, 22,* 233–250. https://doi.org/10.1080/1092648070135766

Keller, J. E., & Keating, L. C. (1993). *Aesop's fables: with a life of Aesop.* University Press of Kentucky. https://uknowledge.uky.edu/upk_classics/1/

Kellett, M. (2007). *Conflict dialogue: Working with layers of meaning for productive relationships,* 12–15. Sage.

Kellett, P. M., & Dalton, D. G. (2001). *Managing Conflict in a Negotiated World: A Narrative Approach to Achieving Dialogue and Change.* Sage.

Kimpell, J. L. (2015). Republican civic virtue, enlightened self-interest and Tocqueville. *European Journal of Political Theory, 14*(3), 345–367. https://doi.org/10.1177/1474885114546139

Kini, P., Wong, J., McInnis, S., Gabana, N., & Brown, J. W. (2016). The effects of gratitude expression on neural activity. Neuroimage, 128, 1–10. https://doi,org/10.1016/j.neuroimage.2015.12.040

Kock, N. (2005). Media richness or media naturalness? The evolution of our biological communication apparatus and its influence on our behavior toward e-communication tools. *IEEE Transactions on Professional Communication, 48*(2), 117–130. https://doi.org/10.1109/tpc.2005.849649

Kohlberg, L. (1976). Moral stages and moralization: The cognitive-developmental approach. In T. Lickona (Ed.), *Moral development and behavior: Theory, research and social issues,* 31–53. Rinehart and Winston. https://doi.org/10.1287/mnsc.32.5.554

Kunkel, D., Carnevale, J., & Henderson, D. (2015). Examining instrument issues in workplace incivility: Measurement or mutation? *Journal of Organizational Culture, Communications and Conflict, 19*(1), 102.

Kvale, S., & Brinkmann, S. (2009). *Interviews: Learning the craft of qualitative research.* Sage.

Lambert, N. M., Clark, M. S., Durtschi, J., Fincham, F. D., & Graham, S. M. (2010). Benefits of expressing gratitude: Expressing gratitude to a partner changes one's view of the relationship. *Psychological Science, 21,* 574–580.

Lazar, M. M. (2005). *Feminist critical discourse analysis: Gender, power and ideology in discourse.* Palgrave Macmillan.

Lengel, R. H., & Daft, R. L. (1988). The selection of communication media as an executive skill. *The Academy of Management Executive, 2*(3), 225–232.

Lim, S., & Lee, A. (2011). Work and nonwork outcomes of workplace incivility: Does family support help? *Journal of Occupational Health Psychology, 16*(1), 95–111. https://doi.org/10.1037/a0021726

Lombardi, M. (2018, June 29). Here's the letter Dan Gilbert wrote Cavaliers fans after Lebron James opted out in 2010. The Spun. https://thespun.com/news/dan-gilbert-lebron-james-letter-comic-sans-2010

Lopez, S. J., & Gallagher, M. W. (2009). A case for positive psychology. In S. J. Lopez & C.R. Snyder (Eds.), *Oxford handbook of positive psychology,* 3–6. Oxford University Press.

Manusov, V. L. & Harvey, J. H. (2001). *Attribution, communication behavior, and close relationships.* Cambridge University Press.

Maslach, C., Schaufeli, W. B., & Leiter, M. P. (2001). Job burnout. *Annual Review of Psychology, 52*(1), 397–422. https://doi.org/10.1146/annurev.psych.52.1.397

Maslow, A. H. (1943). A theory of human motivation. *Psychological Review, 50*(4), 370–96.

McNamara, R. (1967). "Mutual Deterrence" Speech by Secretary of Defense Robert McNamara. September 18, 1967. http://www.atomicarchive.com/Docs/Deterrence/Deterrence.shtml

McPhee, R. D., Poole, M. S., & Iverson, J. (2014) Structuration Theory. In D. K. Mumby & L. Putnum (Eds). *The Sage handbook of organizational communication: advances in theory, research, and methods (3rd ed.),* 75–100. Sage.

Merchant, A., Ford, J., Sargeant, A. (2010). 'Don't forget to say thank you': The effect of an acknowledgement on donor relationships. *Journal of Marketing Management, 26,* 593–611. https://doi.org/10.1080/02672571003780064

Mitchell, R. K., Agle, B. R., & Wood, D. J. (1997). Toward a theory of stakeholder identification and salience: Defining the principle of who and what really counts. *The Academy of Management Review, 22*(4), 853–886.

Moody, P. R. (2008). Rational choice analysis in classical Chinese political thought: The "Han Feizi". *Polity,* 40 (1). 95–119. https://doi.org/10.1057/palgrave.polity.230068

Moore, G. E. (1965). Cramming more components onto integrated circuits. *Electronics*, April 19, 114–117.

Murthy, V. (2017). Work and the loneliness epidemic. *Harvard Business Review*. https://hbr.org/cover-story/2017/09/work-and-the-loneliness-epidemic

Niedhammer, I., David, S., & Degioanni, S. (2006). Association between workplace bullying and depressive symptoms in the French working population. *Journal of Psychosomatic Research, 61*(2), 251–259. https://doi.org/10.1016/j.jpsychores.2006.03.051

Ohashi, J. (2008). Linguistic rituals for thanking in Japanese: Balancing obligations. *Journal of Pragmatics 40*, 2150–2174.

Olsen, R. B., Olsen, J., Gunner-Svensson, F., & Waldstrøm, B. (1991). Social networks and longevity. A 14 year follow-up study among elderly in Denmark. *Social Science & Medicine, 33*(10), 1189–1195. https://doi/org10.1016/0277-9536(91)90235-5

O'Shaughnessy, H. (2018, June 5). A brief history of the complicated relationship between LeBron James and Dan Gilbert. The Ringer. https://www.theringer.com/nba/2018/6/5/17429588/lebron-james-dan-gilbert-relationship-faq

Pearson, C., & Porath, C. (2009). *The cost of bad behavior: How incivility is damaging your business and what to do about it.* Penguin.

Penninx, B. W. J. H., van Tilburg, T., Kriegsman, D. M. W., Deeg, D. J. H., Boeke, A. J. P., & van Eijk, J.T.M. (1997). Effects of social support and personal coping resources on mortality in older age: The longitudinal aging study Amsterdam. *American Journal of Epidemiology, 146*(6), 510–519. https://doi.org/10.1093/oxfordjournals.aje.a009305

Peplau, L. A., & Perlman, D. (1982). Perspectives on loneliness. In L. A. Peblau & D. Perlman (Eds.), *Loneliness: A Sourcebook of Current Theory, Research and Therapy*, 1–18. Wiley.

Petronio, S. (2002). *Boundaries of Privacy: Dialectics of Disclosure*. State University of New York Press.

Petronio, S. (2007). Translational research endeavors and the practices of communication privacy management. *Journal of Applied Communication Research, 35*, 218–222. https://doi.org/10.1080/00909880701422443

Petronio, S. (2009). Privacy management theory. In S. W. Littlejohn & K. A. Foss (Eds.), *Encyclopedia of communication theory* (pp. 796–798). Sage. http://dx.doi.org/10.4135/9781412959384

Pomerantz, A. (1978). *Compliment responses: Notes on the co-operation of multiple constraints. Studies in the Organization of Conversational Interaction*, 79–112. Academic Press. https://doi.org/10.1016/B978-0-12-623550-0.50010-0

Porath, C. L., & Erez, A. (2007). Does rudeness really matter? The effects of rudeness on task performance and helpfulness. *The Academy of Management Journal, 50*(5), 1181–1197. https://doi.org/10.2307/20159919

Porath, C. L., & Erez, A. (2009). Overlooked but not untouched: How rudeness reduces onlookers' performance on routine and creative tasks. *Organizational Behavior and Human Decision Processes, 109*(1), 29–44. https://doi.org/10.1016/j.obhdp.2009.01.003

Porath, C. L., & Pearson C. (2013). The price of incivility. *Harvard Business Review, 91*(1–2), 115–121.

Preskill, H., & Catsambas, T. (2006). *Reframing evaluation through appreciative inquiry.* Sage.

Putnam, R. D. (2000). *Bowling alone: The collapse and revival of American community.* Simon & Schuster.

Pütz, M., Neff-van Aertselaer, J., & Dijk, T. A. v. (2004). Communicating ideologies: Multidisciplinary perspectives on language, discourse, and social practice. Paper presented at the, Bd. 53;Bd. 53. This volume grew out of the 29th International LAUD Symposium, held on March 27-29, 2002 at the University of Koblenz-Landau in Landau.

Rand, A. (2005). *The virtue of selfish*ness. Signet/New American Library. (Original work published 1964).

Reagan, R. (1994). Text of letter written by President Ronald Reagan announcing he has Alzheimer's disease. Ronald Reagan Presidential Library and Museum. https://www.reaganlibrary.gov/sreference/reagan-s-letter-announcing-his-alzheimer-s-diagnosis

Roberts, R. C. (1991). Virtues and rules. *Philosophy and Phenomenological Research, 51*, 325–343. https://doi.org/10.2307/2108130

Roberts, R. C. (1984). Will power and the virtues. *The Philosophical Review, 93*, 227–247.

Romani, S., Grappi, S., & Bagozzi, R. P. (2013). Explaining consumer reactions to corporate social responsibility: The role of gratitude and altruistic values. *Journal of Business Ethics, 114*, 193–206. https://doi.org/10.1007/s10551-012-1337-z

Rubin, R. (2014, August 24). 100 years of gratitude. *The New York Times.* https://www.nytimes.com/2014/08/24/travel/100-years-of-gratitude.html

Saks, A. M. & Gruman, J. A. (2014). What do we really know about employee engagement? *Human Resource Development Quarterly 25*(2), 155–182. https://doi.org/10.1002/hrdq.21187

Salanova, M., Agut, S., & Peiro, J. M. (2005). Linking organizational resources and work engagement to employee performance and customer loyalty: The mediation of service climate. *Journal of Applied Psychology 90*, 1217–1227.

Saldana, J. (2013). *The coding manual for qualitative researchers.* Sage.

Saldana, J. (2016). *The coding manual for qualitative researchers (3rd ed.).* Sage.

Schaufeli, W. B., & Salanova, M. (2010). How to improve work engagement? In S. L. Albrecht & C. L. Cooper (Eds.), *Handbook of employee engagement: Perspectives, issues, research, and practice*, 399–415. Edward Elgar.

Schaufeli, W. B., Leiter, M. P., & Maslach, C. (2009). Burnout: 35 years of research and practice. *Career Development International, 14*(3), 204–220.

Schilling, D. (2013, April 19) Knowledge doubling every 12 months, soon to be every 12 hours. *Industry tap.* https://www.industrytap.com/knowledge-doubling-every-12-months-soon-to-be-every-12-hours/3950

Schilpzand, P., De Pater, I. E., & Erez, A. (2016). Workplace incivility: A review of the literature and agenda for future research. *Journal of Organizational Behavior, 37*(S1), S57-S88. https://doi.org/10.1002/job.1976

Scholten, A. (2005). Workplace bullying: A threat to health and well-being. https://www.excelahealth.org/health-library/article?chunkid=22634&db=hlt

Schumann, K., Zaki, J., & Dweck, C. S. (2014). Addressing the empathy deficit: Beliefs about the malleability of empathy predict effortful responses when empathy is challenging. *Journal of Personality and Social Psychology, 107*(3), 475–493. http://doi.org/10.1037/a0036738

Scott, S. (2015). *Negotiating identity: Symbolic interactionist approaches to social identity.* Polity.

Seligman, M., & Csikszentmihalyi, M. (2000). Positive psychology: An introduction. *American Psychologist, 55,* 5–14. https://doi.org/10.1037/0003-066X.55.1.5

Sheer, V. C., & Chen, L. (2004). Improving media richness theory: A study of interaction goals, message valence, and task complexity in manager-subordinate communication. *Management Communication Quarterly, 18*(1), 76–93. https://doi.org/10.1177/0893318904265803

Shimanoff, S. B. (2009). Facework theories. In *Encyclopedia of Communication Theory* J. S. W. Littlejohn and K. A. Foss. (Eds.). 374–377. Sage.

Shulman, D. (2017). *The presentation of self in contemporary social life.* Sage.

Skowronski, J. (2010). Gilbert fined $100,000 for LeBron rant. The Street, July 13, 2010. https://www.thestreet.com/personal-finance/gilbert-fined-100000-lebron-rant-12806646

Smith, S. A. (2017). Job-searching expectations, expectancy violations, and communication strategies of recent college graduates. *Business and Professional Communication Quarterly, 80*(3), 296–320. https://doi.org/10.1177/2329490617723116

Spitz, B. (2018). *Reagan: An American journey.* Penguin.

Taylor, C. (1985). *Human agency and language.* Cambridge University Press.

Toepfer, S. M., Cichy, C., & Peters, P. (2012). Letters of gratitude: Further evidence for author benefits. *Journal of Happiness Studies, 13,* 187–201. https://doi.org/10.1007/s10902-011-9257-7

United States in World War I. (2020, June 15). In *Wikipedia*. https://en.wikipedia.org/wiki/United_States_in_World_War_I

Valtorta, N. K., Kanaan, M., Gilbody, S., Ronzi, S., & Hanratty, B. (2016). Loneliness and social isolation as risk factors for coronary heart disease and stroke: Systematic review and meta-analysis of longitudinal observational studies. *Heart (British Cardiac Society), 102*(13), 1009–1016. https://doi.org/10.1136/heartjnl-2015-308790

Wall, A. E., Smith, R. A., & Nodoushani, O. (2017). Workplace bullying: A growing epidemic. *Competition Forum, 15*(2), 251–258.

Waters, L. (2012). Predicting job satisfaction: Contributions of individual gratitude and institutional gratitude. *Psychology, 3,* 1174–1176.

Watkins, P. C., Scheer, J., Ovnicek, M., & Kolts, R. (2006). The debt of gratitude: Dissociating gratitude and indebtedness. *Cognition & Emotion, 20,* 217–241. https://doi.org/10.1080/02699930500172291

Watkins, P. C., Van Gelder, M., & Frias, A. (2009). Furthering the science of gratitude. In S. J. Lopez & C.R. Snyder (Eds.), *Oxford Handbook of Positive Psychology,* 437–445. Oxford University Press.

White, P. (2016). Appreciation at work training and the motivating by appreciation inventory: Development and validity. *Strategic HR Review, 15*(1), 20–24. https://doi.org/10.1108/SHR-11-2015-0090

White, P., Chapman, G., & Myra, H. (2014) *Rising above a toxic workplace: Taking care of yourself in an unhealthy environment.* Northfield.

Whitney, D. K. & Trosten-Bloom, A. (2010). *The power of appreciative inquiry: A practical guide to positive change (2nd ed.).* Berrett-Koehler.

Wong, M. L. (2010). Expressions of gratitude by Hong Kong speakers of English: Research from the international corpus of English in Hong Kong (ICE-HK). *Journal of Pragmatics, 42*(5), 1243–1257. https://doi.org/10.1016/j.pragma.2009.09.022

Wood, A. M., Froh, J. J., & Geraghty, A. W. A. (2010). Gratitude and well-being: A review and theoretical integration. *Clinical Psychology Review, 30,* 890–905. https://doi.org/10.1016/j.cpr.2010.03.005

Wood, A. M., Maltby, J., Stewart, N., & Joseph, S. (2008). Conceptualizing gratitude and appreciation as a unitary personality trait. *Personality and Individual Differences, 44,* 621–632. https://doi.org/10.1016/j.paid.2007.09.028

Yeager, D. S., & Dweck, C. S. (2012). Mindsets that promote resilience: When students believe that personal characteristics can be developed. Educational Psychologist 47(4), 302–314. https://doi.org/10.1080/00461520.2012.722805

Zapf, D., Einarsen, S., Hoel, H. and Vartia, M. (2003). Empirical findings on bullying in the workplace. In S. Einarsen, H. Hoel, D. Zapf, & C. L. Cooper, (Eds.), *Bullying and Emotional Abuse in the Workplace,* 75–96. Taylor and Francis.

Index

CPSIA information can be obtained
at www.ICGtesting.com
Printed in the USA
LVHW040332290322
714624LV00007B/45